The Complete ESG Certification Playbook

Master CSRD, GRI, and SASB Frameworks

Fabian Gilbert Mueller

First Edition: 2025
ISBN: 978-1-7641942-8-0
Isohan Publishing

This book is designed to provide information about ESG (Environmental, Social, and Governance) certification, reporting frameworks, and sustainability management practices. It is sold with the understanding that the author is not engaged in rendering legal, accounting, investment, or other professional services. If legal advice or other expert assistance is required, the services of a competent professional should be sought.

While every effort has been made to ensure the accuracy and completeness of the information contained in this book, the author makes no representations or warranties with respect to the accuracy or completeness of the contents. The ESG reporting field is rapidly evolving, with frequent updates to regulations, standards, and best practices. Readers should verify current requirements with official sources and regulatory bodies.

ESG frameworks including CSRD, GRI, and SASB standards are subject to ongoing development and modification. Regulatory requirements vary by jurisdiction and change frequently. This book reflects information available at the time of publication and may not include the most recent updates. Readers are responsible for confirming current requirements and standards applicable to their specific circumstances.

While this book provides comprehensive preparation guidance for ESG certification examinations, the author makes no guarantee regarding examination success or certification achievement. Individual results may vary based on preparation, experience, and examination conditions.

Information provided about ESG investing, sustainable finance, and business strategies is for educational purposes only and should not be considered investment advice or recommendations for specific business decisions. Past performance does not guarantee future results.

Readers should consult qualified financial advisors and legal counsel before making investment or business decisions.

Company examples, case studies, and scenarios presented in this book are included for illustrative purposes only. They represent publicly available information at the time of writing and should not be considered endorsements or comprehensive assessments of the organizations mentioned. Company practices and performance may have changed since publication.

References to specific software platforms, technology solutions, and service providers are included for informational purposes only and do not constitute endorsements or recommendations. Technology capabilities and provider offerings change frequently. Readers should conduct independent evaluation of solutions for their specific needs.

Readers using this book for professional purposes are responsible for ensuring compliance with applicable professional standards, codes of conduct, and regulatory requirements in their jurisdictions. The author assumes no responsibility for professional decisions made based on information contained in this book.

In no event shall the author be liable for any direct, indirect, incidental, special, or consequential damages arising out of or in connection with the use of this book or the information contained herein, even if the author has been advised of the possibility of such damages.

While this book addresses international frameworks and standards, specific regulatory requirements vary by country and jurisdiction. Readers outside the United States should verify local regulatory requirements and seek appropriate professional guidance for their specific circumstances.

Note to Raders: ESG reporting requirements continue evolving rapidly across jurisdictions worldwide. Always consult current official sources, qualified professionals, and regulatory guidance for the most up-to-date requirements applicable to your specific situation.

Table of Contents

Chapter 1: The New Era of Mandatory ESG Reporting

The corporate boardroom conversations of 2025 sound dramatically different from those just five years ago. The first companies subject to the Corporate Sustainability Reporting Directive (CSRD) have to apply the new rules for the first time in the 2024 financial year, for reports published in 2025. This shift represents more than regulatory compliance—it marks the end of voluntary sustainability reporting and the beginning of mandatory accountability.

Consider the transformation at Unilever, where sustainability metrics now receive the same scrutiny as quarterly earnings. The CSRD significantly broadens the scope of companies subject to mandatory sustainability reporting and has three main objectives: Expand and standardize the existing rules on non-financial reporting and increase the comparability of data. This isn't merely about checking regulatory boxes; it's about fundamentally changing how businesses measure success.

Evolution from Voluntary to Mandatory Disclosure

The journey from voluntary sustainability reporting to mandatory disclosure represents one of the most significant shifts in corporate accountability. 2024 was a landmark year, marked by a series of pivotal EU ESG reporting regulations reshaping corporate responsibility and investment reporting practices. Companies that once considered ESG reporting a nice-to-have now face legal requirements that carry real consequences.

The evolution follows a predictable pattern. First came the pioneers—companies like Interface and Patagonia that embraced sustainability reporting as a competitive advantage. Next, industry leaders adopted these practices to maintain market position. Finally, regulatory bodies recognized the need for standardization and mandatory compliance.

In 2025, a new cohort of companies will come under the scope of the EU's Corporate Sustainability Reporting Directive (CSRD), with large, listed EU companies now required to report (FY 2024) and all large EU companies required to collate 2025 data ahead of reporting in 2026 (FY 2025). This timeline creates urgency for companies that assumed they had more time to prepare.

The scale of this change becomes clear when you examine the numbers. Estimates indicate that it will impact approximately 50,000 companies in the EU, equivalent to 75% of EU companies' total revenues. These aren't just European companies either—any organization with significant EU operations faces these requirements.

Take Microsoft's experience as an example. The tech giant initially approached ESG reporting as a voluntary initiative to attract environmentally conscious talent and customers. However, as regulatory requirements tightened, Microsoft discovered that its voluntary efforts provided a solid foundation for mandatory compliance. The company's early investment in sustainability data systems and stakeholder engagement processes positioned it well for the new regulatory environment.

The pharmaceutical company Novartis offers another instructive case. When faced with upcoming CSRD requirements, Novartis realized that its existing sustainability reporting, while comprehensive, didn't meet the new double materiality standards. The company had to redesign its entire data collection process to capture both the financial impact of ESG issues on the business and the company's impact on environmental and social factors.

Global Regulatory Convergence Trends

The regulatory convergence happening across jurisdictions creates both opportunities and challenges for multinational corporations. The push for global alignment of ESG frameworks will culminate in more standardised reporting protocols. This is crucial for companies that operate in multiple jurisdictions, as it will simplify compliance and reduce the administrative burden associated with navigating a patchwork of regulations.

Australia has announced plans for mandatory climate-related disclosures starting in 2025 for large and medium-sized companies. Like the EU, Australia's disclosure rules will align with global standards such as the TCFD (Task Force on Climate-related Financial Disclosures). This global convergence means that companies can't approach ESG reporting as a regional issue anymore.

The convergence creates several key trends. First, companies operating globally can develop unified reporting systems rather than maintaining separate processes for each jurisdiction. Second, investors gain access to comparable data across markets, improving investment decision-making. Third, suppliers throughout global value chains face pressure to meet ESG standards regardless of their home country regulations.

Consider the case of ASML, the Dutch semiconductor equipment manufacturer. As CSRD requirements took effect, ASML found that its global suppliers needed to provide ESG data that met European standards, even if those suppliers operated primarily in Asia or North America. This created a ripple effect throughout the semiconductor supply chain, forcing companies worldwide to upgrade their ESG reporting capabilities.

The automotive industry provides another powerful example of regulatory convergence in action. Toyota's global operations now must navigate ESG requirements in Europe, emerging regulations in Japan, and proposed rules in various U.S. states. Rather than maintaining separate reporting systems, Toyota has invested in a unified ESG data platform that can adapt to different regulatory requirements while maintaining consistency across all markets.

Business Case for ESG Excellence Beyond Compliance

The business case for ESG excellence extends far beyond avoiding regulatory penalties. The global focus on sustainable practices has reshaped industries, making ESG jobs essential for finance professionals, corporate governance, and risk management. Companies that view ESG reporting as merely a compliance exercise miss significant value creation opportunities.

Research consistently shows that companies with strong ESG performance enjoy several competitive advantages. They attract and retain top talent more effectively, particularly among younger workers who prioritize purpose-driven employers. They access capital more easily as investors increasingly incorporate ESG factors into their allocation decisions. They build stronger stakeholder relationships that provide resilience during challenging periods.

The financial services firm BlackRock exemplifies this strategic approach. Rather than treating ESG as a separate function, BlackRock integrated sustainability considerations into its core investment processes. This integration allowed the firm to identify new investment opportunities, manage risks more effectively, and meet growing client demand for sustainable investment options. The result has been significant business growth in BlackRock's sustainable investing division.

The energy company Ørsted demonstrates how ESG excellence can transform an entire business model. Originally a fossil fuel-focused utility, Ørsted recognized that the energy transition represented both a regulatory requirement and a massive business opportunity. The company systematically transformed its operations to focus on offshore wind energy, becoming a global leader in renewable energy development. This transformation required excellent ESG reporting to track progress and communicate value to stakeholders.

Consider also the consumer goods company Unilever's Sustainable Living Plan. This initiative went beyond compliance by setting ambitious sustainability targets that required fundamental changes to the company's operations. The plan demanded sophisticated ESG measurement and reporting systems to track progress across dozens of environmental and social metrics. However, the business benefits included improved operational efficiency, stronger brand loyalty, and access to new markets focused on sustainable products.

Career Opportunities in ESG Certification

The demand for ESG professionals has exploded as companies scramble to meet new reporting requirements and build sustainable business practices. In recent years, the ESG job market witnessed a 223% spike in demand. This growth creates exceptional opportunities for professionals who invest in ESG expertise.

ESG careers aren't confined to specific industries; they permeate diverse sectors, including finance, technology, energy, retail, healthcare, and manufacturing. The breadth of opportunities means that professionals from virtually any background can build ESG careers by developing the right skills and certifications.

The salary prospects reflect the high demand for ESG expertise. ESG investment analysts often collaborate with traditional financial analysts to provide a comprehensive view of investment opportunities across diverse sectors. These roles typically command premium salaries due to the specialized knowledge required and the scarcity of qualified professionals.

Over 85% of executives, supervisors, and HR professionals agree that certified individuals bring value, gain credibility, and are seen as top performers. This recognition translates into career advancement opportunities for professionals who invest in formal ESG education and certification.

The Corporate Finance Institute has responded to this demand by developing specialized ESG certification programs. CFI's curriculum includes 14 courses covering finance, reporting, investing, and business strategy. This is an ideal ESG certification for individuals looking to gain practical, real-world skills that will translate to roles at top global institutions.

For professionals considering ESG careers, the timing couldn't be better. Companies need ESG analysts to interpret regulatory requirements, sustainability managers to develop and implement ESG strategies, and ESG consultants to guide transformation efforts. The skills developed through ESG certification programs—data analysis, stakeholder engagement, regulatory compliance, and strategic thinking—transfer well across industries and functions.

How to Use This Book Effectively

This book provides a systematic approach to mastering the three most important ESG frameworks currently shaping corporate reporting: CSRD, GRI, and SASB. Each framework serves different purposes and audiences, but together they form the foundation of modern ESG reporting.

Begin by reading the foundational chapters to understand the ESG ecosystem and develop your competency framework. These chapters provide context that will help you understand why specific requirements exist and how they connect to broader business objectives.

Next, work through each framework section systematically. Don't try to master all three simultaneously—instead, focus on the framework most relevant to your immediate needs. If you work for a European company or a multinational with EU operations, start with CSRD. If you're in investment management, begin with SASB. If you need broad sustainability reporting knowledge, start with GRI.

Use the practical tools and templates provided throughout the book. These resources help translate theoretical knowledge into actionable skills. Complete the exercises and assessments to test your understanding and identify areas that need additional study.

Finally, stay engaged with the evolving regulatory environment. ESG requirements change rapidly as regulators respond to new challenges and stakeholder demands. Use the book's framework to understand new developments rather than simply memorizing current requirements.

The investment in ESG expertise pays dividends throughout your career. Over 75% of CFI learners report improved productivity or competency within weeks. This improvement comes from understanding how ESG factors influence business performance and learning to identify opportunities and risks that others might miss.

Key Insights to Remember

1. **Mandatory Reporting is Here**: The era of voluntary ESG reporting has ended, with regulatory requirements now affecting tens of thousands of companies globally.

2. **Global Convergence Creates Opportunities**: Regulatory alignment across jurisdictions enables unified reporting systems and comparable data for investors.
3. **ESG Excellence Drives Business Value**: Companies that exceed compliance requirements often discover competitive advantages in talent attraction, capital access, and stakeholder relationships.
4. **Career Prospects are Exceptional**: The ESG job market has grown 223% in recent years, creating opportunities across all industries and functional areas.
5. **Systematic Learning Accelerates Success**: A structured approach to mastering ESG frameworks builds practical skills that translate directly to career advancement.

Chapter 2: Understanding the ESG Ecosystem

The ESG ecosystem operates like a complex web of interconnected relationships, data flows, and stakeholder expectations. Understanding this ecosystem becomes crucial as companies navigate the transition from traditional financial reporting to integrated sustainability disclosure. The complexity emerges not from any single component, but from how environmental, social, and governance factors interact with business operations, stakeholder demands, and regulatory requirements.

Consider how Apple's supply chain ESG monitoring system illustrates this complexity. The company doesn't just track its own environmental impact—it monitors carbon emissions, labor practices, and governance standards across hundreds of suppliers in dozens of countries. Each supplier's performance affects Apple's overall ESG rating, which influences investor decisions, customer loyalty, and regulatory compliance. This interconnectedness exemplifies the modern ESG ecosystem.

Stakeholder Theory and Materiality Concepts

Stakeholder theory provides the foundation for understanding why ESG matters in business decision-making. Unlike traditional shareholder-focused models that prioritize financial returns above all else, stakeholder theory recognizes that businesses create value for multiple groups: employees, customers, suppliers, communities, and the environment itself.

The application of stakeholder theory to ESG requires understanding how different groups define value and success. Employees might prioritize workplace safety and diversity initiatives. Customers may focus on product environmental impact and ethical sourcing. Investors increasingly evaluate long-term sustainability risks alongside financial performance. Communities care about local environmental impact and economic development.

Materiality connects stakeholder concerns to business priorities by identifying which ESG issues significantly affect business operations or stakeholder decisions. Central to the debate on global alignment is materiality. In the one camp, broadly speaking, sit the SEC and the ISSB. They both support a materiality assessment based on the potential effect on the company's enterprise value. This approach focuses on how ESG issues influence financial performance.

The pharmaceutical industry provides a clear example of stakeholder theory in action. When Merck develops new medications, the company must balance multiple stakeholder interests. Patients need affordable, effective treatments. Shareholders expect profitable returns on research investments. Regulators require safety and efficacy data. Environmental groups monitor manufacturing impact. Each stakeholder group's concerns contribute to materiality assessments that guide ESG strategy.

Material risks and opportunities are generally derived from the impacts and dependencies on natural, human and social resources. In addition, for most material impacts, a material risk and/or opportunity may emerge over time. This temporal dimension means that materiality assessments must consider both current stakeholder concerns and emerging issues that may become significant in the future.

The technology sector demonstrates how stakeholder priorities can shift rapidly. Five years ago, data privacy received limited attention in tech company ESG reports. Today, it represents a material issue affecting customer trust, regulatory compliance, and business operations. Companies that anticipated this shift through robust stakeholder engagement were better prepared for privacy regulations like GDPR and CCPA.

Double Materiality Explained

Double materiality describes how a business impacts, and is impacted by, the environment. Traditional "single materiality" focuses only on how sustainability issues affect a company's financial performance and value. The double materiality concept represents a fundamental shift in how companies assess ESG significance.

Under the double materiality concept, a sustainability matter can be material from an impact point of view and/or from a risk and opportunity perspective. This bidirectional approach requires companies to evaluate both outside-in effects (how environmental and social issues affect business performance) and inside-out effects (how business operations affect environmental and social systems).

Financial materiality examines traditional business impacts. Climate change might disrupt supply chains, increase raw material costs, or create new market opportunities for sustainable products. Social issues like workforce diversity might affect talent recruitment and retention. Governance failures might trigger regulatory penalties or damage brand reputation.

Impact materiality focuses on how business operations affect external systems. A manufacturing company's carbon emissions contribute to climate change regardless of immediate financial consequences. A retailer's sourcing practices might support or undermine human rights in developing countries. A financial institution's lending decisions might promote or hinder sustainable development.

This assessment requires viewing materiality from two perspectives. Financial materiality: This "outside in" view focuses on how sustainability matters may pose either a prospective material risk or opportunity that could affect a company's financial performance and position over the short, medium and long term.

Consider IKEA's approach to forest sourcing as an example of double materiality in practice. From a financial materiality perspective, sustainable forestry practices affect IKEA's raw material costs, brand reputation, and regulatory compliance. From an impact materiality perspective, IKEA's sourcing decisions influence deforestation rates, biodiversity protection, and community livelihoods in forest regions. Both perspectives are material and require disclosure under CSRD requirements.

Impact materiality: This "inside out" view focuses on the actual or potential short, medium and long-term impacts on people or the environment that are directly linked to a company's operations and its value chain. This perspective requires companies to understand their role in broader environmental and social systems.

The automotive industry illustrates double materiality complexity. Electric vehicle manufacturers like Tesla must consider both how battery mining affects local communities (impact materiality) and how mineral price volatility affects production costs (financial materiality). Both perspectives influence investment decisions, regulatory responses, and stakeholder relationships.

Banks face similar double materiality challenges with lending decisions. Supporting fossil fuel projects might generate short-term profits (financial materiality) while contributing to climate change (impact materiality). These competing considerations require sophisticated analysis to determine overall materiality and appropriate disclosure.

Relationship Between ESG Ratings, Rankings, and Reporting

ESG ratings and rankings create a feedback loop with corporate reporting that influences investor decisions, stakeholder perceptions, and business strategy. Understanding this relationship helps companies optimize their ESG communication and performance.

ESG rating agencies like MSCI, Sustainalytics, and S&P Global use company-reported data to evaluate ESG performance. However, these agencies also consider external data sources, regulatory filings, news reports, and stakeholder feedback. The result is that reported ESG data represents only one input into rating methodologies.

The relationship between reporting and ratings creates several dynamics. Companies that provide detailed, transparent ESG data often receive better ratings because rating agencies have more information to evaluate. However, comprehensive reporting might also reveal negative information that hurts ratings. This tension encourages companies to balance transparency with strategic communication.

Consider the experience of ExxonMobil, which historically provided limited ESG disclosure. As investor pressure mounted, the company began publishing detailed sustainability reports and engaging more actively with ESG rating agencies. While this transparency revealed challenges in the company's energy transition strategy, it also demonstrated management attention to ESG issues and improved the quality of ESG analysis.

The technology company Microsoft illustrates how strategic ESG reporting can influence ratings and investor perceptions. Microsoft's detailed climate reporting includes scope 1, 2, and 3 emissions data, carbon reduction targets, and progress metrics. This transparency enables rating agencies to assess the company's climate strategy accurately and provides investors with data needed for ESG-focused portfolios.

Rating methodologies vary significantly across agencies, creating challenges for companies trying to optimize their ESG performance. MSCI emphasizes relative performance within industry groups, while Sustainalytics focuses on absolute ESG risks. S&P Global considers both current performance and future outlook. These differences mean that companies might receive varying ratings from different agencies based on the same ESG data.

The influence of ESG ratings extends beyond investment decisions. Companies increasingly use ESG ratings in executive compensation, supplier evaluation, and strategic planning. High ESG ratings can reduce financing costs, improve customer loyalty, and attract top talent. Poor ratings might trigger stakeholder engagement, regulatory scrutiny, or activist investor attention.

Integration with Financial Reporting

The integration of ESG and financial reporting represents one of the most significant changes in corporate disclosure. The CSRD and ESRS are closely interlinked, but they serve different purposes. The CSRD sets the legal framework of the reporting directive. The ESRS, on the other hand, establishes common guidelines for the disclosure of ESG information and serves as the foundation for auditors to provide credible assurance.

This integration requires companies to demonstrate how ESG factors affect financial performance and business strategy. Climate risks might influence asset valuations, depreciation schedules, and impairment assessments. Social factors might affect workforce costs, productivity metrics, and market access. Governance issues might influence risk management, internal controls, and stakeholder relations.

The insurance industry exemplifies successful ESG-financial integration. Companies like AXA and Allianz integrate climate risk analysis into their underwriting processes, investment decisions, and financial reporting. Climate change affects both sides of insurance business models—increasing claims from extreme weather events while creating investment risks in climate-vulnerable assets.

The CSRD also embraces "double materiality," which requires that companies report information necessary to understand how sustainability matters affect their business development and performance and the impact they have on a range of sustainability matters. This integration ensures that ESG information connects directly to business strategy and financial performance.

The energy sector demonstrates the complexity of ESG-financial integration. Oil and gas companies must consider how carbon pricing, stranded asset risks, and energy transition policies affect their financial statements. Companies like Shell and BP have written down billions of dollars in fossil fuel assets while investing heavily in renewable energy projects. These decisions require sophisticated analysis of ESG factors and their financial implications.

Financial institutions face unique integration challenges because their ESG impacts occur primarily through lending, investing, and underwriting activities. Banks like JPMorgan Chase and Bank of America have committed to net-zero financing goals that require fundamental changes to credit policies, risk management, and business strategy. These commitments affect loan portfolio composition, capital allocation, and financial performance.

Technology and Data Management Foundations

Technology infrastructure provides the foundation for effective ESG reporting and management. Many companies captured in new reporting requirements, such as ISSB and CSRD, won't have gone through an assurance process before, engaged with an audit firm to scrutinise their data or have robust data-collection processes in place. For these regulations, Excel simply won't work.

ESG data management requires systems that can collect, validate, analyze, and report information from across global operations and value chains. Unlike financial data, which follows standardized accounting principles, ESG data comes in multiple formats from various sources with different quality levels and verification standards.

The complexity of ESG data management becomes apparent when examining scope 3 emissions reporting. Companies must collect greenhouse gas data from potentially thousands of suppliers, customers, and business partners. This data must be converted to consistent units, validated for accuracy, and aggregated to calculate total value chain emissions. The process requires automated systems that can handle data quality issues and provide audit trails for verification.

Software platforms like Workiva, Diligent, and specialized ESG solutions have emerged to address these challenges. These platforms integrate with existing enterprise systems to automate data collection, provide workflow management for ESG reporting processes, and enable collaboration between different departments and external stakeholders.

Consider how Walmart approaches ESG data management for its sustainability goals. The company collects environmental data from thousands of stores, distribution centers, and transportation providers. Social metrics come from employee surveys, community programs, and supplier assessments. Governance data includes board composition, executive compensation, and compliance metrics. Walmart's technology platform aggregates this information to track progress against sustainability targets and prepare regulatory reports.

The automotive manufacturer BMW demonstrates advanced ESG data management through its integrated sustainability reporting system. The platform connects production data with environmental impact metrics, supplier ESG assessments with procurement decisions, and employee satisfaction surveys with human capital reporting. This integration enables BMW to understand connections between ESG performance and business operations.

Artificial intelligence and machine learning increasingly support ESG data management by automating data collection, identifying anomalies, and predicting future trends. These technologies help companies process large volumes of unstructured ESG data from news sources, social media, and stakeholder feedback to supplement traditional reporting metrics.

Moving Forward in the ESG Ecosystem

Understanding the ESG ecosystem requires recognizing that environmental, social, and governance factors don't operate in isolation. They interact with each other, influence business performance, and respond to stakeholder pressures in complex ways. Companies that master this complexity gain competitive advantages through better risk management, stronger stakeholder relationships, and more effective resource allocation.

The successful navigation of this ecosystem demands sophisticated thinking about stakeholder needs, materiality assessments, data management, and strategic integration. Companies must move beyond compliance to create value through ESG excellence. This requires investment in people, processes, and technology that support continuous improvement in ESG performance.

The foundation built through understanding the ESG ecosystem prepares companies for the specific requirements of individual frameworks like CSRD, GRI, and SASB. Each framework reflects different aspects of the ecosystem while contributing to the overall goal of transparent, comparable, and useful ESG disclosure.

Closing Thoughts

The ESG ecosystem will continue evolving as stakeholder expectations change, regulatory requirements expand, and business practices adapt. Companies that invest time in understanding these fundamental dynamics will be better positioned to navigate future changes and capture emerging opportunities. The complexity of the ecosystem shouldn't discourage engagement—instead, it should motivate systematic learning and strategic thinking about how ESG factors create value for businesses and society.

Key Insights to Remember

1. **Stakeholder Theory Drives ESG Strategy**: Understanding diverse stakeholder needs and concerns provides the foundation for effective ESG strategy and reporting.
2. **Double Materiality Requires Bidirectional Thinking**: Companies must assess both how ESG issues affect business performance and how business operations affect environmental and social systems.
3. **ESG Ratings Influence Multiple Business Outcomes**: The relationship between reporting, ratings, and business performance creates incentives for transparency and continuous improvement.

4. **Integration with Financial Reporting is Essential**: ESG factors must connect clearly to business strategy, risk management, and financial performance to provide value to stakeholders.
5. **Technology Infrastructure Enables Success**: Robust data management systems are essential for collecting, validating, and reporting ESG information at the scale and quality required by modern stakeholders.

Chapter 3: Building Your ESG Competency Framework

The development of ESG competencies requires a systematic approach that builds from foundational knowledge to advanced application skills. Think of ESG competency development like learning a new language—you start with basic vocabulary and grammar, then progress to complex communication and nuanced interpretation. The difference is that ESG competency directly influences business outcomes, career progression, and organizational success.

Professional competency frameworks provide structure for this development process. They define the knowledge, skills, and abilities required for success while creating pathways for continuous learning and advancement. In the rapidly evolving ESG field, these frameworks help professionals stay current with changing regulations, emerging best practices, and stakeholder expectations.

Core Skills for ESG Professionals

ESG professionals need a unique combination of technical knowledge, analytical skills, and stakeholder management capabilities. The technical foundation includes understanding regulatory requirements, measurement methodologies, and reporting standards. However, technical knowledge alone isn't sufficient—ESG professionals must also interpret complex data, communicate with diverse stakeholders, and influence organizational change.

Data analysis and interpretation represent core competencies for ESG professionals. ESG data analysts are responsible for collecting, processing, and analyzing vast amounts of ESG-related data. This role is crucial across various organizations, including corporations, financial institutions, investment firms, and regulatory bodies, as the demand for reliable and comparable ESG data continues to grow.

The analytical skills required go beyond basic data manipulation. ESG professionals must understand statistical concepts, identify trends and patterns, and translate complex information into actionable insights. They need to work with both quantitative metrics (like carbon emissions and diversity ratios) and qualitative assessments (like governance effectiveness and stakeholder satisfaction).

Consider the skills required for carbon footprint analysis. ESG professionals must understand greenhouse gas accounting principles, emission factor databases, and verification standards. They need to collect activity data from multiple sources, apply appropriate calculation methodologies, and identify opportunities for emission reductions. The analysis must then be communicated to technical teams, executives, and external stakeholders in formats appropriate for each audience.

Stakeholder engagement skills are equally important for ESG success. The objective of stakeholder engagement is to understand how people may be impacted by the organization and to get input and feedback on (material) sustainability matters. Effective stakeholder engagement requires understanding different groups' priorities, communication preferences, and decision-making processes.

ESG professionals must engage with internal stakeholders (executives, employees, and board members) and external groups (investors, customers, communities, and NGOs). Each group brings different perspectives, concerns, and expectations to ESG issues. Successful engagement requires adapting communication style, technical depth, and focus areas to match stakeholder needs.

The pharmaceutical industry illustrates stakeholder engagement complexity. ESG professionals at companies like Novartis must engage with patients and patient advocacy groups about drug access and pricing. They work with investors on long-term sustainability strategy. They collaborate with suppliers on responsible sourcing practices. They communicate with regulators about compliance and transparency. Each engagement requires different skills and approaches.

Strategic thinking capabilities distinguish senior ESG professionals from entry-level analysts. ESG strategy requires understanding business models, competitive dynamics, and industry trends. Professionals must identify how ESG factors create risks and opportunities, develop action plans to address material issues, and measure progress against strategic objectives.

ESG investment analysts evaluate companies and investment opportunities through an ESG lens, assessing how these factors may impact financial performance and long-term sustainability. This evaluation requires understanding how ESG factors interact with traditional business drivers like revenue growth, cost management, and capital allocation.

Project management skills enable ESG professionals to implement complex initiatives across organizational boundaries. ESG projects often involve multiple departments, external partners, and lengthy timelines. Professionals must coordinate resources, manage competing priorities, and deliver results despite organizational complexity.

Consider the project management skills required for CSRD implementation. ESG professionals must assess current reporting capabilities, identify data gaps, design new collection processes, train staff across multiple locations, and coordinate with external auditors. The project involves legal, finance, operations, and communications teams while meeting strict regulatory deadlines.

Certification Pathways and Career Progression

The ESG certification landscape offers multiple pathways for professional development, each targeting different career goals and expertise areas. The Sustainable Investing Certificate builds foundational knowledge and a broad understanding of the issues across topics including environmental, social, and governance (ESG) factors. Understanding these pathways helps professionals choose appropriate certifications for their career objectives.

CFA Institute: Offers resources, webinars, and publications related to ESG investing and sustainability. The CFA Institute's sustainable investing certificate (formerly ESG Investing Certificate) provides credibility for investment professionals integrating ESG factors into financial analysis and portfolio management.

Investment professionals who want to learn more about how to analyze and integrate material ESG factors into their day-to-day roles. Professionals working in front or back offices and adjacent roles, including sales and distribution, wealth management, product development, financial advice, consulting, and risk benefit from this certification.

The Corporate Finance Institute offers specialized ESG training focused on practical business applications. CFI's curriculum includes 14 courses covering finance, reporting, investing, and business strategy. This is an ideal ESG certification for individuals looking to gain practical, real-world skills that will translate to roles at top global institutions.

Different certifications serve different career goals. Investment professionals typically pursue CFA Institute credentials to demonstrate expertise in ESG integration for portfolio management and security analysis. Corporate sustainability professionals often choose broader certifications that cover reporting, strategy, and stakeholder engagement. Consultants might select specialized certifications in specific frameworks like GRI or SASB.

Career progression in ESG typically follows several pathways. Entry-level positions include ESG analyst, sustainability coordinator, and junior consultant roles. These positions focus on data collection, basic analysis, and project support. Mid-level roles include ESG manager, sustainability strategy lead, and senior analyst positions that involve strategy development, stakeholder engagement, and team leadership.

Senior ESG positions include Chief Sustainability Officer, ESG investment director, and sustainability consulting partner roles. These positions require strategic thinking, organizational leadership, and external relationship management. They often involve board-level reporting, investor relations, and industry thought leadership.

ESG certifications such as the CFA ESG Certificate and the GARP SCR Certificate equip investment practitioners with the skills to navigate complex sustainability challenges and align with governance factors. The progression through these certifications can accelerate career advancement by demonstrating expertise and commitment to professional development.

Consider the career progression of a sustainability professional at a major bank. Starting as an ESG analyst, they might earn a foundational ESG certificate while supporting sustainable finance initiatives. Moving to ESG manager, they could pursue specialized training in climate risk assessment and sustainable finance frameworks. Advancing to ESG director, they might complete executive education in sustainability strategy and stakeholder engagement.

Creating Organizational ESG Capabilities

Building organizational ESG capabilities requires more than individual training—it demands systematic development of processes, systems, and culture that support sustainable business practices. Organizations must assess current capabilities, identify gaps, and create development plans that align with business strategy and stakeholder expectations.

ESG capability assessment begins with understanding current organizational strengths and weaknesses across different ESG domains. Environmental capabilities might include energy management, waste reduction, and supply chain sustainability. Social capabilities could cover workforce diversity, community engagement, and human rights protection. Governance capabilities might encompass board oversight, risk management, and ethical business practices.

The assessment process should examine both technical capabilities (data systems, measurement processes, reporting mechanisms) and soft capabilities (leadership commitment, employee engagement, stakeholder relationships). This comprehensive view identifies priority areas for capability development and investment.

Consider how IBM approached ESG capability development during its sustainability transformation. The company started by assessing existing environmental programs, social impact initiatives, and governance structures. The assessment revealed strong technical capabilities in environmental management but gaps in social impact measurement and stakeholder engagement. IBM then developed targeted capability-building programs to address these gaps.

Capability development requires investment in people, processes, and technology. People development includes training existing staff, hiring specialized talent, and engaging external expertise. Process development involves creating new workflows, updating policies, and establishing governance structures. Technology development might include implementing ESG management systems, upgrading data collection capabilities, and integrating with existing business systems.

The pharmaceutical company Merck demonstrates systematic capability building through its sustainability program. The company invested in ESG training for employees across all functions, not just sustainability teams. They developed new processes for integrating ESG considerations into business decisions. They implemented technology platforms that support data collection, analysis, and reporting across global operations.

Organizational culture plays a crucial role in ESG capability development. Technical systems and processes can't succeed without cultural support that values sustainability, transparency, and stakeholder engagement. Building this culture requires leadership commitment, employee engagement, and alignment with organizational values and incentives.

The retailer Target illustrates how culture supports ESG capabilities. The company's commitment to diversity and inclusion goes beyond compliance requirements to create a culture that values different perspectives and experiences. This cultural foundation supports Target's ability to engage diverse stakeholders, understand community needs, and develop inclusive business practices.

Change Management for Sustainability Transformation

Sustainability transformation often requires fundamental changes to business models, operational processes, and organizational culture. Change management principles help organizations navigate these transformations while maintaining business performance and stakeholder support.

ESG transformation typically faces several common challenges. Resistance might come from employees who don't understand sustainability benefits or fear changes to their roles. Resource constraints might limit investment in new systems and processes. Technical complexity might overwhelm organizations without specialized expertise. Stakeholder skepticism might question the authenticity or effectiveness of transformation efforts.

Successful change management addresses these challenges through clear communication, stakeholder engagement, and systematic implementation. Communication should explain why transformation is necessary, what changes will occur, and how different groups will be affected. Stakeholder engagement should involve employees, customers, investors, and communities in planning and implementation processes.

The energy company Ørsted provides an exemplary case of sustainability transformation and change management. Originally a fossil fuel utility, Ørsted transformed into a global leader in offshore wind energy. This transformation required fundamental changes to business strategy, technical capabilities, and organizational culture.

Ørsted's change management approach included several key elements. Leadership provided clear vision and commitment to renewable energy transition. The company invested heavily in employee training and development to build new technical capabilities. They engaged stakeholders throughout the transformation to maintain support and credibility. They celebrated early wins to build momentum and demonstrate progress.

The automotive industry faces similar transformation challenges as companies shift toward electric vehicles and sustainable mobility. Tesla pioneered this transformation, but traditional manufacturers like General Motors and Volkswagen now follow similar paths. These transformations require changing manufacturing processes, developing new supply chains, and retraining workers for different production requirements.

Change management for ESG transformation must also address external stakeholder concerns. Investors need confidence that transformation efforts will create long-term value. Customers need assurance that sustainability initiatives won't compromise product quality or service levels. Communities need evidence that transformation efforts will benefit local economic and environmental conditions.

The success of sustainability transformation depends on systematic planning, consistent execution, and continuous adaptation. Organizations must set clear goals, measure progress regularly, and adjust strategies based on results and changing conditions. This requires robust project management, performance monitoring, and stakeholder feedback systems.

Self-Assessment: Your ESG Readiness Scorecard

Personal ESG readiness assessment helps professionals identify strengths, gaps, and development priorities. This assessment should cover technical knowledge, practical skills, and professional experience across different ESG domains. Regular self-assessment supports continuous learning and career planning in the rapidly evolving ESG field.

Technical knowledge assessment should evaluate understanding of key frameworks, regulations, and standards. This includes familiarity with CSRD, GRI, SASB, and other relevant frameworks. It should assess knowledge of measurement methodologies, data quality standards, and reporting requirements. The assessment should also cover understanding of industry-specific ESG issues and best practices.

Rate your current knowledge in each area on a scale of 1-5, where 1 represents basic awareness and 5 represents expert-level understanding. Focus on frameworks most relevant to your industry and career goals, but maintain basic familiarity with all major standards.

For environmental knowledge, assess your understanding of climate science, greenhouse gas accounting, renewable energy, waste management, and biodiversity protection. For social knowledge, evaluate your knowledge of human rights, labor standards, diversity and inclusion, community engagement, and stakeholder relations. For governance knowledge, consider your understanding of board oversight, risk management, business ethics, compliance systems, and transparency requirements.

Practical skills assessment should evaluate your ability to apply ESG knowledge in real-world situations. This includes data collection and analysis capabilities, stakeholder engagement experience, project management skills, and communication abilities. Consider your experience with ESG software platforms, reporting processes, and verification procedures.

Assess your data analysis skills including statistical analysis, data visualization, and trend identification. Evaluate your stakeholder engagement experience across different groups and communication channels. Consider your project management experience with ESG initiatives, cross-functional teams, and external partnerships.

Professional experience assessment should consider your current role, industry background, and career trajectory. This includes your exposure to ESG issues, leadership experience, and external recognition. Consider the size and complexity of organizations where you've worked and the scope of ESG challenges you've addressed.

Document specific ESG projects you've led or supported, including objectives, scope, outcomes, and lessons learned. Identify gaps between your current capabilities and requirements for target roles or responsibilities. Develop action plans to address priority gaps through training, certification, experience, or mentoring.

The assessment should also consider soft skills that support ESG success. These include critical thinking, problem-solving, creativity, emotional intelligence, and cultural awareness. ESG professionals often work with diverse stakeholders on complex, ambiguous issues that require these broader capabilities.

Use assessment results to create a personal development plan that aligns with your career goals and market opportunities. Prioritize areas where you can achieve the greatest impact with available time and resources. Consider both formal learning opportunities (certifications, courses, conferences) and experiential learning (projects, mentoring, volunteering).

Update your assessment regularly as your knowledge and experience grow. The ESG field evolves rapidly, so continuous learning and adaptation are essential for long-term success. Use the assessment to track progress, identify emerging gaps, and adjust development priorities based on changing market conditions and career goals.

Summary Reflections

Building ESG competency requires systematic development of technical knowledge, practical skills, and professional experience. The investment in ESG expertise pays dividends through career advancement, organizational impact, and contribution to sustainable development. Success requires understanding current capabilities, setting clear development goals, and committing to continuous learning in this dynamic field.

The competency framework provides structure for this development while maintaining flexibility to adapt to changing requirements and opportunities. Whether you're beginning an ESG career or advancing to senior leadership, the principles of systematic capability building, stakeholder engagement, and change management support success across different roles and industries.

Key Insights to Remember

1. **Core Skills Span Technical and Soft Competencies**: ESG professionals need data analysis, stakeholder engagement, strategic thinking, and project management capabilities to succeed.
2. **Multiple Certification Pathways Serve Different Goals**: Choose certifications based on career objectives, industry focus, and current expertise levels to maximize development impact.
3. **Organizational Capabilities Require Systematic Development**: Building ESG capabilities demands investment in people, processes, and technology supported by appropriate organizational culture.
4. **Change Management Enables Transformation Success**: Sustainability transformation requires careful planning, stakeholder engagement, and systematic implementation to overcome resistance and achieve goals.
5. **Regular Self-Assessment Supports Continuous Development**: Personal readiness assessment helps

identify strengths, gaps, and development priorities while tracking progress toward career goals.

Chapter 4: CSRD Fundamentals and Scope

The corporate world stood at a crossroads in 2022 when the European Commission adopted what would become the most significant sustainability reporting regulation in business history. The Corporate Sustainability Reporting Directive (CSRD) was published in the Official Journal on 16 December 2022, entering into force 20 days after publication. This wasn't just another regulatory update—it represented a fundamental shift in how businesses must account for their impact on society and the environment.

Understanding the CSRD requires grasping its ambitious scope and the regulatory changes that continue to reshape its implementation. On February 26, 2025, the European Commission published its Omnibus Simplification Package with proposed amendments to the Corporate Sustainability Reporting Directive. These developments show how dynamic this regulatory environment remains, making it essential for businesses to understand both current requirements and emerging changes.

Legislative Background and Objectives

The CSRD emerged from the European Commission's recognition that existing sustainability reporting was fundamentally inadequate. Before the CSRD, the Non-Financial Reporting Directive (NFRD) established the reporting principles for large companies. However, the European Commission discovered that the information reported by companies was insufficient: "Reports often omit information that investors and other stakeholders think is important".

The legislative foundation builds on the European Green Deal's ambitious climate goals. The Green Deal is the new growth strategy of the Union. It aims to transform the Union into a modern, resource-efficient and competitive economy with no net emissions of greenhouse gases (GHG) by 2050. This context explains why the CSRD goes far beyond simple disclosure requirements to drive fundamental business transformation.

The Commission's Action Plan on Sustainable Finance provided the strategic framework for the CSRD. In its Communication of 8 March 2018 entitled 'Action Plan: Financing Sustainable Growth', the Commission set out measures to achieve the following objectives: reorient capital flows towards sustainable investment in order to achieve sustainable and inclusive growth, manage financial risks stemming from climate change, resource depletion, environmental degradation and social issues, and foster transparency and long-termism in financial and economic activity.

Consider how Unilever approached the transition from NFRD to CSRD requirements. The company had been publishing sustainability reports for over a decade under the NFRD framework, but discovered that their existing reporting didn't meet the new double materiality requirements. Unilever needed to completely redesign their data collection systems to capture both how climate change affects their business operations and how their operations impact global climate systems. This required new partnerships with suppliers, enhanced monitoring systems across their value chain, and sophisticated data analytics capabilities.

The pharmaceutical giant Novartis faced similar challenges during CSRD preparation. Their existing sustainability reporting focused primarily on environmental metrics like energy consumption and waste reduction. However, CSRD requirements demanded detailed disclosure about social impacts including patient access to medicines, clinical trial diversity, and supply chain labor practices. Novartis invested over €15 million in new data systems and hired 40 additional sustainability professionals to meet these expanded requirements.

The automotive manufacturer BMW provides another instructive example of CSRD transformation. The company's existing sustainability reporting under NFRD covered factory operations and product lifecycle assessments. CSRD requirements expanded this scope to include detailed reporting on raw material sourcing, dealer network sustainability practices, and end-of-life vehicle recycling. BMW created cross-functional teams spanning procurement, manufacturing, sales, and recycling operations to gather the necessary data and coordinate reporting across their entire value chain.

Scope Determination and Thresholds

The CSRD's scope represents one of the most significant expansions in corporate reporting requirements in European history. Starting in the financial year 2024 (and reporting in 2025) Compliance is mandated for organizations (or 'entities') already mandated to comply with the NFRD. This includes all organizations listed in an EU-regulated market with 500 or more employees. However, recent proposals have dramatically altered these thresholds.

The 2025 Omnibus changes have fundamentally reshaped CSRD scope requirements. Under the new proposal, only companies with 1,000+ employees and €50 million+ turnover must report. This is an 80% reduction in mandatory coverage. These changes reflect ongoing political tensions between sustainability ambitions and business competitiveness concerns.

The original CSRD thresholds created broad coverage across European businesses. In the past, the balance sheet limit was €20 million, the net turnover limit was €40 million, and the employee count limit was 250. These adjustments are expected to lower the number of companies classified as significant from 82,986 to 71,372. The Omnibus proposals would reduce this number even further.

The EC launched the Omnibus sustainability rules simplification package on 26 February 2025. This is the first step of an ambitious simplification agenda to enhance European economic competitiveness. It aims to reduce administrative and reporting burdens on companies and unlocking businesses' investment potential. This represents a significant policy shift responding to business concerns about regulatory burden.

For listed small and medium enterprises, the changes are particularly dramatic. Listed SMEs were previously within CSRD's scope, with simplified reporting standards. Under the Omnibus, all SMEs (listed or not) become out of scope for mandatory reporting. This change eliminates reporting requirements for thousands of smaller European companies.

The practical implications of these threshold changes vary significantly by industry and business model. Technology companies often exceed the employee thresholds while maintaining relatively modest physical assets. Manufacturing companies typically meet asset and turnover thresholds with fewer employees. Service companies may fall above or below the new thresholds depending on their specific business model and geographic footprint.

Consider the impact on different company types. A software company with 1,200 employees and €60 million turnover would remain in scope under the Omnibus proposals. However, a family-owned manufacturing business with 800 employees but €75 million turnover would be excluded from mandatory reporting despite its significant environmental footprint. This creates potential inconsistencies in coverage based on business model rather than actual sustainability impact.

Timeline and Phased Implementation

The CSRD implementation follows a carefully structured timeline designed to allow companies adequate preparation time while ensuring regulatory objectives are met. Companies already subject to the NFRD must begin reporting in 2025 on their 2024 financial year. This aggressive timeline reflects the urgency of climate action and sustainability transformation.

The original implementation schedule created a predictable rollout across different company categories. For companies not previously subject to NFRD, such as listed small and medium-sized enterprises or those outside of the EU, the directive will apply for fiscal years starting on or after January 1, 2026. However, recent developments have significantly altered these timelines.

On April 3rd 2025, the EU Commission voted to postpone CSRD compliance by two years for all companies, except for those in the first wave of the previous NFRD. This vote related to the "stop-the-clock" proposal. This postponement provides additional preparation time but creates uncertainty for companies already investing in compliance systems.

The revised timeline now includes these key phases:

First wave companies continue reporting as originally planned. First wave: Companies that were already reporting under the NFRD (i.e., large listed companies and public-interest entities with over 500 employees) still need to report according to CSRD as planned for FY2024 (in 2025). These companies cannot benefit from the delay and must maintain their implementation schedules.

Second wave companies receive a two-year extension. Second wave: Large companies with more than 250 employees that previously needed to report in 2026 (FY 2025) will now report in 2028 (FY 2027). This change affects thousands of European companies and their global subsidiaries.

Third wave companies also receive extended timelines. Third wave: Listed SMEs that previously needed to report in 2027 (FY 2026) will now report in 2029 (FY 2028). However, many of these companies may be entirely excluded from CSRD scope under the Omnibus proposals.

The implementation timeline creates several practical challenges for businesses. Companies must balance investment in CSRD compliance systems against the uncertainty of changing requirements. Early movers who invested heavily in compliance infrastructure may find their systems over-engineered for simplified requirements. Companies that delayed preparation may struggle to meet even extended deadlines.

The automotive industry provides a clear example of timeline complexity. Volkswagen Group, as a large listed company, must continue with original CSRD implementation timelines. However, many of their European suppliers who were expected to report starting in 2026 now have until 2028, creating coordination challenges across the value chain. Volkswagen needs supplier ESG data to complete their own value chain reporting, but suppliers may lack incentives to accelerate their own compliance preparations.

Extraterritorial Application for Non-EU Companies

The CSRD's extraterritorial reach represents one of the most significant aspects of the regulation for global businesses. Though it's an EU directive, the CSRD also applies to companies based abroad that have a presence in the EU. This means that a hypothetical U.S.-based company with dozens of subsidiaries has to abide by the CSRD if even one of those subsidiaries is in the EU.

The scope of extraterritorial application depends on specific threshold criteria that capture companies with substantial EU operations. Companies in this category, CSRD compliance is required if the company – or any of its their subsidiaries – meet two or more of the following criteria: Have an annual EU revenue exceeding €150 million in each of the last two consecutive financial years, Have an EU branch that generates a net turnover exceeding €40 million, Have an EU subsidiary that meets two or more of specific criteria.

The practical implications for non-EU companies vary significantly based on their European business structure and revenue levels. The directive is aimed at driving change in the business behavior of companies that operate in the EU, which includes US companies with EU subsidiaries that meet certain criteria. This creates compliance obligations for thousands of international companies.

The extraterritorial provision kicks in starting in FY 2028: If you have a branch or subsidiary in Europe with €40M EUR in annual revenue, and you earn €150M EUR in annual revenue from your total operations in Europe, your subsidiary will have to file a report covering its global parent. This timeline provides international companies with additional preparation time compared to EU-based entities.

However, the Omnibus proposals may significantly alter these requirements. These companies must generate, in the EU, at the group level, a net turnover of at least EUR 450 million and have at least one large EU subsidiary. This represents a tripling of the revenue threshold, potentially excluding many international companies from CSRD scope.

Consider the impact on major US technology companies. Microsoft generates well over €450 million in EU revenue and maintains substantial European operations including development centers, sales offices, and data centers. Under both original and proposed CSRD requirements, Microsoft would need to provide CSRD-compliant reporting covering their global operations. The company has invested significantly in sustainability data systems and stakeholder engagement processes to meet these requirements.

Apple presents another instructive case. The company's European operations include retail stores, distribution centers, and significant sales volumes across EU member states. Apple's EU revenue clearly exceeds the extraterritorial thresholds, requiring CSRD compliance. However, Apple's existing sustainability reporting already covers many CSRD requirements, making the compliance transition more manageable than for companies with less mature ESG programs.

Japanese automotive manufacturers like Toyota and Honda face similar extraterritorial requirements due to their substantial European manufacturing and sales operations. These companies must coordinate CSRD reporting with existing sustainability disclosure requirements in Japan and other markets, creating complex multi-jurisdictional compliance challenges.

Key Differences from NFRD

The transformation from NFRD to CSRD represents a fundamental shift in corporate sustainability reporting requirements. Put simply: the EU believes that consumers and investors deserve to know the sustainability impact of businesses, and the CSRD was created because the existing legislation wasn't cutting it. Understanding these differences helps companies appreciate the magnitude of change required for compliance.

The scope expansion represents the most visible difference between NFRD and CSRD. The CSRD notably expands the scope, sustainability disclosures and reporting requirements of its predecessor, the Non-Financial Reporting Directive (NFRD). While NFRD covered approximately 11,000 large companies, CSRD originally planned to cover nearly 50,000 entities across Europe.

Double materiality requirements represent a conceptual shift from NFRD approaches. The CSRD – like the NFRD – requires "double materiality," which means that businesses will have to disclose not only the risks they face from a changing climate, but also the impacts they may cause to the climate and to society. However, CSRD provides much more detailed guidance on implementing double materiality assessments.

Standardization and digitalization requirements differ dramatically between the frameworks. The CSRD will require company sustainability data to be submitted in a standardized digital format. This is meant to provide a clear format for company sustainability reporting – which is currently rife with many idiosyncratic formats – allowing for better understandability and easier comparison between companies.

Assurance requirements under CSRD are more rigorous than NFRD mandates. The CSRD requires a third party to audit and assure the sustainability information and data included in the report. Initially, compliance will require the auditor to provide limited assurance, mainly based on the organization's own statements. NFRD assurance requirements were much less prescriptive and often voluntary.

The reporting location and integration requirements also differ significantly. Under NFRD, companies often published separate sustainability reports with varying formats and timing. CSRD requires integration of sustainability information within management reports, ensuring simultaneous publication with financial information and consistent formatting standards.

Value chain reporting represents another major difference between the frameworks. NFRD focused primarily on direct operations with limited value chain coverage. CSRD requires detailed reporting on upstream and downstream value chain impacts, risks, and opportunities, significantly expanding the scope of data collection and stakeholder engagement required.

Consider how these differences affected Deutsche Bank's reporting transformation. Under NFRD, the bank published an annual sustainability report covering environmental initiatives, community programs, and governance practices. CSRD requirements demanded much more detailed disclosure including climate risk assessments for loan portfolios, biodiversity impact assessments for financing activities, and social impact evaluations for all business lines. The bank invested over €20 million in new data systems and hired 60 additional professionals to meet CSRD requirements.

The CSRD represents a fundamental shift in corporate accountability that extends far beyond European borders. The key objective is to reduce sustainability-related reporting obligations by 25%; for small and medium-sized enterprises ("SMEs"), reductions of up to 35% are envisaged. These ongoing changes demonstrate that CSRD implementation remains a dynamic process requiring continuous attention and adaptation.

Companies must balance investment in compliance infrastructure with the uncertainty of evolving requirements. The Omnibus proposals may reduce immediate compliance burdens, but the underlying trend toward mandatory sustainability reporting continues across global markets. Organizations that develop robust ESG data systems and stakeholder engagement processes will be better positioned for future regulatory developments regardless of specific CSRD requirements.

Essential Takeaways

1. **CSRD Scope Remains Dynamic**: The Omnibus proposals significantly reduce the number of companies required to report, but extraterritorial applications still affect many global businesses.
2. **Timeline Extensions Provide Breathing Room**: The two-year delay for second and third wave companies

allows additional preparation time but creates coordination challenges across value chains.

3. **Extraterritorial Reach Affects Global Companies**: Non-EU companies with substantial European operations face the same reporting requirements as EU-based entities.
4. **Double Materiality Represents Fundamental Change**: Companies must assess both how they impact society and how social issues affect their business performance.
5. **Integration and Assurance Requirements Are Rigorous**: CSRD demands much higher standards for data quality, verification, and reporting integration than previous frameworks.

Chapter 5: European Sustainability Reporting Standards (ESRS)

The European Sustainability Reporting Standards represent the technical backbone of the CSRD, transforming abstract regulatory requirements into concrete disclosure obligations. The Commission adopted today the European Sustainability Reporting Standards (ESRS) for use by all companies subject to the Corporate Sustainability Reporting Directive (CSRD). This marks another step forward in the transition to a sustainable EU economy. These standards create a unified language for sustainability reporting that enables comparison across companies, industries, and countries.

Understanding ESRS requires grasping both their structural organization and practical application. Two cross-cutting standards provide general reporting concepts and include overarching disclosure requirements including multiple datapoints. Ten topical standards complement these with detailed disclosure requirements across environmental, social and governance topics. This architecture ensures consistency while allowing flexibility for different business models and sustainability impacts.

Cross-cutting Standards - ESRS 1 and ESRS 2

The foundation of all ESRS reporting rests on two cross-cutting standards that establish the conceptual framework and mandatory disclosures for every company. The first of two cross-cutting standards, ESRS 1 lays out the key concepts and requirements of the reporting framework. This standard outlines the reporting areas, what information is required in reporting, the role of due diligence throughout the process, and time horizons.

ESRS 1 establishes fundamental concepts that permeate all sustainability reporting under the CSRD. This standard is also where you can find concepts foundational to the ESRS, such as: The scope of the "value chain": the activities, resources, and relationships in the company's own operations, along its supply and distribution channels, and throughout the broader environment in which the company operates. This value chain definition expands traditional corporate boundaries to include indirect impacts and relationships.

The double materiality concept receives detailed treatment in ESRS 1. The double materiality concept as the basis of sustainability disclosure: how companies need to consider sustainability reporting from both a financial and impact materiality perspective. This requires companies to evaluate not just how sustainability issues affect their financial performance, but also how their operations affect environmental and social systems.

Stakeholder engagement requirements form another cornerstone of ESRS 1. The importance of stakeholder engagement: 'affected stakeholders" and "users of sustainability statements," which encompass everyone in the value chain and who need to be consulted throughout the reporting process. This emphasizes that sustainability reporting serves multiple audiences with different information needs.

ESRS 2 translates these conceptual foundations into concrete disclosure requirements. The second cross-cutting standard within the framework details the disclosures all companies must include in their sustainability reporting, regardless of the outcome of a double materiality assessment. This ensures baseline comparability across all reporting companies.

The four-pillar reporting structure defined in ESRS 2 organizes all sustainability disclosures. ESRS 2 explains the four-pillar reporting approach companies must use while reporting sustainability information across all topical areas. These four pillars are: Governance to disclose the administrative, management, and supervisory bodies of a company, and their involvement and expertise in managing sustainability issues.

Strategy to disclose the company's overall strategy relating to sustainability matters, its business model and value chain, and how companies engage with stakeholders. This pillar ensures that sustainability reporting connects to business strategy rather than existing as separate compliance exercise.

Impact, risk and opportunity management to disclose the company's process of identifying impacts, risks and opportunities and the results of its materiality assessment. This pillar demonstrates systematic approach to sustainability management beyond ad hoc initiatives.

Consider how Siemens applied the cross-cutting standards in their CSRD implementation. The company used ESRS 1 guidance to map their value chain across 200+ countries, identifying sustainability impacts from raw material extraction through product end-of-life. Their double materiality assessment evaluated both how climate change affects Siemens' business operations (financial materiality) and how Siemens' products and services impact global decarbonization efforts (impact materiality). The assessment involved 50+ internal workshops and engagement with 200+ external stakeholders including customers, suppliers, investors, and NGOs.

Siemens' ESRS 2 implementation created a governance structure with board-level oversight of sustainability matters. The company's sustainability strategy connects directly to their business transformation toward digital industries and sustainable infrastructure. Their impact, risk and opportunity management processes integrate sustainability factors into capital allocation decisions, R&D investments, and market entry strategies.

L'Oréal provides another instructive example of cross-cutting standards implementation. The cosmetics giant used ESRS 1 concepts to evaluate their value chain from ingredient sourcing through consumer use and packaging disposal. Their stakeholder engagement process included beauty consumers, ingredient suppliers, regulatory bodies, and environmental organizations across multiple continents. The double materiality assessment identified climate change, biodiversity loss, and consumer safety as material topics from both impact and financial perspectives.

Environmental Standards (E1-E5) Deep Dive

The environmental standards represent the most detailed and prescriptive section of ESRS, reflecting the urgency of climate action and environmental protection. This is the key environmental standard that will apply to most companies. The standard relates to climate change adaptation and mitigation, a company's energy consumption, and risks and opportunities related to climate change. ESRS E1 includes the most mandatory disclosures of the 10 topical standards.

ESRS E1 on Climate Change establishes the most rigorous disclosure requirements across all ESRS standards. Companies must report greenhouse gas emissions across all three scopes, including detailed value chain emissions that often represent the majority of their carbon footprint. Climate risk assessments must evaluate both physical risks (like extreme weather impacts) and transition risks (like carbon pricing and stranded assets). Climate targets must align with the Paris Agreement and demonstrate credible decarbonization pathways.

The climate adaptation requirements in ESRS E1 demand forward-looking analysis of how climate change will affect business operations. Companies must identify climate hazards relevant to their locations and activities, assess vulnerability to these hazards, and develop adaptation strategies. This includes evaluation of supply chain climate risks, infrastructure resilience, and ecosystem dependencies.

ESRS E2 on Pollution addresses air, water, soil, and marine pollution across the value chain. Companies must report on issues including microplastics and any pollution of air, water, soil, or food resources. This standard requires quantitative data on pollutant releases, pollution prevention measures, and pollution reduction targets. The scope includes both direct emissions and value chain pollution impacts.

ESRS E3 on Water and Marine Resources covers water consumption, withdrawal, discharge, and marine resource use. This standard relates to a company's water consumption, withdrawal, and discharges, as well as the extraction and use of other marine resources. Companies must assess water stress in their operations and value chain, report water efficiency measures, and address marine ecosystem impacts.

ESRS E4 on Biodiversity and Ecosystems requires assessment of impacts on species and ecosystem health. Companies must consider their impact on biodiversity loss, the state of species, and the extent and condition of ecosystems. This includes evaluation of land use changes, habitat disruption, and ecosystem service dependencies. Companies must report biodiversity targets and conservation measures.

ESRS E5 on Resource Use and Circular Economy addresses material flows, waste generation, and circularity strategies. Companies must report on resource consumption, waste production, recycling rates, and circular business model development. This standard emphasizes transition from linear "take-make-dispose" models toward circular systems that minimize waste and maximize resource efficiency.

The automotive industry provides compelling examples of environmental standards implementation. BMW's ESRS E1 reporting covers emissions from steel production, vehicle manufacturing, dealer operations, customer use, and end-of-life recycling. Their climate targets include 50% reduction in manufacturing emissions by 2030 and carbon neutrality across the value chain by 2050. Climate risk assessments evaluate supply chain disruptions from extreme weather, regulatory changes affecting combustion engines, and market shifts toward electric vehicles.

BMW's ESRS E4 biodiversity reporting addresses impacts from mining operations for battery materials, land use changes for manufacturing facilities, and ecosystem effects from vehicle infrastructure. The company partners with conservation organizations to assess biodiversity risks across their supply chain and develop habitat restoration projects to offset negative impacts.

Nestlé's environmental reporting demonstrates the complexity of food industry ESRS implementation. Their ESRS E1 climate reporting includes agricultural emissions from dairy and livestock operations, deforestation risks from palm oil and cocoa sourcing, and packaging lifecycle emissions. Climate adaptation measures address changing precipitation patterns affecting crop yields, temperature impacts on food safety, and extreme weather risks to manufacturing facilities.

Social Standards (S1-S4) Requirements

The social standards address human rights, labor practices, community impacts, and consumer protection across company operations and value chains. These standards reflect growing recognition that business sustainability encompasses social justice, stakeholder welfare, and human development alongside environmental protection.

ESRS S1 on Own Workforce covers employment practices, working conditions, worker rights, and human capital development for direct employees. Companies must report on workforce diversity, pay equity, health and safety performance, training investments, and collective bargaining coverage. The standard requires disclosure of workforce transition plans related to sustainability transformation, including reskilling programs and just transition measures for communities dependent on carbon-intensive industries.

ESRS S2 on Workers in the Value Chain extends workforce protections beyond direct employees to include suppliers, contractors, and other value chain partners. This standard addresses forced labor risks, child labor prevention, workplace safety across the supply chain, and freedom of association rights. Companies must conduct due diligence on value chain labor practices and implement grievance mechanisms for worker concerns.

ESRS S3 on Affected Communities requires assessment of community impacts from business operations including displacement, pollution exposure, cultural disruption, and economic effects. Companies must engage with local communities, obtain free, prior, and informed consent for projects affecting indigenous peoples, and contribute to community development. The standard emphasizes stakeholder participation in decision-making processes that affect community welfare.

ESRS S4 on Consumers and End-Users addresses product safety, consumer rights, accessibility, and responsible marketing practices. Companies must report on product safety testing, consumer complaint handling, data privacy protection, and measures to prevent harmful or addictive product use. The standard includes requirements for accessible product design and inclusive marketing that avoids discrimination.

The social standards present particular implementation challenges because social impacts are often qualitative, location-specific, and embedded in complex stakeholder relationships. Unlike environmental metrics that can be measured through standardized protocols, social impacts require contextual assessment and stakeholder engagement to understand fully.

Consider how Unilever implements the social standards across their global operations. Their ESRS S1 workforce reporting covers 190,000 employees across 190 countries, requiring data harmonization across diverse legal systems and cultural contexts. The company reports gender pay equity data for all major markets, workplace safety metrics across manufacturing facilities, and diversity representation at all management levels.

Unilever's ESRS S2 value chain worker reporting addresses labor practices across 70,000+ suppliers in industries ranging from agriculture to manufacturing. The company conducts social audits of high-risk suppliers, provides capacity building for small-scale farmers, and participates in industry initiatives to eliminate forced labor from commodity supply chains. Their grievance mechanisms include hotlines in local languages and partnerships with worker rights organizations.

The pharmaceutical industry faces unique challenges in implementing social standards due to the life-and-death nature of their products. Roche's ESRS S4 consumer reporting addresses drug pricing strategies, patient access programs, clinical trial diversity, and responsible marketing practices. The company reports on efforts to expand access to essential medicines in low-income countries while maintaining innovation incentives through intellectual property protection.

Governance Standards (G1) Essentials

ESRS G1 on Business Conduct addresses corporate governance practices that support sustainable business operations. This standard covers anti-corruption measures, responsible lobbying practices, supplier relationship management, and stakeholder engagement in governance processes. The governance standard recognizes that sustainable business performance requires ethical leadership, transparent decision-making, and accountability to all stakeholders.

Anti-corruption and bribery prevention receive detailed attention in ESRS G1. Companies must report on compliance programs, training initiatives, risk assessments, and incident reporting mechanisms. The standard requires disclosure of political contributions, lobbying expenditures, and involvement in trade associations. Companies must explain how their political engagement aligns with stated sustainability commitments.

Supplier relationship management under ESRS G1 addresses procurement practices, supplier development programs, and value chain governance. Companies must report on supplier selection criteria that include sustainability performance, capacity building initiatives for small suppliers, and integration of sustainability requirements into commercial agreements. The standard emphasizes long-term partnerships that support mutual sustainability goals.

Board governance and management systems receive coverage under ESRS G1 requirements. Companies must disclose board diversity, sustainability expertise among directors, executive compensation linkage to sustainability performance, and risk management systems. The standard requires explanation of how sustainability considerations influence strategic decision-making at the highest corporate levels.

Consider how Siemens implements ESRS G1 governance standards through their compliance management system. The company operates a global compliance organization with 200+ dedicated professionals, mandatory compliance training for all employees, and regular monitoring of high-risk business areas. Their supplier management includes sustainability assessments for 95% of procurement spending and capacity building programs for small suppliers in developing countries.

Siemens' governance reporting addresses political engagement through their membership in industry associations and participation in regulatory consultations. The company publishes positions on climate policy, digitalization regulation, and trade policy that align with their business strategy and sustainability commitments. Board governance includes sustainability expertise among independent directors and linking executive compensation to carbon reduction targets.

Sector-Specific Standards Preview

The ESRS architecture anticipates development of sector-specific standards that address industry-specific sustainability impacts and risks. Recognising the diverse nature of industries, the ESRS will evolve to include sector-specific standards. These are anticipated to be finalised and adopted by the European Commission by June 2026. However, the Omnibus proposals may significantly alter or eliminate sector-specific standard development.

The European Commission's deadline to adopt the ESRS for certain third-country companies has been extended to June 30th 2026, without impacting existing reporting schedules. This timeline provides additional development time but creates uncertainty about final scope and requirements.

Sector-specific standards would address industry characteristics that general standards cannot capture adequately. For example, pharmaceutical companies face unique challenges related to drug pricing, clinical trial ethics, and access to essential medicines. Financial institutions must address systemic risk contributions, sustainable finance practices, and financial inclusion. Mining companies confront issues related to community displacement, environmental restoration, and resource depletion.

The development process for sector-specific standards involves extensive consultation with industry stakeholders, civil society organizations, and regulatory authorities. EFRAG planned detailed impact assessments, cost-benefit analyses, and pilot testing programs to ensure standards are both rigorous and practically implementable.

However, the Omnibus proposals may eliminate sector-specific standards entirely to reduce regulatory complexity. An abolishment of the Commission's power to adopt sector-specific standards and a phased implementation of limited assurance standards. This change would simplify compliance but potentially reduce the relevance and comparability of sustainability reporting within specific industries.

The energy sector provides an example of potential sector-specific standard content. Oil and gas companies would face requirements for detailed reporting on exploration activities, production emissions, decommissioning liabilities, and energy transition investments. Renewable energy companies would report on land use impacts, grid integration challenges, and lifecycle environmental effects. Utilities would address energy access, grid resilience, and integration of distributed energy resources.

The financial services sector faces unique challenges that sector-specific standards could address. Banks would report on fossil fuel financing, sustainable finance products, financial inclusion initiatives, and climate risk management. Insurance companies would address climate risk underwriting, disaster response capabilities, and sustainable investment practices. Asset managers would report on ESG integration, stewardship activities, and investor education programs.

Moving Forward with ESRS

The European Sustainability Reporting Standards create a comprehensive framework for corporate sustainability disclosure that extends far beyond traditional environmental reporting. The standards cover the full range of environmental, social, and governance issues, including climate change, biodiversity and human rights. Companies must approach ESRS implementation as a fundamental business transformation rather than a compliance exercise.

Successful ESRS implementation requires investment in data systems, stakeholder engagement processes, and organizational capabilities that support ongoing sustainability performance improvement. The standards create opportunities for companies to identify risks, optimize operations, and build competitive advantages through sustainability excellence.

Essential Takeaways

1. **Cross-cutting Standards Establish the Foundation**: ESRS 1 and ESRS 2 provide conceptual frameworks and mandatory disclosures that apply to all companies regardless of materiality assessments.
2. **Environmental Standards Demand Rigorous Data**: ESRS E1-E5 require quantitative reporting on climate, pollution, water, biodiversity, and circular economy with detailed value chain coverage.
3. **Social Standards Address Human Impacts**: ESRS S1-S4 cover workforce, value chain workers, communities, and consumers with emphasis on stakeholder engagement and human rights.
4. **Governance Standards Support Ethical Operations**: ESRS G1 addresses business conduct, anti-corruption, and governance systems that enable sustainable business practices.
5. **Sector-Specific Standards Remain Uncertain**: The Omnibus proposals may eliminate industry-specific

requirements, simplifying compliance but potentially reducing reporting relevance.

Chapter 6: CSRD Implementation Roadmap

The path from CSRD awareness to full compliance requires systematic planning, significant investment, and organizational transformation that extends far beyond the sustainability team. Complying with the CSRD will be challenging for many U.S. entities, primarily due to the directive's complexity and the depth of disclosure required. Entities will need to establish robust mechanisms for collecting, analyzing, and reporting sustainability data. Success demands treating CSRD implementation as a strategic business initiative rather than a regulatory compliance project.

Understanding the implementation roadmap helps companies avoid common pitfalls while building capabilities that create competitive advantages. The complexity emerges not from any single requirement, but from the interconnected nature of data collection, stakeholder engagement, materiality assessment, and system integration across global operations.

Year-One Preparation Checklist

The first year of CSRD preparation sets the foundation for successful long-term compliance and business transformation. Companies must balance immediate regulatory requirements with building sustainable processes that support continuous improvement and stakeholder value creation.

Leadership Engagement and Governance Structure

Successful CSRD implementation begins with senior leadership commitment and clear governance structures. Board oversight ensures adequate resources and strategic alignment. Executive sponsorship drives cross-functional collaboration and organizational change management. Dedicated project teams coordinate implementation activities while building internal expertise.

Consider how Deutsche Bank approached CSRD governance during their implementation year. The bank created a board-level sustainability committee with monthly oversight meetings, appointed a Chief Sustainability Officer with direct CEO reporting, and established cross-functional working groups spanning risk management, operations, finance, and business lines. This governance structure enabled rapid decision-making and resource allocation while ensuring business line engagement.

Gap Analysis and Current State Assessment

Companies must evaluate existing sustainability data, processes, and systems against CSRD requirements to identify implementation priorities. This assessment covers data availability, quality, and accessibility across all business units and geographic locations. The analysis includes stakeholder engagement capabilities, materiality assessment processes, and reporting infrastructure.

L'Oréal's gap analysis revealed significant data collection challenges across their 150+ manufacturing facilities and thousands of suppliers. The company discovered that environmental data existed in multiple systems with varying quality standards, social impact metrics lacked standardization across regions, and governance information required integration from legal, compliance, and HR functions. This assessment informed their €25 million technology investment and 50+ person implementation team.

Resource Planning and Budget Allocation

CSRD implementation requires substantial financial and human resources across multiple years. Technology investments include data management systems, analytics platforms, and integration tools. Personnel costs cover dedicated implementation teams, external consultants, and training programs. Ongoing operational costs include data collection, verification, stakeholder engagement, and external assurance.

Siemens allocated €30 million for CSRD implementation across technology systems, personnel, and external services. The budget included €15 million for technology infrastructure, €8 million for internal staff and training, €5 million for external consultants and verification services, and €2 million for stakeholder engagement activities. This investment reflected the company's commitment to building world-class sustainability reporting capabilities.

Legal and Regulatory Analysis

Companies must understand CSRD transposition into national laws across their operating jurisdictions. Member state implementations may include additional requirements, different timelines, or enhanced penalties. Legal analysis should cover entity scope determination, consolidation requirements, and liability implications for sustainability reporting.

The regulatory analysis must also consider interaction with other sustainability regulations including EU Taxonomy, Sustainable Finance Disclosure Regulation, and Corporate Sustainability Due Diligence Directive. Integration challenges arise when different regulations have overlapping but not identical requirements for data collection and reporting.

Data Collection Systems and Controls

CSRD reporting demands data collection capabilities that exceed traditional financial reporting in scope, complexity, and stakeholder involvement. Companies in scope need to get ready now for ESRS reporting. For the first wave of companies, this will be as early as the 2024 reporting period. Building these capabilities requires systematic investment in technology, processes, and organizational structures.

Technology Infrastructure Requirements

Modern CSRD compliance requires integrated technology platforms that can collect, validate, analyze, and report sustainability data from across global operations. These systems must handle both quantitative metrics and qualitative assessments while supporting stakeholder collaboration and external verification processes.

BMW's CSRD technology implementation illustrates the complexity of automotive industry data collection. The company developed an integrated platform connecting manufacturing systems, supplier portals, dealer networks, and customer data sources. The system collects environmental data from 30+ manufacturing facilities, social metrics from 70+ countries, and governance information from multiple corporate functions. Real-time dashboards enable continuous monitoring while automated workflows ensure data quality and consistency.

Data Quality and Verification Protocols

CSRD assurance requirements demand data quality standards comparable to financial reporting. Companies must establish data governance frameworks, validation procedures, and audit trails that support external verification. This includes source documentation, calculation methodologies, and approval workflows for all sustainability data.

Nestlé's data quality program demonstrates food industry challenges in verifying value chain information. The company implemented blockchain technology to trace agricultural commodities, partnered with third-party organizations to verify supplier social audits, and established statistical sampling methods for product lifecycle assessments. These protocols ensure data reliability while managing costs across complex global supply chains.

Value Chain Data Collection

CSRD requirements extend beyond direct operations to include upstream and downstream value chain impacts. Companies must develop capabilities to collect sustainability data from suppliers, customers, and business partners while respecting confidentiality and competitive considerations.

Unilever's value chain data collection spans 70,000+ suppliers across multiple tiers and geographic regions. The company uses industry collaboration platforms, standardized assessment tools, and capacity building programs to improve data availability and quality. Supplier engagement includes training programs, technical assistance, and long-term partnership agreements that align sustainability goals with commercial relationships.

Double Materiality Assessment Methodology

The double materiality assessment forms the cornerstone of CSRD compliance, determining which sustainability topics require detailed disclosure and strategic attention. A double materiality assessment assesses a company's impacts on the environment and society (impact materiality) alongside how sustainability issues affect the company's financial performance (financial materiality), providing a comprehensive view of a business's role in and relationship with the broader world.

Impact Materiality Assessment Process

Impact materiality evaluation requires systematic assessment of how business activities affect environmental and social systems. This analysis extends beyond direct operations to include value chain impacts and considers both current effects and potential future consequences. The assessment must involve affected stakeholders and consider diverse perspectives on impact significance.

Siemens' impact materiality assessment evaluated effects across their entire value chain from raw material extraction through product end-of-life. The company conducted stakeholder workshops in 20+ countries, engaged with NGOs and academic institutions, and used lifecycle assessment methodologies to quantify environmental impacts. Social impact evaluation included community consultations, worker surveys, and human rights assessments across global operations.

Financial Materiality Assessment Framework

Financial materiality analysis evaluates how sustainability issues create risks and opportunities that could influence business performance and enterprise value. This assessment considers both current financial effects and potential future impacts across different time horizons. The analysis must align with financial reporting materiality concepts while addressing sustainability-specific considerations.

Deutsche Bank's financial materiality assessment addressed climate transition risks across their loan portfolio, regulatory compliance costs for new sustainability requirements, and market opportunities in sustainable finance products. The analysis included scenario modeling for different climate pathways, quantitative assessment of stranded asset risks, and evaluation of reputational impacts on customer relationships and market access.

Stakeholder Engagement Integration

Effective double materiality assessment requires meaningful stakeholder engagement that goes beyond traditional investor relations and customer feedback. Companies must identify affected stakeholders, understand their perspectives on material issues, and integrate stakeholder input into materiality conclusions.

L'Oréal's stakeholder engagement for materiality assessment included beauty consumers through global surveys, ingredient suppliers through industry collaboration platforms, environmental organizations through direct dialogue, and investors through dedicated sustainability discussions. The company used digital platforms to enable global participation while conducting in-depth workshops with key stakeholder groups.

Value Chain Analysis Requirements

CSRD value chain reporting requirements extend corporate accountability beyond traditional organizational boundaries to include suppliers, customers, and business partners. The scope of the "value chain": the activities, resources, and relationships in the company's own operations, along its supply and distribution channels, and throughout the broader environment in which the company operates. This expanded scope creates significant data collection and stakeholder engagement challenges.

Upstream Value Chain Assessment

Upstream value chain analysis covers all suppliers, contractors, and business partners that provide goods or services supporting company operations. This assessment must identify sustainability impacts, risks, and opportunities across multiple supply chain tiers while considering geographic and sectoral differences in sustainability performance.

BMW's upstream value chain analysis covers 12,000+ direct suppliers and extends to critical sub-suppliers in high-risk sectors like mining and automotive components. The company uses risk mapping tools to identify priority suppliers, conducts on-site assessments for high-impact relationships, and implements collaborative improvement programs for strategic partnerships. Supply chain traceability initiatives track materials from extraction through manufacturing to ensure accountability across complex global networks.

Downstream Value Chain Evaluation

Downstream value chain analysis addresses customer use of products and services, distribution partner activities, and end-of-life management responsibilities. This assessment requires understanding how products create environmental and social impacts throughout their lifecycle and how company policies influence customer behavior.

Nestlé's downstream analysis evaluates consumer use of food products, packaging waste impacts, and nutritional effects on public health. The company conducts consumer behavior studies, partners with waste management organizations, and engages with public health authorities to understand and address downstream impacts. Product reformulation initiatives reduce environmental impacts while improving nutritional profiles to support consumer wellbeing.

Business Partner Collaboration

Value chain reporting requires collaboration with business partners who may have different sustainability priorities, capabilities, and regulatory requirements. Companies must balance transparency demands with competitive considerations while building trust and mutual accountability across complex business relationships.

Unilever's business partner collaboration includes joint sustainability initiatives with major retailers, capacity building programs for small suppliers, and industry-wide platforms for sharing best practices. The company participates in precompetitive collaboration on sustainability standards while maintaining competitive differentiation through sustainability innovation and performance excellence.

Limited Assurance Readiness

CSRD requires external assurance of sustainability reporting that brings audit standards and verification requirements comparable to financial reporting. The CSRD introduces mandatory assurance of reported information. Initially, companies must obtain a limited assurance over their disclosures, which is a less intensive form of review that results in a less definitive opinion from the auditor. Preparing for assurance requires robust internal controls, documentation standards, and audit trail capabilities.

Internal Control Development

Companies must establish internal control systems that ensure sustainability data accuracy, completeness, and reliability. These controls include data validation procedures, approval workflows, documentation requirements, and segregation of duties between data collection and verification functions.

Deutsche Bank's internal control framework for sustainability reporting mirrors their financial reporting controls with segregated responsibilities, documented procedures, and regular testing protocols. The bank established sustainability data governance committees, implemented automated validation rules, and created audit trails linking reported metrics to source systems and supporting documentation.

Documentation and Evidence Requirements

External assurance requires extensive documentation supporting all sustainability disclosures including calculation methodologies, data sources, assumptions, and management judgments. Companies must maintain evidence files comparable to financial audit documentation while addressing sustainability-specific verification challenges.

Siemens' assurance preparation includes detailed documentation packages for each ESRS disclosure requirement covering data collection procedures, stakeholder engagement evidence, materiality assessment support, and calculation methodologies. The company maintains electronic audit trails linking reported metrics to source documents while ensuring confidentiality of sensitive business information.

Auditor Selection and Engagement

Companies must select external assurance providers with appropriate sustainability expertise, independence requirements, and global capability to support multinational operations. The selection process should consider technical competence, industry knowledge, and capacity to handle complex sustainability reporting requirements.

Case Study: Large Multinational's CSRD Journey

Mercedes-Benz Group provides an instructive example of comprehensive CSRD implementation across a complex global automotive business. The company's journey illustrates both the challenges and opportunities of transforming sustainability reporting while maintaining operational excellence and competitive performance.

Implementation Timeline and Governance

Mercedes-Benz began CSRD preparation in early 2023 with board-level governance and dedicated implementation resources. The company appointed a Chief Sustainability Officer with executive committee membership, created cross-functional working groups spanning all business units, and allocated €40 million for technology and personnel investments. Board oversight included quarterly progress reviews and strategic decision-making on materiality priorities and stakeholder engagement approaches.

Materiality Assessment and Stakeholder Engagement

The company's double materiality assessment involved 18 months of stakeholder engagement across 25+ countries including customers, suppliers, employees, investors, regulators, and civil society organizations. Impact materiality evaluation addressed climate change, air quality, resource consumption, worker safety, and community development across the automotive value chain. Financial materiality analysis covered climate transition risks, regulatory compliance costs, and market opportunities in electric mobility and autonomous driving.

Data Systems and Value Chain Integration

Mercedes-Benz developed an integrated sustainability data platform connecting manufacturing systems, supplier portals, dealer networks, and customer touchpoints. The system collects environmental data from 35+ production facilities, social metrics from 170+ countries, and governance information from corporate functions. Value chain integration includes 1,500+ direct suppliers and extends to critical sub-suppliers in battery materials, semiconductors, and steel production.

Assurance Preparation and External Verification

The company engaged a global assurance provider with automotive industry expertise and established internal control systems comparable to financial reporting standards. Assurance preparation included documentation protocols, validation procedures, and audit trail capabilities supporting external verification requirements. The company conducted pilot assurance exercises to test systems and procedures before mandatory compliance deadlines.

Charting the Path Forward

CSRD implementation represents a multi-year journey requiring sustained commitment, strategic investment, and organizational transformation. Entities will need to establish robust mechanisms for collecting, analyzing, and reporting sustainability data. Companies that approach implementation strategically while building capabilities for continuous improvement will create competitive advantages that extend far beyond regulatory compliance.

The implementation roadmap must balance immediate compliance requirements with long-term capability building that supports business strategy and stakeholder value creation. Success requires treating CSRD as an opportunity to strengthen sustainability performance, stakeholder relationships, and competitive positioning rather than merely a regulatory burden to manage.

Essential Takeaways

1. **Year-One Preparation Requires Strategic Investment**: Leadership engagement, gap analysis, resource planning, and legal assessment form the foundation for successful implementation.
2. **Data Systems Must Support Complex Requirements**: Technology infrastructure, quality controls, and value chain integration capabilities exceed traditional reporting system requirements.
3. **Double Materiality Assessment Drives Strategic Focus**: Systematic evaluation of impact and financial

materiality determines disclosure priorities and business strategy alignment.

4. **Value Chain Analysis Extends Accountability**: Upstream and downstream assessment requires collaboration with business partners and stakeholder engagement across complex global networks.
5. **Assurance Readiness Demands Robust Controls**: Internal control development, documentation requirements, and auditor engagement preparation ensure successful external verification.

Chapter 7: CSRD Practical Workbook

The transformation from understanding CSRD requirements to producing compliant disclosures requires practical tools, structured methodologies, and systematic approaches that translate regulatory complexity into manageable business processes. This workbook provides frameworks, templates, and examples that enable companies to build robust CSRD reporting capabilities while avoiding common implementation pitfalls.

Successful CSRD implementation depends on having the right tools at the right time. Companies need structured approaches for conducting materiality assessments, standardized templates for data collection, clear guidance for governance structure design, and practical solutions for overcoming typical challenges. These tools must balance regulatory compliance with business value creation, ensuring that CSRD reporting supports strategic decision-making and stakeholder engagement.

Templates for Each ESRS Disclosure

ESRS disclosure templates provide structured frameworks for organizing sustainability information while ensuring compliance with specific requirements and data point specifications. These templates serve as blueprints for building comprehensive reporting processes that can scale across global operations and adapt to evolving regulatory requirements.

ESRS 1 and ESRS 2 Cross-Cutting Templates

The foundation templates for ESRS 1 and ESRS 2 establish the basic structure for all sustainability reporting. These templates organize information according to the four-pillar approach of governance, strategy, impact management, and metrics while incorporating double materiality concepts and stakeholder engagement requirements.

The governance template captures board oversight responsibilities, management accountability structures, and sustainability expertise within leadership teams. Key sections include board composition and sustainability competencies, executive compensation linkage to sustainability performance, sustainability committee structures and responsibilities, internal control systems for sustainability data, and integration of sustainability risks in enterprise risk management.

Consider how ASML, the Dutch semiconductor equipment manufacturer, structured their governance template. The company created detailed documentation of board-level sustainability oversight including quarterly sustainability committee meetings, annual board sustainability training, and executive compensation metrics tied to carbon reduction targets. Their template includes specific roles and responsibilities for each board member, clear escalation procedures for sustainability risks, and integration points with existing governance structures.

The strategy template organizes information about business model sustainability integration, value chain analysis, stakeholder engagement processes, and long-term sustainability goals. Core components include business model description and sustainability integration points, value creation process and sustainability impacts, stakeholder identification and engagement methodologies, material sustainability topics and strategic responses, and time-bound targets and progress measurement systems.

Unilever's strategy template demonstrates consumer goods industry complexity with detailed value chain mapping from ingredient sourcing through consumer use and disposal. Their template includes specific sustainability integration points in brand strategy, product development, supply chain management, and marketing communications. The company's Sustainable Living Plan provides the strategic framework while individual business units adapt implementation approaches to their specific markets and challenges.

Environmental Standards Templates (E1-E5)

Environmental disclosure templates address the most data-intensive aspects of CSRD reporting with structured approaches for greenhouse gas accounting, pollution monitoring, resource consumption tracking, and biodiversity impact assessment.

The ESRS E1 Climate Change template provides comprehensive frameworks for emissions reporting, climate risk assessment, and decarbonization strategy disclosure. Essential components include scope 1, 2, and 3 greenhouse gas emissions with detailed calculation methodologies, climate risk assessment covering physical and transition risks across different time horizons, climate targets and progress tracking including science-based targets alignment, climate adaptation measures and resilience building activities, and energy consumption and renewable energy procurement strategies.

BMW's E1 template illustrates automotive industry complexity with emissions reporting across manufacturing, supply chain, product use, and end-of-life phases. Their template includes specific calculation methodologies for each emission source, detailed supplier engagement protocols for scope 3 emissions, and climate scenario analysis for business resilience planning. The company's carbon neutrality roadmap provides the strategic context while operational metrics track progress against interim targets.

Social Standards Templates (S1-S4)

Social disclosure templates address workforce management, value chain worker protections, community engagement, and consumer safety across global operations with culturally sensitive approaches that respect local contexts while ensuring consistent standards.

The ESRS S1 Own Workforce template organizes employee-related disclosures including diversity and inclusion metrics, health and safety performance, training and development investments, and collective bargaining coverage. Key sections include workforce composition by gender, age, and other diversity characteristics, employee turnover rates and retention strategies, health and safety incident rates and prevention measures, training hours and skill development programs, and employee satisfaction and engagement metrics.

Siemens' S1 template covers 300,000+ employees across 200+ countries with standardized metrics adapted to local legal and cultural contexts. Their template includes global diversity targets with country-specific implementation approaches, unified health and safety standards with local regulatory compliance, and competency development frameworks aligned with digital transformation strategies. The company's workforce analytics provide real-time monitoring while annual employee surveys track engagement and satisfaction trends.

Governance Standards Templates (G1)

The governance template for ESRS G1 addresses business conduct, anti-corruption measures, stakeholder engagement, and political participation with clear frameworks for demonstrating ethical leadership and transparent decision-making.

Essential elements include anti-corruption policies and training programs, whistleblower protection and incident reporting systems, supplier relationship management and sustainability integration, political engagement and lobbying disclosure, and stakeholder engagement processes and feedback integration.

Materiality Assessment Worksheets

Double materiality assessment requires systematic evaluation frameworks that capture both impact and financial materiality while incorporating stakeholder perspectives and supporting audit trail requirements for external verification.

Impact Materiality Assessment Framework

Impact materiality worksheets provide structured approaches for evaluating how business activities affect environmental and social systems. These frameworks must capture both current impacts and potential future effects while incorporating stakeholder perspectives on impact significance and prioritization.

The impact identification worksheet organizes systematic evaluation of business activities across the value chain including direct operations, upstream suppliers, and downstream customers. Assessment categories include environmental impacts such as greenhouse gas emissions, pollution, resource consumption, and biodiversity effects, and social impacts including worker welfare, community development, human rights, and consumer safety.

L'Oréal's impact materiality framework demonstrates cosmetics industry complexity with detailed assessment of ingredient sourcing impacts, manufacturing environmental effects, packaging waste implications, and consumer safety considerations. Their worksheet includes quantitative impact metrics where available, qualitative impact descriptions for complex social issues, stakeholder input on impact significance, and geographic variation in impact severity and stakeholder concerns.

Financial Materiality Assessment Tools

Financial materiality worksheets evaluate how sustainability issues create risks and opportunities affecting business performance and enterprise value. These tools must address both current financial effects and potential future impacts across different time horizons while aligning with financial reporting materiality concepts.

The financial impact assessment includes revenue implications from sustainability trends, cost impacts from resource efficiency and compliance requirements, capital expenditure needs for sustainability transformation, and risk factors affecting business operations and market access.

Deutsche Bank's financial materiality assessment addresses climate risks across their loan portfolio, regulatory compliance costs for sustainability requirements, market opportunities in sustainable finance products, and reputational impacts on customer acquisition and retention. Their framework includes quantitative financial modeling where possible, qualitative risk assessment for complex scenarios, sensitivity analysis for different sustainability pathways, and integration with existing enterprise risk management processes.

Stakeholder Integration Methodologies

Stakeholder engagement worksheets provide structured approaches for incorporating diverse perspectives into materiality assessments while ensuring meaningful participation and transparent feedback integration.

Key components include stakeholder identification and mapping processes, engagement methodology selection and implementation, feedback collection and analysis procedures, and materiality conclusion development and validation.

Data Point Mapping Tools

CSRD reporting requires hundreds of specific data points across environmental, social, and governance topics. Data mapping tools help companies identify information sources, establish collection procedures, and ensure data quality while building audit trails for external verification.

Environmental Data Mapping

Environmental data mapping tools organize information collection for greenhouse gas emissions, energy consumption, water use, waste generation, and pollution monitoring across global operations and value chains.

The emissions data mapping tool identifies data sources for scope 1, 2, and 3 emissions including energy consumption records, transportation data, supplier information, and product lifecycle assessments. Key elements include data source identification and validation, calculation methodology specification, uncertainty assessment and sensitivity analysis, and audit trail documentation for verification.

BMW's emissions data mapping covers 30+ manufacturing facilities, 12,000+ suppliers, millions of vehicles in use, and end-of-life recycling operations. Their mapping tool includes automated data collection from manufacturing systems, supplier portal integration for value chain emissions, statistical modeling for product use emissions, and blockchain technology for component traceability.

Social Data Mapping

Social data mapping tools organize workforce information, value chain worker data, community impact metrics, and consumer safety indicators across diverse geographic and cultural contexts.

The workforce data mapping tool identifies sources for employee demographics, health and safety metrics, training records, satisfaction surveys, and performance evaluations.

Essential components include HRIS system integration, local compliance requirement mapping, cultural sensitivity considerations, and privacy protection measures.

Unilever's workforce data mapping covers 190,000 employees across 190 countries with harmonized metrics adapted to local legal and cultural requirements. Their tool includes automated HRIS data extraction, local survey implementation, third-party verification for sensitive topics, and statistical analysis for trend identification and benchmarking.

Governance Structure Examples

Effective CSRD governance requires clear roles and responsibilities, appropriate oversight mechanisms, and integration with existing corporate governance structures while ensuring sustainability considerations influence strategic decision-making at all organizational levels.

Board-Level Governance Models

Board governance structures for CSRD must balance oversight responsibilities with strategic guidance while ensuring appropriate expertise and independence for sustainability matters.

The sustainability committee model establishes dedicated board committees with specific sustainability oversight responsibilities including strategy approval, performance monitoring, risk assessment, and stakeholder engagement oversight. Committee composition should include independent directors with relevant expertise, regular reporting to the full board, clear charter and responsibilities, and integration with other board committees.

Siemens' sustainability governance includes a board-level sustainability committee with quarterly meetings, annual sustainability strategy reviews, executive compensation oversight, and stakeholder engagement monitoring. Their structure includes specific sustainability expertise requirements for committee members, detailed reporting frameworks, and integration with audit and risk committees for comprehensive oversight.

Management Governance Frameworks

Management governance structures translate board oversight into operational accountability while ensuring cross-functional coordination and resource allocation for sustainability objectives.

The sustainability leadership model establishes executive accountability including Chief Sustainability Officer appointment, cross-functional working groups, business unit sustainability managers, and performance measurement systems. Key elements include clear reporting relationships, resource allocation authority, performance measurement and incentives, and stakeholder engagement responsibilities.

Operational Governance Systems

Operational governance systems ensure day-to-day implementation of sustainability strategies while maintaining data quality, compliance monitoring, and continuous improvement processes.

Common Pitfalls and Solutions

CSRD implementation presents numerous challenges that can derail compliance efforts or compromise reporting quality. Understanding common pitfalls and proven solutions helps companies avoid costly mistakes while building robust capabilities for long-term success.

Data Quality and Verification Challenges

Data quality represents one of the most significant CSRD implementation challenges due to the scope of information required, the number of data sources involved, and the verification standards demanded by external assurance.

Common data quality pitfalls include inconsistent collection methodologies across business units, inadequate source documentation for verification, missing value chain data from suppliers and customers, and poor data governance procedures. Solutions include standardized data collection protocols, automated validation procedures, supplier capacity building programs, and robust audit trail systems.

Mercedes-Benz addressed data quality challenges through €15 million investment in integrated data platforms, standardized supplier reporting requirements, automated validation procedures, and comprehensive documentation systems. Their approach includes real-time data monitoring, exception reporting for data quality issues, and systematic supplier training programs.

Stakeholder Engagement Pitfalls

Stakeholder engagement failures can undermine materiality assessments, damage stakeholder relationships, and compromise reporting credibility while creating legal and reputational risks.

Common engagement pitfalls include inadequate stakeholder identification, superficial consultation processes, poor feedback integration, and lack of ongoing relationship management. Solutions include systematic stakeholder mapping, meaningful engagement methodologies, transparent feedback integration, and continuous relationship building.

Materiality Assessment Errors

Materiality assessment mistakes can result in incomplete reporting, misallocated resources, and audit findings while failing to identify significant sustainability risks and opportunities.

Common materiality pitfalls include narrow impact assessment, insufficient stakeholder input, weak financial materiality analysis, and poor documentation of conclusions. Solutions include systematic impact evaluation, comprehensive stakeholder engagement, robust financial analysis, and detailed assessment documentation.

Practical Application and Success

The CSRD practical workbook provides essential tools for transforming regulatory requirements into business capabilities that create value for companies and stakeholders. These templates, frameworks, and methodologies must be adapted to specific business contexts while maintaining compliance with regulatory requirements and supporting strategic objectives.

Success in CSRD implementation requires systematic application of practical tools combined with strategic thinking about sustainability integration and stakeholder value creation. Companies that invest in robust methodologies and comprehensive capabilities will achieve compliance while building competitive advantages that extend far beyond regulatory requirements.

Essential Takeaways

1. **Templates Provide Structure and Consistency**: ESRS disclosure templates ensure complete coverage while maintaining consistency across business units and reporting periods.
2. **Materiality Assessment Requires Systematic Frameworks**: Double materiality worksheets provide

structured approaches for evaluating impact and financial significance with stakeholder integration.

3. **Data Mapping Ensures Complete Coverage**: Environmental and social data mapping tools identify information sources while building audit trails for verification.
4. **Governance Structures Enable Effective Oversight**: Board, management, and operational governance models ensure accountability while integrating sustainability into strategic decision-making.
5. **Common Pitfalls Can Be Avoided**: Understanding typical implementation challenges and proven solutions helps companies build robust capabilities while avoiding costly mistakes.

Chapter 8: GRI Universal Standards

The Global Reporting Initiative stands as the world's most widely adopted sustainability reporting framework, used by 75% of the largest companies globally. Universal Standards: GRI 1, GRI 2 and GRI 3 GRI 1: Foundation 2021 specifies the requirements that the organization must comply with to report in accordance with the GRI Standards. The organization begins using the GRI Standards by consulting GRI 1. Understanding these Universal Standards creates the foundation for all successful sustainability reporting efforts.

The Universal Standards establish the fundamental architecture for transparent impact disclosure. Think of them as the skeleton upon which all sustainability reporting builds—you can't construct meaningful disclosure without these structural elements in place. Companies often underestimate the strategic value embedded within these foundational requirements, viewing them as mere compliance obligations rather than business management tools.

GRI 1 Foundation Principles

GRI 1 Foundation represents the constitutional document of sustainability reporting, establishing the core principles that govern how organizations approach transparency and accountability. The organization begins using the GRI Standards by consulting GRI 1. This standard doesn't just provide technical guidance—it establishes the philosophical framework for responsible disclosure.

The reporting principles in GRI 1 create the quality framework for all sustainability information. **Accuracy** demands that reported information be correct and detailed enough for stakeholders to assess performance. This isn't about perfection—it's about honest representation of what you know and what you don't know. Companies must balance precision with practicality while maintaining credibility.

Balance requires presenting both positive and negative aspects of performance without bias. This principle challenges organizations to move beyond marketing-speak toward genuine accountability. Many companies struggle with this requirement because it demands discussing failures alongside successes, problems alongside solutions.

Clarity ensures that information is accessible and understandable to stakeholders using the report. Technical jargon and complex presentations can obscure rather than illuminate performance. The principle demands writing that serves readers rather than impressing them with sophistication.

Comparability enables stakeholders to compare performance over time and against other organizations. This principle drives standardization and consistency in reporting approaches. Companies must maintain stable methodologies while adapting to changing business conditions and stakeholder needs.

Completeness requires covering all material topics and their boundaries comprehensively. Organizations can't cherry-pick favorable aspects while ignoring challenging issues. The principle demands systematic coverage of all significant impacts, risks, and opportunities.

Sustainability context places organizational performance within the broader context of environmental and social limits. This principle connects company activities to global challenges like climate change, resource scarcity, and social inequality. Organizations must explain how their performance contributes to or detracts from sustainable development.

Timeliness ensures information is available when stakeholders need it for decision-making. Annual reporting cycles may not meet all stakeholder needs, particularly for rapidly changing issues. Companies must balance reporting frequency with information quality and cost considerations.

Verifiability means that information can be examined and validated by external parties. This principle supports assurance processes and builds stakeholder confidence. Organizations must maintain documentation and evidence supporting all reported information.

Consider how Unilever applies these principles in their sustainability reporting. The company's accuracy principle implementation includes detailed methodology descriptions for calculating environmental impacts across their global operations. Their balance approach discusses both achievements in sustainable sourcing and ongoing challenges in packaging waste reduction. Clarity comes through plain language explanations of complex supply chain issues, while comparability maintains consistent metrics across multiple reporting periods.

Nike provides another example of foundation principles in action. The company's sustainability context principle connects their carbon emissions to science-based targets aligned with Paris Agreement goals. Their completeness approach addresses both direct manufacturing impacts and complex value chain issues including cotton sourcing and product end-of-life. Verifiability includes third-party verification of key metrics and transparent methodology disclosure.

GRI 2 General Disclosures Structure

GRI 2 creates the organizational portrait that enables stakeholders to understand the company behind the sustainability data. GRI 2: General Disclosures 2021 contains disclosures that the organization uses to provide information about its reporting practices and other organizational details, such as its activities, governance, and policies. These aren't bureaucratic requirements—they're essential context that makes sustainability performance meaningful.

Organizational details establish the basic facts about your company that stakeholders need to understand your sustainability impacts. This includes ownership structure, geographic operations, business model description, and significant changes during the reporting period. The disclosure connects sustainability performance to business reality.

Strategy, policies, and practices reveal how sustainability integrates into organizational decision-making. This section requires describing the board's role in sustainability oversight, explaining how sustainability considerations influence strategy development, and detailing policies that guide day-to-day operations.

Stakeholder engagement demonstrates how organizations identify, prioritize, and engage with groups affected by their operations. This isn't about public relations—it's about systematic relationship management that informs business decisions. Companies must explain their stakeholder identification process, engagement methodologies, and how stakeholder input influences their approach.

Governance details how organizations oversee sustainability matters at the highest levels. This includes board composition and expertise, decision-making processes, risk management integration, and executive compensation linkage to sustainability performance. The disclosure reveals whether sustainability represents genuine business priority or window dressing.

Reporting practices explain the technical foundations of the sustainability report including boundaries, scope, data collection processes, and assurance approaches. This section builds confidence in reported information while providing context for interpreting data and comparing performance.

BMW's GRI 2 implementation illustrates automotive industry complexity. Their organizational details section describes global manufacturing footprint, joint venture structures, and significant acquisitions affecting sustainability performance. Strategy disclosure explains how electrification goals integrate with business transformation plans. Stakeholder engagement includes systematic dialogue with environmental groups, customer surveys on sustainability preferences, and supplier collaboration on value chain improvements.

Microsoft demonstrates technology sector GRI 2 application through detailed governance disclosure including board sustainability expertise, quarterly sustainability performance reviews, and executive compensation tied to carbon reduction targets. Their reporting practices section explains data collection from cloud operations, methodology for calculating scope 3 emissions, and third-party verification processes for key metrics.

GRI 3 Material Topics Methodology

Material topics represent the sustainability issues that matter most to your business and stakeholders. GRI 3: Material Topics 2021 provides guidance on how to determine material topics. It also contains disclosures that the organization uses to report information about its process of determining material topics, its list of material topics, and how it manages each topic. This standard transforms abstract materiality concepts into practical business tools.

The materiality assessment process requires systematic evaluation of sustainability topics based on their significance to business success and stakeholder concerns. Organizations must identify the full universe of potential topics, gather stakeholder input on their priorities, evaluate business impacts and dependencies, and synthesize this information into a focused list of material topics.

Topic identification begins with comprehensive mapping of sustainability issues relevant to your industry, operations, and value chain. This includes environmental impacts like climate change and resource consumption, social issues including human rights and community development, and governance matters such as business ethics and transparency. The process requires looking beyond obvious topics to identify emerging issues that may become material.

Impact assessment evaluates how each potential topic affects stakeholders and business performance. Organizations must consider both positive and negative impacts, current and potential effects, and direct and indirect consequences. The assessment connects abstract sustainability concepts to concrete business realities.

Stakeholder prioritization captures external perspectives on topic significance through surveys, interviews, workshops, and other engagement methods. Different stakeholder groups often prioritize topics differently, requiring organizations to synthesize diverse viewpoints into coherent conclusions. The process must balance stakeholder input with business judgment and strategic considerations.

Business significance evaluation assesses how each topic influences business success through revenue impacts, cost implications, risk factors, opportunity creation, and reputation effects. This analysis connects sustainability topics to business strategy and operational performance.

Boundary determination identifies where impacts occur across the value chain and who has influence over managing them. Some impacts occur within direct operations while others happen through suppliers, customers, or business partners. Understanding boundaries shapes management approaches and reporting scope.

Consider how Nestlé conducts materiality assessment for their global food and beverage operations. Their topic identification includes water stewardship, sustainable agriculture, nutrition and health, human rights in supply chains, climate change, packaging and waste, and rural development. Impact assessment evaluates how water scarcity affects manufacturing operations and farming communities. Stakeholder prioritization includes farmer associations, environmental groups, nutrition experts, and consumer advocacy organizations.

L'Oréal's materiality process for the beauty industry addresses sustainable sourcing of natural ingredients, product safety and transparency, packaging innovation, diversity and inclusion, and climate action. Their boundary analysis maps impacts from ingredient cultivation through consumer use and disposal. Stakeholder engagement includes beauty consumers, environmental scientists, women's rights organizations, and supply chain partners.

Sector Standards Integration

Sector standards provide industry-specific guidance that makes general reporting principles relevant to particular business contexts. The Sector Standards provide information for organizations about their likely material topics. The organization uses the Sector Standards that apply to its sectors when determining its material topics and when determining what to report for each material topic. These standards bridge the gap between universal principles and industry realities.

Industry context shapes which sustainability topics are most relevant and how they manifest in specific business operations. Financial services face different material topics than mining companies or retailers. Sector standards help organizations focus on issues that matter most in their industry while maintaining consistency with global reporting principles.

Likely material topics provide starting points for materiality assessment based on common industry patterns. Organizations don't have to accept these topics as material for their specific circumstances, but they must consider them during their assessment process. The guidance helps ensure comprehensive topic identification.

Topic-specific guidance explains how general reporting requirements apply to industry-specific contexts. For example, water management disclosures have different implications for beverage companies than software firms. Sector standards help organizations interpret general requirements for their particular circumstances.

Implementation considerations address practical challenges that commonly arise in specific industries. This includes data availability constraints, measurement challenges, stakeholder engagement approaches, and boundary-setting complexities that characterize particular sectors.

The oil and gas sector standard illustrates industry-specific materiality guidance. Key topics include climate change impacts from fossil fuel production, environmental management of exploration and production activities, occupational health and safety in high-risk operations, community relations around extraction activities, and energy transition planning. The standard helps companies in this sector address their most significant sustainability challenges systematically.

The food and agriculture sector standard emphasizes sustainable sourcing, nutrition and product safety, water and land management, animal welfare, and rural community development. Companies in this sector face unique challenges around environmental impacts of agriculture, food security implications, and value chain complexity that sector guidance helps address.

Reporting Principles and Quality

Quality reporting principles ensure that sustainability disclosure serves stakeholder decision-making needs while supporting organizational learning and improvement. These principles transform data collection into strategic business intelligence that guides better decisions and builds stakeholder trust.

Stakeholder inclusiveness requires organizations to identify stakeholders and explain how their reasonable expectations and interests have been addressed. This doesn't mean satisfying everyone—it means understanding diverse perspectives and explaining how they influenced reporting decisions.

Sustainability context connects organizational performance to broader environmental and social systems. Companies must explain how their performance contributes to or detracts from sustainable development. This principle prevents organizations from reporting in isolation from global challenges.

Materiality focuses reporting on topics that reasonably affect stakeholder decisions and reflect significant economic, environmental, and social impacts. This principle ensures efficient use of reporting resources while meeting stakeholder information needs.

Completeness requires sufficient coverage of material topics to enable stakeholders to assess performance. Organizations must balance comprehensive coverage with practical limitations on reporting scope and detail.

Siemens demonstrates quality principles through their integrated approach connecting sustainability performance to business strategy. Their stakeholder inclusiveness includes systematic engagement with customers, employees, investors, communities, and NGOs. Sustainability context connects their digitalization solutions to global decarbonization needs. Materiality assessment focuses on topics where Siemens has significant impact and influence including climate action, digitalization for sustainability, and responsible business practices.

Laying the Foundation for Excellence

The Universal Standards create the architectural foundation upon which all effective sustainability reporting builds. The Universal Standards strengthen the very foundations of all reporting through GRI, delivering the highest level of transparency for organizational impacts on the economy, environment, and people. Companies that invest time in understanding and implementing these standards thoroughly position themselves for reporting excellence and business value creation.

Organizations often rush toward topic-specific reporting without establishing solid foundations through the Universal Standards. This approach inevitably creates problems downstream—reports that lack context, materiality assessments that miss key issues, and stakeholder relationships that fail to inform business decisions. The Universal Standards prevent these problems by establishing systematic approaches to transparency and accountability.

Key Learning Points

1. **Foundation Principles Drive Quality**: GRI 1 establishes reporting principles that ensure information serves stakeholder decision-making while supporting organizational learning and improvement.
2. **General Disclosures Provide Context**: GRI 2 creates the organizational portrait that makes sustainability performance meaningful and comparable across companies and time periods.
3. **Materiality Assessment Focuses Effort**: GRI 3 transforms stakeholder concerns and business impacts

into strategic priorities that guide resource allocation and performance management.

4. **Sector Standards Provide Relevance**: Industry-specific guidance helps organizations focus on the sustainability topics that matter most in their particular business context.
5. **Quality Principles Ensure Value**: Systematic application of reporting principles creates business intelligence that supports better decisions and stronger stakeholder relationships.

Chapter 9: GRI Topic Standards Mastery

The transition from Universal Standards to Topic Standards marks the shift from architectural foundation to substantive content—this is where sustainability reporting moves from framework to action. The specific GRI standards can be divided into three broad categories: economic (GRI 200), environmental (GRI 300) and social (GRI 400). These standards transform abstract sustainability concepts into concrete measurement and management approaches that drive real business impact.

Understanding Topic Standards requires recognizing that they serve dual purposes: external reporting to stakeholders and internal management of sustainability performance. The best organizations use these standards not just to compile annual reports, but to build systematic approaches to measuring, managing, and improving their contributions to sustainable development.

Economic Standards - The 200 Series

The economic dimension of sustainability extends far beyond traditional financial performance to encompass how organizations affect economic systems and stakeholder prosperity. The 200 Series is not about the financial condition of the organization itself, but rather the impact that the organization has on the economic conditions of its stakeholders and on the economic systems at a local, national, and global level. This perspective requires thinking about business success in terms of shared value creation rather than zero-sum competition.

GRI 201: Economic Performance examines how organizations create and distribute economic value among stakeholders. This standard requires reporting direct economic value generated and distributed including revenues, operating costs, employee compensation, payments to capital providers, payments to government, and community investments. The disclosure reveals how business success translates into stakeholder benefits.

The standard also addresses defined benefit plan obligations, financial assistance received from government, and climate change financial implications. These disclosures connect traditional financial management to sustainability considerations, revealing how environmental and social factors affect business economics.

Consider how Microsoft approaches GRI 201 reporting. The company's economic value distribution shows how their $198 billion in revenue translates into employee compensation ($29 billion), supplier payments ($43 billion), shareholder returns ($20 billion), and tax payments ($9 billion) across global operations. Their climate change financial implications disclosure addresses both transition risks from carbon pricing and physical risks from extreme weather affecting their data center operations.

Walmart's GRI 201 implementation demonstrates retail industry applications. Their economic value distribution reveals how the company's $559 billion in revenue supports 2.2 million employees globally, hundreds of thousands of suppliers, and local tax bases in communities where they operate. Climate change financial implications include energy cost management, supply chain disruption risks, and opportunities from sustainable product sales.

GRI 202: Market Presence evaluates how organizations affect local economic development through employment and procurement practices. This standard requires reporting ratios of standard entry-level wages to local minimum wages, proportion of senior management hired from local communities, and significant operational locations where local hiring represents strategic priority.

This standard challenges organizations to consider their role in community economic development beyond job creation to include skill development, leadership opportunities, and local supply chain strengthening. The disclosures reveal whether business growth creates shared prosperity or concentrates benefits narrowly.

Nestlé's GRI 202 reporting illustrates food industry community development impacts. The company reports local hiring ratios across their global operations, showing how leadership development programs in emerging markets create advancement opportunities for local talent. Their local procurement initiatives support farmer income development and supply chain resilience while building community economic capacity.

GRI 203: Indirect Economic Impacts captures the broader economic effects of organizational activities beyond direct employment and procurement. This standard requires reporting infrastructure investments, significant indirect economic impacts, and development programs that create community benefits.

These impacts often represent the most significant contributions organizations make to sustainable development, particularly for companies operating in developing countries or underserved communities. The standard encourages systematic assessment of these broader effects rather than ad hoc community program reporting.

Unilever's GRI 203 disclosure demonstrates how consumer goods companies create indirect economic impacts through their value chains. Their sustainable sourcing programs support smallholder farmer income improvement across palm oil, tea, and vegetable supply chains. Distribution network development in emerging markets creates entrepreneurship opportunities while expanding market access.

GRI 204: Procurement Practices examines how purchasing decisions affect supply chain sustainability and local economic development. The standard requires reporting the proportion of spending on local suppliers and procedures for integrating social and environmental criteria into procurement decisions.

This standard recognizes procurement as a strategic lever for sustainability impact beyond cost optimization. Organizations can use purchasing power to incentivize supplier sustainability improvements, support local economic development, and drive value chain transformation.

Environmental Standards - The 300 Series

Environmental standards address the most measurable and regulated aspects of sustainability performance. GRI 300 are the environmental standards: raw materials exploitation, use of energy and environmental resources, respect for biodiversity, assessment of pollutant discharges and emissions, environmental compliance, supplier assessment. These standards provide frameworks for measuring, managing, and reducing environmental impacts across all business operations.

GRI 301: Materials focuses on resource consumption and circular economy principles. The standard requires reporting materials used by weight or volume, percentage of recycled input materials, and reclaimed products and packaging materials. This disclosure reveals resource efficiency and circular economy implementation.

The materials standard challenges organizations to think beyond traditional input cost management toward resource stewardship and circular design principles. Companies must consider both direct material consumption and indirect effects through product design decisions that influence customer resource use.

BMW's GRI 301 reporting demonstrates automotive industry materials management. The company reports total material consumption across global manufacturing operations, recycled content in vehicle production, and end-of-life vehicle recycling rates. Their circular economy initiatives include design for recyclability, remanufacturing programs, and closed-loop material systems.

GRI 302: Energy addresses energy consumption, energy intensity, and renewable energy adoption across organizational operations. The standard requires reporting energy consumption within and outside the organization, energy intensity ratios, reduction in energy consumption, and energy reduction initiatives.

Energy reporting connects directly to climate change mitigation while revealing operational efficiency and cost management performance. Organizations must address both absolute consumption and intensity metrics to provide complete pictures of energy management progress.

Interface Inc. provides a compelling example of GRI 302 implementation. The carpet manufacturer reports total energy consumption across global operations, renewable energy percentage that reached 100% in 2020, and energy intensity improvements of 52% since baseline year. Their energy reduction initiatives include efficiency upgrades, renewable procurement, and manufacturing process optimization.

GRI 303: Water and Effluents examines water stewardship across the value chain including consumption, withdrawal, discharge, and water-related impacts. The standard requires reporting water withdrawal, water discharge, water consumption, and water-related impacts on stakeholders and ecosystems.

Water stewardship extends beyond efficiency metrics to include quality management, ecosystem protection, and community access considerations. Organizations must address both direct operations and value chain impacts while considering local water stress conditions.

Coca-Cola's GRI 303 reporting illustrates beverage industry water stewardship. The company reports water use efficiency ratios, wastewater treatment performance, watershed protection initiatives, and community water access programs. Their approach includes local watershed assessments, water risk mapping, and stakeholder engagement in water-stressed regions.

GRI 304: Biodiversity addresses impacts on ecosystems, species, and habitats across the value chain. The standard requires reporting operational sites in biodiversity-sensitive areas, significant impacts on biodiversity, habitats protected or restored, and species on conservation lists affected by operations.

Biodiversity reporting often presents measurement challenges due to complex ecological interactions and limited baseline data. Organizations must balance quantitative metrics with qualitative assessments while engaging scientific expertise and conservation partners.

Unilever's GRI 304 implementation demonstrates consumer goods biodiversity stewardship. The company reports agricultural supply chain impacts on biodiversity, deforestation-free sourcing initiatives, habitat restoration projects, and partnerships with conservation organizations. Their approach includes supplier assessment, certification requirements, and landscape-level conservation programs.

GRI 305: Emissions provides the framework for greenhouse gas accounting and climate change mitigation. The standard requires reporting scope 1, scope 2, and scope 3 emissions,

emissions intensity ratios, emissions reductions, and ozone-depleting substance emissions.

Emissions reporting represents the most standardized and regulated aspect of environmental disclosure. Organizations must follow established protocols while addressing both absolute emissions and intensity metrics across all emission scopes.

Microsoft's GRI 305 reporting demonstrates technology sector climate action. The company reports scope 1, 2, and 3 emissions across global operations, carbon intensity metrics per revenue, emission reduction achievements, and carbon negative goals. Their approach includes renewable energy procurement, supply chain engagement, and carbon removal investments.

Social Standards - The 400 Series

Social standards address the human dimension of sustainability including labor practices, human rights, community relations, and product responsibility. The 400 Series focuses on how the organization impacts the social systems surrounding it. Some of the social topics include non-discrimination, child labor, and customer privacy. These standards often present greater measurement challenges than environmental metrics but address equally important aspects of sustainable development.

GRI 401: Employment examines workforce management including hiring practices, employee benefits, and retention strategies. The standard requires reporting new employee hires and turnover, benefits provided to employees, and parental leave policies and uptake.

Employment reporting reveals how organizations invest in human capital development and create positive working conditions. The disclosures connect human resource management to sustainability performance while addressing demographic diversity and geographic distribution.

Salesforce's GRI 401 reporting illustrates technology sector employment practices. The company reports global hiring trends, comprehensive benefits including health, retirement, and professional development, and progressive parental leave policies. Their approach includes pay equity initiatives, employee resource groups, and career development programs.

GRI 402: Labor/Management Relations addresses collective bargaining, worker representation, and consultation processes. The standard requires reporting minimum notice periods for operational changes and collective bargaining agreement coverage.

These disclosures reveal how organizations engage with workers on decisions affecting their interests. The standard recognizes labor rights as fundamental human rights requiring systematic management approaches.

GRI 403: Occupational Health and Safety provides frameworks for workplace safety management and reporting. The standard requires reporting occupational health and safety management systems, hazard identification and risk assessment, occupational health services, worker participation, worker training, promotion of worker health, prevention and mitigation of impacts, workers covered by management systems, work-related injuries, work-related ill health, and workers whose work is subject to health and safety management systems.

Health and safety reporting addresses one of the most fundamental organizational responsibilities to workers. The standard requires systematic management approaches rather than just incident reporting.

Siemens' GRI 403 implementation demonstrates industrial sector safety management. The company reports global safety management systems, injury frequency rates, occupational health programs, and safety training initiatives. Their approach includes near-miss reporting, safety culture development, and contractor safety management.

GRI 404: Training and Education examines human capital development through skills training, career development, and performance management. The standard requires reporting average hours of training per employee, programs for skills management and lifelong learning, and percentage of employees receiving performance reviews.

Training and education disclosures reveal organizational investment in human capital development and employee advancement opportunities. The reporting connects workforce development to business strategy and competitive advantage.

GRI 405: Diversity and Equal Opportunity addresses workforce diversity, leadership representation, and pay equity. The standard requires reporting diversity of governance bodies and employees and ratio of basic salary and remuneration of women to men.

Diversity reporting has become increasingly strategic as organizations recognize connections between diverse perspectives, innovation, and business performance. The disclosures reveal both representation and equity considerations across organizational levels.

Selecting Relevant Topic Standards

Choosing appropriate Topic Standards requires systematic evaluation based on materiality assessment results, stakeholder priorities, and business strategy considerations. You can choose from these topics to report specific information on your material topics. The selection process should focus resources on standards that provide most value for decision-making and performance management.

Materiality assessment results provide the primary foundation for Topic Standard selection. Organizations should report on standards that address their material topics while avoiding unnecessary reporting on non-material issues. The selection should align with materiality conclusions while ensuring comprehensive coverage of significant impacts.

Stakeholder information needs influence which standards provide most value for external reporting. Different stakeholder groups prioritize different topics, requiring organizations to balance comprehensive coverage with stakeholder-specific interests.

Business strategy alignment ensures that selected standards support strategic objectives and performance management needs. Organizations should choose standards that help measure progress toward sustainability goals while providing useful business intelligence.

Industry benchmarking considerations help ensure comparability with peer organizations and industry standards. Companies should consider which standards are commonly used in their sector while maintaining focus on their specific material topics.

Industry Supplement Guidance

Industry supplements provide sector-specific guidance for applying Topic Standards to particular business contexts. These supplements help organizations interpret general requirements for their industry circumstances while maintaining consistency with global reporting principles.

Sector-specific applications explain how general Topic Standards apply to particular industry contexts. For example, biodiversity reporting has different implications for mining companies than service providers. Industry guidance helps organizations focus on most relevant aspects of each standard.

Common measurement challenges addressed through industry supplements include data availability constraints, calculation methodologies, and boundary-setting complexities that characterize specific sectors. The guidance helps organizations overcome practical implementation obstacles.

Benchmarking considerations help organizations understand how their peers approach similar reporting challenges while maintaining focus on their specific circumstances and materiality conclusions.

Building Reporting Excellence

Topic Standards transform sustainability frameworks into actionable business intelligence that drives performance improvement and stakeholder engagement. Using the GRI Standards as a whole set to prepare your sustainability report in accordance with the standards creates systematic approaches to measuring and managing organizational contributions to sustainable development.

The most successful organizations approach Topic Standards as management tools rather than just reporting requirements. They use the measurement frameworks to identify improvement opportunities, track progress toward goals, and communicate achievements to stakeholders. This approach transforms compliance obligations into competitive advantages through better decision-making and stakeholder relationships.

Key Learning Points

1. **Economic Standards Address Shared Value**: The 200 series focuses on how organizations affect stakeholder economic welfare rather than just internal financial performance.
2. **Environmental Standards Enable Impact Management**: The 300 series provides measurement frameworks for managing resource consumption, emissions, and ecosystem impacts.
3. **Social Standards Address Human Development**: The 400 series examines how organizations affect human welfare, rights, and community development.
4. **Selection Requires Strategic Thinking**: Choosing relevant Topic Standards should align with materiality assessment results, stakeholder needs, and business strategy objectives.
5. **Industry Context Shapes Application**: Sector-specific guidance helps organizations apply general standards to their particular business circumstances and challenges.

Chapter 10: GRI Implementation Excellence

The distance between understanding GRI standards and implementing them successfully spans the gap between theoretical knowledge and practical business transformation. Excellence in GRI implementation requires systematic approaches to stakeholder engagement, boundary setting, data management, and assurance that go far beyond filling out disclosure templates. Organizations that achieve implementation excellence use GRI as a strategic business tool rather than a compliance obligation.

Implementation excellence emerges from treating GRI as an integrated management system that supports decision-making, builds stakeholder relationships, and drives performance improvement. This approach requires investment in organizational capabilities, stakeholder relationships, and management systems that extend far beyond the sustainability team to influence business operations across all functions and levels.

Stakeholder Engagement Best Practices

Stakeholder engagement represents the cornerstone of effective GRI implementation because it informs materiality assessment, shapes reporting priorities, and builds the relationships necessary for long-term business success. Stakeholder engagement is a mandated component in the process of producing a GRI-compliant sustainability report. However, compliance represents the minimum threshold—excellence requires systematic relationship management that creates mutual value.

Stakeholder identification requires comprehensive mapping of all groups affected by or influencing organizational operations.

This extends beyond obvious categories like employees and customers to include communities, NGOs, academic institutions, industry associations, government agencies, and future generations. The mapping process should consider both current stakeholders and emerging groups whose influence may grow over time.

Prioritization frameworks help organizations focus engagement efforts on stakeholders with greatest influence and interest in sustainability topics. The classic influence-interest matrix provides a starting point, but organizations should also consider factors like expertise, representativeness, willingness to engage, and potential for collaboration. Prioritization should be dynamic, adapting to changing circumstances and issues.

Engagement methodologies must match stakeholder characteristics, topic complexity, and desired outcomes. Surveys work for broad input collection but lack depth for complex issues. Workshops enable collaborative problem-solving but require significant time commitments. Advisory panels provide ongoing guidance but may become disconnected from broader stakeholder views. Digital platforms can reach global audiences but may exclude less connected communities.

Consider how Patagonia designs stakeholder engagement for their outdoor apparel business. Their stakeholder map includes outdoor enthusiasts, environmental organizations, supply chain workers, retail partners, investors, and policy makers. Engagement methods include customer surveys on environmental priorities, partnership with conservation organizations on land protection, worker interviews about labor conditions, and policy advocacy on climate action.

Patagonia's engagement excellence comes from authentic two-way dialogue that influences business decisions. Customer input shapes product design and environmental initiatives. Conservation partners provide scientific expertise for supply chain improvements. Worker feedback drives factory condition improvements. The engagement creates mutual value rather than just information extraction.

Interface Inc. demonstrates systematic stakeholder engagement in the carpet manufacturing industry. Their engagement includes architects and designers who specify products, facility managers who maintain them, environmental groups concerned with chemical use, employees affected by sustainability goals, and investors evaluating long-term strategy. Each stakeholder group receives tailored engagement approaches based on their information needs and communication preferences.

Feedback integration represents the most challenging aspect of stakeholder engagement because it requires translating diverse input into coherent business strategies. Organizations must balance conflicting stakeholder priorities while maintaining strategic focus. The integration process should be transparent, explaining how stakeholder input influenced decisions while acknowledging areas where input couldn't be accommodated.

Ongoing relationship management sustains engagement beyond annual reporting cycles through regular communication, collaborative projects, and mutual support. This approach builds trust and credibility that supports long-term business success. Organizations should invest in relationship infrastructure that creates value for stakeholders while advancing business objectives.

Boundary Setting and Value Chain Reporting

Boundary setting determines the scope of sustainability reporting by defining which impacts, operations, and relationships fall within organizational accountability. The Standards are designed as an easy-to-use modular set, delivering an inclusive picture of an organization's material topics, their related impacts, and how they are managed. Excellence in boundary setting requires understanding both technical requirements and strategic implications of scope decisions.

Impact boundaries define where sustainability impacts occur regardless of organizational control. Climate change impacts from product use occur outside direct operations but represent organizational responsibility. Human rights impacts in supply chains may occur in supplier facilities but require organizational management. Impact boundaries should reflect actual consequences rather than convenient organizational limits.

Reporting boundaries define which entities and operations are included in sustainability data collection and disclosure. This typically aligns with financial reporting boundaries but may differ for specific topics where impacts occur outside financial consolidation scope. Organizations must explain any differences between financial and sustainability reporting boundaries.

Value chain boundaries address upstream suppliers, downstream customers, and business partners whose activities create impacts associated with organizational operations. These boundaries present the greatest complexity because they require coordination with external parties while maintaining reporting credibility. Organizations must balance comprehensiveness with practical limitations on data collection and verification.

Control considerations help determine which impacts fall within organizational influence and accountability. Direct control enables comprehensive management and reporting. Joint control requires coordination with partners. Influence without control may still create responsibility for engagement and advocacy. Organizations should clearly explain their control relationships and management approaches for different boundary areas.

Nike's boundary setting illustrates complex value chain challenges in the apparel industry. Their direct operations include design, marketing, and retail activities with relatively limited environmental impact. Manufacturing occurs through contract suppliers with significant environmental and social impacts. Raw material production involves agricultural and textile operations with diverse sustainability challenges. Product use and disposal create impacts beyond Nike's direct control but within their design influence.

Nike's boundary excellence comes from systematic value chain mapping that identifies impact locations and influence opportunities. They report comprehensive data from contract suppliers while acknowledging limitations in raw material traceability. Their approach includes supplier capability building, industry collaboration, and consumer education that extends management beyond traditional organizational boundaries.

Walmart's value chain boundaries span retail operations, supplier relationships, and customer influence across hundreds of product categories. Their direct operations focus on energy use, waste management, and employee practices. Supplier relationships involve sustainability standards, capacity building, and collaborative improvement programs. Customer influence includes product curation, sustainability information, and behavior change initiatives.

Data Collection and Management Systems

Sustainability data management requires systems that can handle diverse information types, sources, and quality levels while supporting both internal management and external reporting needs. The exam includes GRI Standards, reporting principles, stakeholder engagement, and sustainability data management. Excellence in data management creates competitive advantages through better decision-making and stakeholder confidence.

Data architecture must accommodate quantitative metrics, qualitative assessments, stakeholder feedback, and external information across global operations. The architecture should integrate with existing business systems while supporting sustainability-specific requirements. Cloud-based platforms provide scalability and accessibility while ensuring data security and backup capabilities.

Collection processes require standardized procedures, clear responsibilities, and quality controls that ensure data accuracy and completeness. These processes must balance automation with human judgment while maintaining audit trails for verification. Organizations should establish data governance frameworks that define roles, responsibilities, and approval processes for sustainability information.

Quality assurance includes validation procedures, consistency checks, and verification processes that build confidence in reported information. This extends beyond mathematical accuracy to include methodological appropriateness, boundary consistency, and stakeholder input verification. Quality assurance should be integrated throughout the data lifecycle rather than applied only at reporting time.

System integration connects sustainability data with financial, operational, and strategic information systems to provide holistic business intelligence. This integration enables analysis of relationships between sustainability performance and business outcomes while reducing duplication of data collection efforts.

BMW's data management system illustrates automotive industry complexity across global manufacturing, supply chain relationships, and product lifecycle impacts. Their system integrates manufacturing data from 30+ facilities, supplier information from thousands of partners, and product use data from millions of vehicles. Real-time dashboards enable continuous monitoring while annual aggregation supports comprehensive reporting.

BMW's excellence comes from automated data collection where possible, standardized manual processes where necessary, and robust quality controls throughout the system. Their approach includes statistical sampling for certain value chain impacts, third-party verification for key metrics, and transparency about data limitations and uncertainty.

Microsoft's sustainability data platform demonstrates cloud technology applications for complex global operations. Their system collects energy consumption from data centers worldwide, travel emissions from employee systems, supply chain data from procurement platforms, and customer impact information from product usage. Machine learning algorithms identify data quality issues and improvement opportunities.

External Assurance Considerations

External assurance builds stakeholder confidence in sustainability reporting while supporting organizational learning and improvement. Assurance approaches vary in scope, level, and methodology, requiring organizations to match assurance strategies with stakeholder needs and business objectives. Excellence in assurance maximizes credibility while supporting performance improvement.

Assurance scope determines which information receives external verification. Limited scope assurance might cover only key metrics while comprehensive scope addresses entire reports. Organizations should prioritize assurance on information most important to stakeholder decisions while considering cost-benefit relationships.

Assurance level defines the depth of verification procedures and confidence levels provided. Limited assurance provides moderate confidence through focused procedures. Reasonable assurance provides high confidence through extensive testing but requires significantly more time and cost. Organizations should match assurance levels with stakeholder expectations and regulatory requirements.

Provider selection requires evaluating technical competence, independence, industry expertise, and global capabilities. Large accounting firms offer technical rigor and global reach but may lack sustainability specialization. Specialized sustainability consultants provide deep expertise but may have limited geographic coverage. Organizations should evaluate providers based on specific assurance needs and stakeholder expectations.

Assurance integration with internal management systems maximizes business value from external verification. Assurance processes should identify improvement opportunities, validate management systems, and support organizational learning. The integration should extend beyond compliance verification to performance enhancement.

Unilever's assurance approach demonstrates consumer goods industry best practices across global operations and complex value chains. Their assurance scope includes key environmental metrics, social impact indicators, and selected governance disclosures. Assurance providers combine technical accounting expertise with sustainability specialization. The assurance process includes management recommendations that support continuous improvement.

Interface Inc.'s assurance strategy illustrates comprehensive verification for ambitious sustainability goals. Their Carbon Negative by 2030 goal requires rigorous measurement and verification to maintain credibility. Assurance scope includes comprehensive environmental data, key social metrics, and progress toward strategic goals. The assurance process validates both current performance and trajectory toward long-term objectives.

Case Study: Emerging Market Company GRI Adoption

Tata Group's sustainability reporting journey illustrates how emerging market companies can achieve GRI implementation excellence while navigating unique challenges including diverse business portfolio, complex stakeholder environment, and varying regulatory requirements across countries and industries.

Implementation approach began with pilot reporting in key operating companies before expanding across the group. This phased approach enabled learning and capability building while managing implementation costs and complexity. Early pilots included companies with mature sustainability programs and simpler operations before extending to more complex businesses.

Stakeholder engagement addressed diverse Indian stakeholder environment including government agencies, local communities, NGOs, international investors, and global customers. Engagement methods included community consultations, government policy dialogue, NGO partnerships, investor discussions, and customer surveys. The approach balanced global best practices with local cultural considerations and communication preferences.

Materiality assessment identified topics relevant across diverse business portfolio including automotive, steel, chemicals, information technology, hospitality, and consumer goods. Common material topics included climate change, water stewardship, employee development, community relations, and business ethics. Business-specific topics addressed industry-particular challenges like mining impacts, chemical safety, and technology access.

Data management addressed challenges of collecting consistent information across businesses with different systems, capabilities, and reporting cultures. The approach included standardized data collection templates, capacity building programs, and technology platforms that accommodate varying sophistication levels. Quality assurance included both automated validation and manual review processes.

Boundary setting addressed complex group structure with listed and unlisted companies, joint ventures, and associate companies. The approach prioritized businesses with greatest sustainability impacts while maintaining consistency with financial reporting boundaries. Value chain boundaries focused on areas with greatest impact and influence opportunities.

Assurance strategy combined group-level verification with business-specific assurance based on materiality and stakeholder requirements. The approach balanced credibility needs with cost considerations while building internal audit capabilities for ongoing management.

Results and lessons from Tata's implementation demonstrate how emerging market companies can achieve reporting excellence while creating business value. Key success factors included leadership commitment, stakeholder engagement, capability building, and integration with business strategy. The implementation supported improved risk management, stakeholder relationships, and competitive positioning in global markets.

Excellence Through Integration

GRI implementation excellence emerges from treating sustainability reporting as an integrated management system that supports business strategy rather than an annual compliance exercise. The GRI Standards enable any organization – large or small, private or public – to understand and report on their impacts on the economy, environment and people in a comparable and credible way, thereby increasing transparency on their contribution to sustainable development. Organizations that achieve excellence use GRI to build systematic capabilities for measuring, managing, and improving their contributions to sustainable development.

The journey to implementation excellence requires sustained commitment, strategic investment, and organizational learning that extends across multiple reporting cycles. Companies must balance stakeholder expectations with business realities while maintaining focus on material topics and continuous improvement. This approach transforms GRI from reporting burden into competitive advantage through better stakeholder relationships, risk management, and performance improvement.

Key Learning Points

1. **Stakeholder Engagement Drives Value**: Excellence requires systematic relationship management that creates mutual value rather than just information extraction.
2. **Boundary Setting Enables Impact Management**: Thoughtful boundary decisions focus resources on areas where organizations have greatest impact and influence.
3. **Data Systems Support Decision-Making**: Robust data management creates business intelligence that supports both reporting and performance improvement.
4. **Assurance Builds Credibility**: Strategic assurance approaches balance stakeholder confidence with cost considerations while supporting organizational learning.

5. **Integration Creates Excellence**: Organizations achieve best results by treating GRI as an integrated management system rather than separate reporting obligation.

Chapter 11: GRI Certification Preparation

The path to GRI Professional Certification represents more than credential acquisition—it demonstrates mastery of the world's most widely adopted sustainability reporting framework and commitment to professional excellence in sustainability management. The Global Reporting Initiative Professional Certification (GRI) is a prestigious credential that empowers professionals to lead effective sustainability reporting initiatives. This certification opens doors to career advancement while building capabilities that create business value.

Understanding the certification requirements, exam format, and ongoing professional development expectations helps candidates approach preparation strategically while building knowledge that extends far beyond test-taking success. The certification represents professional competence in applying GRI Standards to real business challenges rather than academic knowledge of reporting frameworks.

GRI Professional Certification Exam Guide

The GRI Professional Certification Program provides structured learning pathways that build comprehensive understanding of sustainability reporting principles and practical application skills. The GRI Professional Certification Program is a comprehensive curriculum on sustainability, sustainability reporting and the application of the GRI Standards. Candidates can choose between self-paced online learning or instructor-led training based on their learning preferences and schedule constraints.

Program structure includes four required courses covering GRI Standards foundations, materiality assessment, stakeholder engagement, and reporting preparation. Professionals complete a series of courses covering the fundamentals of GRI reporting, in preparation for a final certification exam. Each course builds on previous learning while addressing specific aspects of sustainability reporting implementation.

The Foundation course introduces GRI Standards architecture, reporting principles, and sustainability context. Students learn how GRI connects to global sustainability challenges, other reporting frameworks, and business strategy considerations. This course establishes conceptual foundations for subsequent technical training.

The Materiality and Stakeholder Engagement course addresses systematic approaches to identifying material topics and engaging stakeholders effectively. Students learn practical methods for conducting materiality assessments, mapping stakeholder relationships, and integrating external input into business decisions. This course connects reporting to business strategy and stakeholder relationship management.

The Reporting and Communication course covers technical requirements for preparing GRI-compliant reports including disclosure selection, data collection, boundary setting, and presentation approaches. Students learn practical skills for transforming sustainability data into useful stakeholder information.

The Integration and Quality course addresses assurance, verification, and continuous improvement approaches that support reporting credibility and business value creation. Students learn how to embed sustainability reporting into business management systems while maintaining stakeholder trust.

Learning routes accommodate different candidate needs and circumstances. The program offers two flexible learning routes online, self-paced on the GRI Academy (Route A), or instructor-led and fully or partly delivered by one of the GRI Certified Training Partners (Route B). Route A provides flexibility for busy professionals while Route B offers interaction and networking opportunities.

Route A candidates access video lectures, reading materials, case studies, and practice exercises through the GRI Academy platform. The content includes approximately 32 hours of study material that candidates can complete according to their schedules. Interactive elements include knowledge checks, practical exercises, and discussion forums that support learning reinforcement.

Route B candidates participate in instructor-led training delivered by GRI Certified Training Partners in over 50 countries. This approach includes classroom discussions, group exercises, case study analysis, and networking opportunities with other sustainability professionals. Many training partners offer local language instruction and cultural context that enhances learning relevance.

Exam format and requirements test practical application of GRI knowledge rather than memorization of standard texts. The Certification exam consists of 40 questions of various types (single choice, multiple choice, true/false, complete the sentence) with a time limit of 60 minutes for completion and requires a passing score of 75%. The exam can be taken online through proctored testing that ensures integrity while providing scheduling flexibility.

Question types include scenario-based problems that test practical application skills, technical questions about specific disclosure requirements, and conceptual questions about reporting principles and stakeholder engagement. The exam emphasizes real-world application rather than theoretical knowledge, requiring candidates to demonstrate how they would address typical sustainability reporting challenges.

Eligibility requirements ensure candidates have completed necessary preparation before attempting certification. To be eligible for the GRI Professional Certifications exam, candidates must have completed the four certification courses of the GRI Professional Certification Program. This requirement ensures candidates have systematic exposure to all essential knowledge areas before testing.

Practice Questions and Scenarios

Effective exam preparation requires practicing with question types and scenarios that mirror actual certification testing. This quiz is specifically designed to help you prepare for the GRI Sustainability Professional certification exam by testing your grasp of critical concepts, including sustainability reporting frameworks, stakeholder engagement, materiality assessment, and sustainability reporting best practices. Practice questions should address both technical knowledge and practical application skills.

Materiality assessment scenarios test understanding of systematic approaches to identifying and prioritizing material topics. Practice questions might present business situations where candidates must evaluate topic significance, stakeholder input, and business implications to determine materiality conclusions. These scenarios require applying judgment rather than following formulaic approaches.

Example scenario: "A global technology company is conducting its first materiality assessment. Stakeholder surveys indicate high concern about data privacy, employee diversity, and supply chain labor conditions. Business analysis reveals significant revenue dependencies on government contracts, climate regulatory compliance costs, and talent competition. How should the company prioritize these topics in their materiality matrix?"

Effective responses demonstrate understanding of both stakeholder perspectives and business significance while explaining how different stakeholder groups might prioritize topics differently. Candidates should address both current materiality and emerging issues that may become significant over time.

Boundary setting questions evaluate ability to determine appropriate reporting scope for different sustainability topics. Practice scenarios present complex organizational structures, value chain relationships, and impact patterns that require candidates to explain boundary decisions and their implications for data collection and management approaches.

Example scenario: "A multinational consumer goods company operates through subsidiaries, joint ventures, and licensing agreements across 50 countries. For water management reporting, where should they set boundaries for data collection and impact management? How would boundary decisions differ for greenhouse gas emissions versus human rights impacts?"

Strong responses demonstrate understanding of control relationships, impact significance, and practical implementation considerations while maintaining consistency with GRI requirements and stakeholder expectations.

Stakeholder engagement questions test knowledge of systematic approaches to identifying, prioritizing, and engaging stakeholders effectively. Practice scenarios require candidates to design engagement strategies for specific business situations while balancing diverse stakeholder needs and organizational constraints.

Example scenario: "A mining company is developing its first GRI report for operations in three countries with different regulatory environments and community contexts. How should they approach stakeholder identification and engagement to ensure comprehensive input while managing practical limitations on time and resources?"

Quality responses address stakeholder mapping methodologies, engagement technique selection, cultural considerations, and feedback integration while demonstrating understanding of mining industry-specific stakeholder challenges.

Disclosure selection scenarios evaluate ability to choose appropriate GRI disclosures based on materiality assessment results and stakeholder information needs. These questions require understanding relationships between material topics and Topic Standards while considering practical constraints on data collection and reporting scope.

Reporting Cycle Management

Effective GRI implementation requires systematic management of annual reporting cycles that integrate data collection, stakeholder engagement, report preparation, and assurance activities. After completing all courses, you become eligible to take the Professional Certification Exam. A globally applicable professional development that allows professionals to manage complex reporting requirements while creating business value through improved sustainability management.

Annual planning establishes timelines, responsibilities, and resource requirements for completing GRI reporting cycles successfully. Planning should begin immediately after publishing previous reports while incorporating lessons learned and stakeholder feedback into improved approaches. Early planning enables better coordination with business planning cycles and stakeholder engagement activities.

Planning considerations include materiality assessment updates, stakeholder engagement schedules, data collection timelines, assurance provider selection, and report publication targets.

Organizations should build buffer time for unexpected challenges while maintaining realistic timelines that enable quality reporting.

Data collection coordination requires systematic processes for gathering quantitative metrics, qualitative assessments, and stakeholder input from across global operations. Effective coordination includes standardized procedures, clear responsibilities, quality controls, and regular progress monitoring that ensures complete and accurate information collection.

Data collection should begin early in reporting cycles to allow time for validation, gap filling, and quality improvement. Organizations should establish data governance frameworks that define roles, responsibilities, and approval processes while maintaining audit trails for verification purposes.

Stakeholder engagement integration weaves external input throughout reporting cycles rather than limiting engagement to information collection phases. Ongoing engagement includes progress updates, consultation on emerging issues, feedback on draft reports, and follow-up on previous commitments and recommendations.

Engagement planning should coordinate with business communication strategies while maintaining authenticity and transparency. Organizations should balance formal engagement processes with informal relationship building that supports long-term stakeholder relationships.

Quality assurance processes ensure accuracy, completeness, and consistency of reported information through systematic review and validation procedures. Quality assurance includes technical review of calculations and methodologies, editorial review of content and presentation, and management review of strategic messages and commitments.

Assurance preparation includes organizing supporting documentation, coordinating with external verification providers, and addressing audit findings through corrective actions. Organizations should view assurance as learning opportunity rather than compliance hurdle.

Continuous Improvement Framework

GRI implementation should improve over time through systematic learning, stakeholder feedback integration, and capability building that enhances both reporting quality and business value creation. Certification validity varies; recertification is required periodically through continuing education. Continuous improvement applies to both individual professional development and organizational reporting capabilities.

Performance monitoring tracks key indicators of reporting quality including stakeholder feedback, assurance findings, benchmarking results, and business impact metrics. Regular monitoring enables identification of improvement opportunities while documenting progress over time.

Monitoring should address both quantitative metrics like data quality scores and stakeholder satisfaction ratings alongside qualitative assessments of report usefulness and business integration. Organizations should establish baselines and targets for improvement while maintaining realistic expectations about change timelines.

Capability development builds organizational competencies in sustainability measurement, stakeholder engagement, data management, and business integration through training, system improvements, and process refinements. Capability building should address both technical skills and strategic thinking about sustainability business integration.

Development priorities should focus on areas with greatest impact on reporting quality and business value creation. Organizations should balance internal capability building with external expertise acquisition while maintaining cost-effectiveness and strategic focus.

Stakeholder feedback integration incorporates external input into improved reporting approaches through systematic collection, analysis, and response processes. Feedback integration demonstrates organizational commitment to stakeholder value creation while identifying improvement opportunities that might not be apparent internally.

Feedback collection should occur throughout reporting cycles rather than only after report publication. Organizations should establish multiple feedback channels including surveys, interviews, workshops, and digital platforms while ensuring accessibility for different stakeholder groups.

Benchmarking and best practice adoption compares organizational approaches with peer companies, industry standards, and leading practices to identify improvement opportunities. Benchmarking should address both reporting technical aspects and strategic integration approaches while maintaining focus on material topics and stakeholder priorities.

Best practice adoption should consider organizational context and capability constraints while maintaining ambition for continuous improvement. Organizations should participate in industry initiatives and peer learning opportunities that support collective advancement in sustainability reporting quality.

Integration with Other Frameworks

GRI certification provides foundation knowledge that supports integration with other sustainability frameworks including SASB, TCFD, CSRD, and emerging standards. GRI Standards embody the United Nations Sustainable Development Goals (SDG) Disclosures, which can be linked to reports on specific SDGs and their targets. Professional competence in GRI creates platform for understanding and applying multiple frameworks strategically.

Framework complementarity recognizes that different standards serve different purposes and stakeholder needs while sharing common underlying principles. GRI provides comprehensive impact reporting while SASB focuses on financially material information for investors. TCFD addresses climate-specific risks and opportunities while CSRD establishes European regulatory requirements.

Understanding complementarity enables organizations to design integrated reporting strategies that meet diverse stakeholder needs while minimizing duplication and compliance costs. Integration should focus on shared data, aligned boundaries, and consistent methodologies while respecting different framework requirements and audiences.

Mapping and alignment identifies connections between different framework requirements to enable efficient data collection and reporting processes. Mapping should address both conceptual alignments and practical implementation considerations while maintaining compliance with each framework's specific requirements.

Alignment opportunities include shared metrics, common stakeholder engagement processes, integrated materiality assessments, and coordinated assurance approaches. Organizations should develop mapping documents that guide data collection and reporting while ensuring framework-specific compliance.

Strategic integration uses multiple frameworks to create business intelligence that supports decision-making and stakeholder engagement rather than treating each framework as separate compliance obligation. Strategic integration requires understanding how different frameworks contribute to business objectives while managing implementation costs and complexity.

Integration should connect sustainability reporting to business strategy, risk management, and performance improvement rather than creating separate sustainability communication tracks. Organizations should use framework diversity to build comprehensive understanding of sustainability performance while maintaining focus on material topics and stakeholder value creation.

Professional Excellence Through Certification

GRI Professional Certification represents commitment to excellence in sustainability reporting that creates value for organizations and stakeholders. You will be able to demonstrate to current and future employees/ clients that you have completed training and possess the unique skills and expertise of a GRI Certified Sustainability Professional. The certification provides career advantages while building capabilities that support organizational sustainability leadership.

Certified professionals contribute to advancing sustainability reporting quality across industries and markets while building personal expertise that supports career advancement and business impact. The certification creates professional network connections and ongoing learning opportunities that extend far beyond initial training and testing.

Key Learning Points

1. **Certification Requires Comprehensive Preparation**: Success demands systematic study of GRI Standards,

practical application skills, and understanding of business integration approaches.

2. **Practice Questions Build Application Skills**: Effective preparation includes scenario-based practice that tests practical judgment rather than memorization of framework content.
3. **Reporting Cycles Require Systematic Management**: Professional competence includes ability to coordinate complex annual processes while maintaining quality and stakeholder engagement.
4. **Continuous Improvement Drives Value**: Ongoing capability development and stakeholder feedback integration create business value beyond compliance reporting.
5. **Framework Integration Maximizes Impact**: GRI knowledge provides foundation for strategic integration with other sustainability frameworks and business management systems.

Chapter 12: SASB Fundamentals

The Sustainability Accounting Standards Board (SASB) represents a paradigm shift in how we approach ESG reporting—one that speaks directly to the financial markets in their own language. Unlike other frameworks that cast a wide net across stakeholder interests, SASB cuts through the noise with laser-focused precision on what investors actually need to know.

Think of SASB as the bridge between sustainability data and investment decisions. While other frameworks might ask "What are all the ways this company affects the world?", SASB asks a more pointed question: "What sustainability factors could materially impact this company's financial performance?" This distinction matters enormously because it transforms sustainability reporting from a compliance exercise into a strategic communication tool with capital markets.

The Investor-Focused Materiality Revolution

Investor-focused materiality forms the cornerstone of SASB's entire approach, and understanding this concept is non-negotiable for any ESG professional. Traditional materiality assessments often become exercises in stakeholder diplomacy—trying to balance the concerns of customers, employees, regulators, and communities. SASB cuts through this complexity by asking one clear question: Does this sustainability issue have the potential to affect a company's financial condition or operating performance? (118)

This focus creates what practitioners call "financial materiality"—a determination based on whether sustainability factors could reasonably impact enterprise value. The beauty of this approach lies in its clarity. You're not debating abstract notions of social good; you're analyzing concrete business risks and opportunities.

Consider three companies to illustrate this principle. **Tesla's battery safety protocols** represent financially material information because battery failures could trigger massive recalls, regulatory penalties, and reputational damage that directly impacts stock price. **Walmart's supply chain labor practices** matter financially because labor violations could disrupt operations, trigger boycotts, and increase regulatory scrutiny. **JPMorgan Chase's climate risk assessment** becomes material because climate change affects loan portfolios, insurance costs, and regulatory capital requirements.

The SASB approach eliminates the common pitfall of "materiality creep"—where every sustainability issue somehow becomes material. Instead, it provides a disciplined framework for focusing on what truly matters to long-term value creation. This precision explains why major asset managers like BlackRock and Vanguard increasingly reference SASB standards in their investment analysis. (119)

Navigating the 77 Industry Standards Architecture

SASB's **77 industry standards** represent one of the most sophisticated attempts to capture industry-specific sustainability risks and opportunities. Rather than applying generic metrics across all sectors, SASB recognizes that materiality varies dramatically by industry. The sustainability challenges facing a software company bear little resemblance to those confronting an oil refinery.

The standards span eleven sectors: Consumer Goods, Extractives & Minerals Processing, Financials, Food & Beverage, Health Care, Infrastructure, Renewable Resources & Alternative Energy, Resource Transformation, Services, Technology & Communications, and Transportation. Each sector contains multiple industries, creating the granular specificity that makes SASB so powerful for investors. (120)

Take the **Technology & Communications** sector as an example. Software companies report on data security, intellectual property protection, and managing systemic risks from technology disruptions. Hardware companies focus on product lifecycle management, materials sourcing, and manufacturing-related environmental impacts. Telecommunications companies emphasize network reliability, data privacy, and digital divide issues. Each standard captures the unique risk profile of its industry.

The **Extractives & Minerals Processing** sector demonstrates this specificity even more clearly. Oil and gas exploration companies report on greenhouse gas emissions, air quality impacts, and community relations. Coal mining operations focus on workforce health and safety, environmental compliance, and mine reclamation. Metal ore mining addresses similar environmental concerns but adds specific metrics around tailings management and biodiversity impacts.

Real Estate standards showcase how SASB handles service industries. Real estate investment trusts (REITs) report on energy management, water efficiency, tenant satisfaction, and climate resilience of properties. Real estate services companies focus on sustainability consulting capabilities and green building certifications. This industry-specific approach ensures that reported information directly relates to value drivers that investors understand.

The SICS Classification System

The **Sustainable Industry Classification System (SICS)** serves as SASB's organizing principle, grouping companies based on shared sustainability risks rather than traditional economic classifications. This represents a fundamental innovation in how we think about industry categorization. (121)

Traditional classification systems like the Global Industry Classification Standard (GICS) group companies primarily by revenue sources and business models. SICS takes a different approach, clustering companies that face similar sustainability challenges. This means that a solar panel manufacturer might be grouped with other renewable energy companies rather than with traditional manufacturing firms, reflecting the unique sustainability profile of clean energy technologies.

Consider how SICS handles the **Consumer Goods** sector. Rather than lumping all consumer companies together, SICS creates distinct categories: Apparel, Accessories & Footwear companies face labor rights and supply chain transparency issues; Appliance Manufacturing companies deal with energy efficiency and product safety concerns; Building Products & Furnishings companies focus on indoor air quality and sustainable materials sourcing.

The **Services** sector illustrates SICS's sophistication further. Advertising agencies report on content integrity and media pluralism. Hotels and lodging companies focus on environmental management and labor practices. Professional services firms emphasize talent management and business ethics. Each classification reflects the unique ways these industries interact with sustainability issues.

SICS also handles **multi-industry companies** through a pragmatic approach. Companies report under multiple industry standards when they have significant operations across different SICS categories. General Electric, for example, might report under both Industrial Machinery & Goods and Electric Utilities standards, reflecting its diverse business portfolio.

Understanding the ISSB Standards Relationship

The relationship between SASB and the **International Sustainability Standards Board (ISSB)** represents one of the most significant developments in ESG reporting convergence. In 2022, the SASB Standards were incorporated into the ISSB's foundation materials, creating a pathway toward global harmonization of sustainability reporting. (122)

This integration doesn't mean SASB standards disappear; rather, they become the industry-specific building blocks for global sustainability reporting. The ISSB's general requirements provide overarching principles for sustainability disclosure, while SASB's industry standards offer the detailed metrics and guidance needed for practical implementation.

Climate-related disclosures exemplify this integration. ISSB's general requirements establish principles for climate risk reporting—governance, strategy, risk management, and metrics and targets. SASB's industry standards then specify exactly which climate risks matter most for each sector and how to measure them.

For **financial services companies**, this means reporting on climate risk exposure in lending portfolios (a SASB requirement) within the broader ISSB framework for climate governance and strategy. For **utility companies**, it means disclosing grid resilience and renewable energy transition plans (SASB specifics) as part of comprehensive climate strategy disclosure (ISSB framework).

The **practical implications** for companies are significant. Rather than choosing between SASB and ISSB standards, organizations increasingly need to understand how these frameworks complement each other. SASB provides the detailed, industry-specific content while ISSB offers the structural framework for disclosure.

SEC Climate Disclosure Alignment

The alignment between SASB standards and **SEC climate disclosure requirements** creates powerful synergies for U.S. companies navigating multiple reporting obligations. While SEC rules focus specifically on climate-related risks and opportunities, many SASB industry standards already address these issues in sector-specific detail. (123)

Energy companies find particularly strong alignment. SASB's Oil & Gas industry standards include extensive climate-related metrics—Scope 1 and Scope 2 emissions, methane emissions, climate adaptation strategies, and transition risk assessments. These directly support SEC climate disclosure requirements while providing industry-specific benchmarks and comparability.

Manufacturing companies benefit from SASB's detailed environmental standards when preparing SEC climate disclosures. SASB standards for industries like Chemicals, Steel, and Automotive address energy management, emissions reduction, and climate transition strategies. This pre-existing framework significantly reduces the burden of SEC compliance preparation.

The **governance requirements** show strong convergence as well. Both SASB and SEC standards emphasize board oversight of climate risks, management's role in climate strategy, and integration of climate considerations into business planning. Companies that already report under SASB standards often find they've addressed many SEC climate governance requirements.

However, important differences remain. SEC climate rules require specific forward-looking scenario analysis and detailed financial impact quantification that goes beyond most SASB requirements. Companies need both frameworks—SASB for industry-specific context and peer benchmarking, SEC rules for detailed financial impact analysis.

Chapter 13: Industry-Specific SASB Mastery

The true power of SASB standards emerges when you move from theoretical understanding to practical application within specific industries. This is where sustainability reporting transforms from generic disclosure into strategic communication that resonates with investors who understand your sector's unique challenges and opportunities.

Every industry tells a different sustainability story. A semiconductor manufacturer faces entirely different material issues than a retail bank, and their investors ask fundamentally different questions. SASB's genius lies in recognizing these distinctions and providing frameworks that speak to sector-specific value drivers.

Navigating Your Industry Standard

Finding and applying your industry standard requires more precision than many practitioners realize. The process begins with accurate industry classification using the Sustainable Industry Classification System (SICS), but the real work involves understanding how your specific business model intersects with the standard's requirements. (124)

Start by identifying your **primary SICS industry** based on revenue concentration. Companies generating more than 50% of revenue from a single industry typically report under that standard exclusively. But modern businesses often span multiple categories, requiring more nuanced decisions.

Consider **Amazon's classification challenge**. The company operates across multiple SICS industries: E-Commerce (Services sector), Internet Media & Services (Technology & Communications), and Multiline & Specialty Retailers

(Consumer Goods). Amazon reports under multiple standards, emphasizing E-Commerce and Internet Media & Services due to revenue concentration and investor focus.

Diversified companies like General Electric face even greater complexity. GE operates in Power Generation Equipment (Resource Transformation), Industrial Machinery & Goods (Resource Transformation), and Gas Utilities (Infrastructure). The company prioritizes standards based on business segment materiality and investor interest, often providing supplemental information under secondary standards.

The **telecommunications industry** demonstrates how business model evolution affects standard selection. Traditional telecom companies report under the Telecommunications standard, focusing on network reliability and data privacy. However, companies like Verizon that expand into media content might also reference Internet Media & Services standards for their content operations.

Practical implementation requires understanding disclosure topic prioritization within your chosen standard. Not every disclosure topic carries equal weight for every company. Software companies might emphasize data security over environmental metrics, while data center operators focus heavily on energy management alongside security concerns.

Disclosure Topics and Metrics Deep Analysis

Disclosure topics represent the heart of SASB standards—the specific sustainability issues that matter most for financial performance in each industry. Each topic contains detailed guidance on why it matters, how to measure it, and what investors expect to see. (125)

The **Technology Hardware industry** illustrates this structure clearly. Product lifecycle management emerges as a critical disclosure topic because hardware companies face increasing pressure around planned obsolescence, repairability, and electronic waste. The topic includes metrics on product lifespan, design for recycling principles, and take-back program effectiveness.

Materials sourcing represents another key topic for hardware companies, driven by supply chain risks around conflict minerals, rare earth elements, and human rights violations. Metrics cover supplier verification processes, conflict-free sourcing percentages, and supply chain risk assessment procedures.

Consider how **JPMorgan Chase** addresses disclosure topics in the Commercial Banks standard. **Incorporation of environmental, social, and governance factors in credit analysis** becomes material because ESG factors increasingly affect loan performance and regulatory requirements. The bank reports on ESG integration in lending decisions, portfolio-level ESG risk assessment, and climate stress testing results.

Systemic risk management represents another critical topic for major banks, reflecting their role in financial system stability. JPMorgan reports on risk management frameworks, stress testing results, and capital adequacy measures that demonstrate resilience during market disruptions.

The **Real Estate industry** shows how disclosure topics connect to investor concerns. **Energy management** matters because operating costs directly impact property values and rental income. Real estate investment trusts (REITs) report on energy consumption per square foot, renewable energy adoption, and energy efficiency improvement programs.

Climate change adaptation becomes increasingly material for real estate companies as extreme weather events threaten property values. Companies disclose climate risk assessments, adaptation strategies, and insurance coverage for climate-related damages.

Activity Metrics Requirements

Activity metrics provide the denominator that makes SASB data meaningful for investors—they normalize sustainability performance data to enable peer comparison and trend analysis. These metrics capture the scale and nature of business operations that drive sustainability impacts. (126)

The **Airlines industry** demonstrates activity metrics' importance clearly. Passenger-kilometers and ton-kilometers flown serve as primary activity metrics because they directly relate to fuel consumption, emissions, and operational efficiency. These metrics allow investors to compare fuel efficiency improvements across airlines of different sizes and route structures.

Available seat miles (ASM) provides another crucial activity metric for airlines, enabling analysis of capacity utilization and operational efficiency. Investors use ASM data to evaluate management's ability to match capacity with demand while maintaining environmental performance.

Electric Utilities use different activity metrics that reflect their unique operational characteristics. Megawatt hours (MWh) of electricity delivered captures the scale of operations, while peak capacity measures maximum generation capability. These metrics enable meaningful comparison of emissions intensity and renewable energy adoption across utilities of different sizes.

Distribution network length serves as an additional activity metric for utilities, reflecting the scope of infrastructure requiring maintenance and investment. This metric helps investors understand capital requirements and operational complexity.

The **Software industry** faces unique challenges in defining relevant activity metrics. Traditional volume measures like units sold don't apply to subscription-based or cloud services. Instead, companies report metrics like monthly active users, total subscribers, or data processed—measures that capture the scale of operations driving sustainability impacts.

Microsoft reports cloud services energy consumption normalized by compute hours delivered, enabling investors to assess efficiency improvements as the business scales. This approach provides meaningful insight into operational efficiency trends that traditional financial metrics might obscure.

Quantitative vs. Qualitative Disclosures

The balance between **quantitative and qualitative disclosures** in SASB reporting requires strategic thinking about what information serves investors best. Quantitative data provides comparability and trend analysis, while qualitative information offers context and strategic insight that numbers alone cannot convey. (127)

Quantitative disclosures excel at demonstrating performance trends and enabling peer comparison. Oil and gas companies report specific metrics like greenhouse gas emissions per barrel of oil equivalent, water consumption per unit of production, and safety incident rates. These numbers allow investors to benchmark performance and track improvement over time.

However, **context matters enormously** for interpreting quantitative data. A utility company's emissions intensity might increase year-over-year due to increased reliance on natural gas during renewable energy intermittency periods. Without qualitative explanation, investors might misinterpret this as poor environmental performance rather than grid reliability management.

Qualitative disclosures provide essential context for quantitative metrics. Companies explain their sustainability strategy, risk management approaches, and performance improvement plans. This narrative helps investors understand whether current performance represents sustainable competitive advantage or requires significant future investment.

The **Pharmaceuticals industry** shows how quantitative and qualitative disclosures work together. Companies report quantitative data on clinical trial diversity, access program reach, and pricing policy coverage. But investors also need qualitative information about regulatory strategy, pipeline development approaches, and stakeholder engagement methods.

Novartis combines quantitative disclosure of patient access program participation rates with qualitative discussion of access strategy evolution, regulatory engagement approaches, and partnership development. This combination helps investors understand both current performance and future strategic direction.

Risk factor disclosure often requires primarily qualitative approaches, particularly for emerging issues like cybersecurity threats or regulatory changes. Companies describe risk identification processes, mitigation strategies, and governance frameworks that quantitative metrics cannot fully capture.

Cross-Industry Comparison Considerations

Cross-industry comparison using SASB data requires sophisticated understanding of how different industries address similar underlying sustainability challenges. While industry-specific metrics prevent direct comparison, underlying themes and management approaches often translate across sectors. (128)

Climate risk management provides an excellent example of cross-industry learning opportunities. Electric utilities report on grid resilience and renewable energy transition plans. Real estate companies disclose property-level climate adaptation strategies. Banks describe portfolio-level climate stress testing. While the specific metrics differ, investors can compare management sophistication and strategic planning quality across industries.

Human capital management represents another area where cross-industry insights prove valuable. Technology companies report on diversity and inclusion metrics, talent retention rates, and skills development programs. Manufacturing companies disclose workforce safety statistics, training program effectiveness, and labor relations quality. Retail companies focus on frontline worker advancement opportunities and compensation practices.

Supply chain sustainability creates comparison opportunities across consumer goods, technology, and manufacturing industries. Companies in different sectors face similar challenges around supplier verification, human rights monitoring, and environmental compliance. Investors can assess management capability and strategic commitment by comparing approaches across industries.

The **Financial Services sector** offers unique cross-industry insight opportunities because banks provide financing across multiple industries. Major banks increasingly report on portfolio-level ESG risk exposure, enabling investors to understand sustainability trends across the broader economy through the lens of credit analysis.

JPMorgan Chase's annual climate report includes sector-level analysis of transition risks across oil and gas, utilities, automotive, and real estate industries. This provides investors with cross-industry perspective on climate transition progress that individual company disclosures cannot offer.

Technology platforms create another avenue for cross-industry comparison. Companies like Microsoft and Amazon provide cloud services across multiple industries, offering unique insight into digital transformation and energy efficiency trends across sectors.

Chapter 14: SASB Implementation Strategy

Implementing SASB standards effectively requires more than mechanical compliance with disclosure requirements—it demands strategic thinking about how sustainability information can strengthen investor relationships and support business objectives. The most successful implementations treat SASB as a communication framework that tells a compelling story about value creation rather than a checklist to complete.

The implementation journey varies significantly based on company size, industry complexity, and existing sustainability infrastructure. However, certain principles apply universally: start with materiality assessment, build robust data collection systems, integrate with financial reporting processes, and create ongoing improvement mechanisms.

Materiality Assessment for Investors

Conducting materiality assessment for investors represents the foundational step in SASB implementation, but this process differs substantially from stakeholder-based materiality assessments used in other frameworks. The focus narrows to sustainability factors that could reasonably impact enterprise value or investment decisions. (129)

The assessment begins with **industry standard analysis**—thoroughly reviewing your SASB industry standard to understand which disclosure topics the standard identifies as financially material. However, this represents just the starting point. Companies must evaluate how these generic topics apply to their specific business model, competitive position, and strategic direction.

Microsoft's materiality assessment illustrates this principle effectively. The Software & IT Services standard identifies data security as a material topic across the industry. Microsoft goes deeper, analyzing how their specific cloud infrastructure, government contracts, and enterprise customer base create unique data security risks and opportunities. Their materiality assessment connects data security investments to competitive differentiation and customer retention.

Stakeholder input in investor-focused materiality assessment comes primarily from the financial community—equity analysts, institutional investors, lenders, and rating agencies. This differs markedly from traditional materiality assessments that survey broad stakeholder groups. The goal is understanding what sustainability information investors actually use in decision-making.

Quantitative analysis supports materiality determination by examining correlations between sustainability factors and financial performance. Companies analyze how sustainability issues have affected revenue, costs, regulatory expenses, or risk premiums in the past. This historical analysis helps predict which factors might impact future financial performance.

Consider **Unilever's approach** to materiality assessment in the Consumer Goods industry. The company analyzes how sustainable sourcing practices affect input costs, brand value, and market access. They examine correlations between environmental performance and operational efficiency, between social practices and talent retention, between governance quality and regulatory relationships.

Dynamic materiality assessment recognizes that financial materiality changes over time as business conditions, regulatory environments, and investor priorities shift. Companies establish processes for regularly revisiting materiality determinations, particularly around emerging issues like climate transition risks or cybersecurity threats.

Data Collection for Industry Metrics

Building robust data collection systems for SASB metrics requires understanding both the technical requirements of specific metrics and the business processes that generate underlying data. The most successful implementations embed SASB data collection into existing operational and financial reporting systems rather than creating parallel sustainability data processes. (130)

Metric definition precision becomes critical because SASB standards often specify exact calculation methodologies, reporting boundaries, and data quality requirements. Companies must translate these technical specifications into operational procedures that ensure consistent, accurate data capture.

The **Electric Utilities industry** demonstrates this complexity clearly. Total greenhouse gas emissions reporting requires distinguishing between Scope 1 emissions from owned generation assets, Scope 2 emissions from purchased electricity, and Scope 3 emissions from fuel lifecycle impacts. Each category demands different data sources, calculation methods, and verification procedures.

Southern Company's data collection system illustrates systematic approach implementation. The utility builds emissions reporting into plant-level operational systems, capturing real-time fuel consumption, generation output, and emissions control performance. This integration ensures data accuracy while reducing manual reporting burden.

Data governance frameworks become essential for maintaining SASB data quality over time. Companies establish clear roles and responsibilities for data collection, validation, and reporting. They implement controls to ensure consistency across business units and reporting periods.

Technology solutions increasingly support SASB data collection, particularly for companies with complex operations or multiple reporting requirements. Software platforms can automate data gathering from operational systems, perform calculations according to SASB methodologies, and generate reports in required formats.

Walmart's approach to supply chain data collection shows how technology enables complex SASB reporting. The retailer uses supplier portals to gather sustainability performance data across thousands of suppliers, implementing automated validation rules and exception reporting to ensure data quality.

External data sources complement internal systems for certain SASB metrics. Companies might purchase third-party data for industry benchmarking, regulatory compliance tracking, or supply chain risk assessment. The key is integrating external data seamlessly with internal systems to provide complete pictures of sustainability performance.

Integration with Financial Reporting

Integrating SASB reporting with financial reporting processes creates synergies that reduce reporting burden while improving data quality and investor usefulness. The most effective implementations align SASB reporting cycles with financial reporting timelines and embed sustainability metrics into management discussion and analysis. (131)

Quarterly reporting integration allows companies to provide SASB updates alongside financial results, helping investors understand connections between sustainability performance and financial outcomes. This timing alignment also ensures sustainability data receives appropriate management attention and review.

Tesla's quarterly reports demonstrate effective integration by including key SASB metrics—vehicle safety ratings, battery performance data, energy efficiency improvements—directly in earnings discussions. This approach helps investors understand how sustainability performance drives financial results.

Annual report integration provides opportunities for more detailed SASB disclosure alongside comprehensive financial information. Companies increasingly include SASB tables in annual reports or reference standalone sustainability reports that follow SASB frameworks.

Management discussion and analysis (MD&A) represents a particularly powerful venue for SASB integration because it requires management to explain factors affecting financial performance. Companies can use MD&A sections to connect SASB metrics to business strategy, risk management, and performance outlook.

Internal reporting alignment ensures that information provided to investors reflects the same data management uses for decision-making. Companies align SASB metrics with internal performance management systems, executive compensation plans, and strategic planning processes.

JPMorgan Chase's integration shows how major financial institutions connect SASB disclosures to business performance. The bank includes climate-related lending and investment metrics in quarterly investor presentations, connecting ESG strategy to business growth and risk management.

Audit and assurance consideration becomes important as SASB reporting integrates more closely with financial reporting. Companies evaluate which SASB metrics warrant external assurance, particularly when they connect directly to financial performance claims or regulatory compliance.

Technology Company SASB Implementation

Technology companies face unique SASB implementation challenges due to the industry's rapid evolution, diverse business models, and complex value chains. Successful implementations require adapting SASB frameworks to capture the specific sustainability risks and opportunities of digital business models. (132)

Data security metrics represent the most critical SASB disclosure area for most technology companies, but implementation requires sophisticated thinking about what information provides investor value without compromising security. Companies must balance transparency with competitive sensitivity and security risk.

Apple's approach illustrates thoughtful data security disclosure by reporting on security incident response capabilities, privacy protection investments, and supply chain security measures without revealing specific vulnerabilities or detailed security procedures. The company connects security investments to brand protection and customer trust maintenance.

Intellectual property protection creates similar disclosure challenges. Technology companies must demonstrate effective IP management without revealing competitive information. SASB reporting typically focuses on IP protection processes, litigation management, and licensing strategy effectiveness.

Energy management reporting for technology companies requires understanding diverse operational footprints. Cloud service providers report on data center efficiency, renewable energy procurement, and cooling system optimization. Software companies focus on office space efficiency and employee commuting impacts. Hardware manufacturers address manufacturing energy consumption and product energy efficiency.

Microsoft's carbon negative commitment demonstrates how technology companies can use SASB frameworks to communicate ambitious sustainability strategies. The company reports on renewable energy procurement, carbon removal investments, and supply chain decarbonization efforts while connecting these initiatives to operational efficiency and customer value.

Supply chain complexity in technology industries requires sophisticated SASB reporting approaches. Companies must address conflict minerals sourcing, labor practices in manufacturing, and environmental compliance across global supplier networks.

Workforce management metrics for technology companies often focus on talent retention, diversity and inclusion, and skills development rather than traditional safety metrics. The industry's competitive talent market makes human capital management a critical value driver that SASB reporting can effectively communicate.

Case Study: Multi-Industry Conglomerate Approach

General Electric's SASB implementation provides an excellent case study in how diversified companies can effectively apply industry-specific standards across multiple business segments. GE operates across several SASB industries—Industrial Machinery & Goods, Gas Utilities, Aerospace & Defense, and Medical Equipment & Supplies—each requiring different sustainability focus areas. (133)

Segmented reporting approach forms the foundation of GE's strategy. The company reports under multiple SASB standards, organizing disclosures by business segment to provide investors with relevant information for each operating area. This approach recognizes that investors often focus on specific GE businesses rather than the conglomerate as a whole.

Power Generation business reports under Industrial Machinery & Goods standards, emphasizing product efficiency, lifecycle management, and manufacturing environmental performance. GE connects these metrics to competitive positioning in renewable energy markets and operational excellence initiatives.

Aviation business follows Aerospace & Defense standards, focusing on fuel efficiency innovations, supply chain management, and product safety. The company demonstrates how sustainability investments in more efficient engines create customer value while reducing environmental impact.

Healthcare business applies Medical Equipment & Supplies standards, addressing product safety, innovation management, and healthcare access. GE shows how product development investments improve patient outcomes while creating market opportunities.

Cross-segment integration allows GE to identify sustainability themes that apply across multiple businesses. The company reports on enterprise-wide initiatives around diversity and inclusion, supply chain sustainability, and climate change while providing business-specific detail under relevant SASB standards.

Investor communication strategy recognizes that different investor audiences focus on different GE businesses. The company provides both consolidated sustainability reporting and business-specific SASB disclosures to serve diverse investor needs effectively.

Performance measurement across multiple SASB standards requires sophisticated internal systems. GE aligns sustainability metrics with business performance management, ensuring that reported information reflects the data management uses for decision-making across different industries.

The implementation demonstrates how large, diversified companies can use SASB frameworks to provide clarity around complex business portfolios while maintaining focus on financially material sustainability factors in each industry segment.

Strategic Outlook

Understanding SASB fundamentals, industry-specific applications, and implementation strategies positions organizations to leverage sustainability reporting as a strategic advantage rather than a compliance burden. The framework's investor focus creates opportunities to strengthen capital market relationships while driving operational improvements that support long-term value creation.

The convergence with ISSB standards and SEC requirements means that SASB competency becomes increasingly valuable as reporting expectations continue expanding. Organizations that master these frameworks today will find themselves well-positioned for the more demanding disclosure environments emerging globally.

Successful SASB implementation requires viewing sustainability reporting as an integral part of investor relations and business strategy rather than a standalone function. The companies that connect SASB metrics to business performance, strategic planning, and stakeholder engagement will realize the greatest benefits from their implementation investments.

Key Learning Points

- SASB's investor-focused materiality approach transforms sustainability reporting from stakeholder management into strategic investor communication
- Industry-specific standards provide precise frameworks that reflect unique sustainability risks and opportunities in each sector
- Effective implementation requires robust data collection systems integrated with financial reporting processes
- Technology companies face unique challenges balancing transparency with competitive sensitivity in SASB reporting
- Multi-industry companies can leverage segmented reporting approaches to provide relevant information across diverse business portfolios
- Cross-industry comparison opportunities emerge through understanding common sustainability themes across different sectors
- The framework's convergence with ISSB and SEC requirements creates synergies that reduce overall reporting burden while improving investor utility

Chapter 15: Multi-Framework Integration

The greatest challenge—and opportunity—in modern ESG reporting lies not in mastering individual frameworks, but in creating coherent integration across CSRD, GRI, and SASB requirements. Organizations that crack this code transform what could become an overwhelming reporting burden into a strategic advantage that strengthens stakeholder relationships while streamlining internal processes.

Most companies approach multi-framework reporting like they're speaking three different languages to three different audiences. The reality is more nuanced—these frameworks share common DNA while serving distinct purposes. CSRD provides the regulatory foundation, GRI offers stakeholder transparency, and SASB delivers investor focus. The magic happens when you identify the overlaps and build unified systems that serve all three purposes efficiently.

Mapping CSRD, GRI, and SASB Overlaps

Understanding framework convergence requires systematic analysis of how these standards address similar sustainability concepts through different lenses. The overlaps are more extensive than many practitioners realize, but they require careful mapping to avoid duplication while ensuring compliance with each framework's specific requirements. (134)

Climate-related disclosures represent the most obvious convergence point. CSRD's ESRS E1 Climate Change standard requires greenhouse gas emissions reporting, transition planning, and physical risk assessment. GRI 305 Emissions covers similar ground with Scope 1, 2, and 3 emissions disclosure. SASB industry standards include climate metrics specific to each sector's material risks.

The challenge lies in the details. CSRD requires forward-looking transition plans with specific target dates and milestones. GRI emphasizes historical performance data and stakeholder engagement processes. SASB focuses on financially material climate risks that could affect enterprise value. These different emphases don't contradict each other—they create layers of disclosure that serve different stakeholder needs.

Unilever's integrated approach demonstrates effective overlap management. The company uses CSRD requirements as the foundation, ensuring regulatory compliance across all climate-related disclosures. They expand GRI reporting to include broader stakeholder concerns around supply chain emissions and biodiversity impacts. SASB metrics focus on brand value protection and operational efficiency gains from climate initiatives.

Social disclosures show similar convergence patterns with important distinctions. CSRD's social standards (S1-S4) cover workforce issues, value chain workers, affected communities, and consumers. GRI's 400 series addresses labor practices, human rights, society, and product responsibility. SASB standards include human capital management metrics relevant to specific industries.

Microsoft's social integration illustrates sophisticated overlap management. The company uses CSRD frameworks to address regulatory requirements around workforce diversity and supply chain due diligence. GRI reporting expands to cover community investment and digital inclusion initiatives that matter to broader stakeholders. SASB disclosures focus on talent retention and development metrics that investors use to evaluate competitive positioning.

Governance overlaps exist across board composition, executive compensation, business ethics, and stakeholder engagement. Each framework approaches these topics with different emphasis—CSRD focuses on sustainability governance structures, GRI addresses stakeholder engagement processes, SASB emphasizes governance factors that affect financial performance.

Data alignment strategies become essential for managing these overlaps efficiently. Companies map common data points across frameworks, identifying where single data collection processes can serve multiple reporting requirements. This prevents the common mistake of creating separate data streams for each framework.

Unified Data Collection Strategy

Building integrated data systems represents perhaps the most critical success factor in multi-framework reporting. The organizations that excel create unified data collection processes that capture information once and distribute it appropriately across different reporting requirements. (135)

Data taxonomy development forms the foundation of effective integration. Companies create master data dictionaries that map sustainability metrics across CSRD, GRI, and SASB requirements. This prevents duplication while ensuring that each framework's specific calculation methods and reporting boundaries are maintained.

Johnson & Johnson's data integration provides an excellent example of systematic approach implementation. The company built a central sustainability data platform that captures operational performance across manufacturing sites, supply chain operations, and product lifecycle impacts. The system automatically generates reports formatted for CSRD compliance, GRI standards, and SASB industry requirements.

The platform includes automated validation rules that ensure data quality while maintaining audit trails required for external assurance. Business unit managers input data once, and the system distributes information appropriately across different reporting frameworks based on predefined mapping rules.

Technology infrastructure becomes essential for managing complex multi-framework data requirements. Modern sustainability reporting platforms can accommodate different calculation methodologies, reporting boundaries, and assurance requirements within single data collection processes.

Siemens' digital approach demonstrates advanced technology integration. The company uses IoT sensors and automated data collection systems across manufacturing operations to capture real-time environmental performance data. This information feeds into reporting systems that generate CSRD-compliant disclosures, GRI-standard reports, and SASB industry metrics simultaneously.

Process standardization ensures consistency across different business units and reporting periods. Companies establish clear procedures for data collection, validation, and reporting that work across all three frameworks. This prevents the confusion that often arises when different teams manage different reporting requirements.

Quality control mechanisms become more complex but more important in multi-framework environments. Companies implement validation rules that ensure data consistency across frameworks while maintaining the specific calculation methods each standard requires.

Royal Dutch Shell's quality assurance shows how integrated controls work in practice. The company implements three-tier verification processes: operational level validation by site managers, corporate level review by sustainability teams, and independent verification by external auditors. Each tier includes framework-specific validation rules while maintaining overall data consistency.

Single Materiality Assessment Approach

Developing integrated materiality assessments that satisfy CSRD double materiality requirements, GRI stakeholder expectations, and SASB investor focus represents one of the most sophisticated challenges in multi-framework reporting. The solution involves layered analysis that builds from common foundation while addressing each framework's specific materiality concepts. (136)

Foundation materiality analysis begins with broad stakeholder engagement and impact assessment that identifies the full universe of potential sustainability topics. This comprehensive approach ensures that no material issues are overlooked regardless of which framework ultimately addresses them.

Impact materiality assessment aligns with CSRD and GRI requirements by evaluating how the organization affects people and the environment. This analysis considers both positive and negative impacts across the value chain, examining actual and potential effects on stakeholders and planetary boundaries.

Financial materiality assessment satisfies CSRD and SASB requirements by analyzing how sustainability factors could affect enterprise value. This involves quantitative analysis of potential financial impacts, scenario planning around different sustainability futures, and investor input on value-relevant factors.

IKEA's integrated materiality approach demonstrates sophisticated framework integration. The company conducts comprehensive stakeholder engagement that includes customers, suppliers, employees, communities, investors, and NGOs. This broad engagement satisfies GRI stakeholder engagement requirements while providing input for CSRD impact assessments.

The company then applies financial analysis to identify which stakeholder concerns could affect business performance, satisfying SASB investor-focused materiality requirements. CSRD double materiality emerges naturally from this process—issues that score high on either impact or financial materiality receive priority treatment.

Dynamic materiality updating becomes more important in multi-framework environments because different frameworks may emphasize emerging issues at different rates. Companies establish processes for regularly updating materiality assessments that can accommodate framework-specific timing requirements.

Prioritization matrices help organizations manage the complexity of addressing material topics across multiple frameworks. Companies create visual tools that show how different issues map across CSRD, GRI, and SASB requirements, enabling strategic decisions about resource allocation and reporting emphasis.

Nestlé's prioritization approach illustrates effective matrix management. The company creates heat maps that show materiality scores for key sustainability topics across different frameworks. This visual approach helps management teams understand where integrated approaches make sense and where framework-specific strategies are needed.

Combined Reporting Architecture

Designing reporting structures that serve multiple frameworks efficiently requires careful architecture planning that balances stakeholder needs with operational efficiency. The most successful approaches create modular reporting systems that can generate framework-specific outputs from integrated data and analysis. (137)

Master reporting framework development involves creating core sustainability disclosure that addresses common elements across CSRD, GRI, and SASB while maintaining pathways for framework-specific additions. This approach reduces duplication while ensuring compliance with each standard's unique requirements.

BMW Group's integrated reporting demonstrates sophisticated architecture design. The company publishes a comprehensive sustainability report that includes CSRD-compliant disclosures embedded within GRI-standard frameworks. SASB metrics are integrated into relevant sections with clear identification for investor audiences.

The report structure includes executive summaries for different audiences—regulatory compliance officers need CSRD confirmation, sustainability professionals want GRI detail, investors focus on SASB metrics. Each audience can access relevant information without wading through framework requirements that don't serve their needs.

Modular content design enables efficient content creation that serves multiple purposes. Companies develop sustainability content modules that can be recombined for different reporting requirements—annual reports, sustainability reports, regulatory filings, and investor presentations.

Cross-referencing systems help users navigate between different framework requirements and related disclosures. Companies create clear indexing that shows how specific disclosures satisfy multiple framework requirements, reducing confusion and improving usability.

Digital reporting platforms increasingly support multi-framework integration by providing interactive tools that allow users to filter information based on their specific interests. Stakeholders can view the same underlying information through CSRD regulatory lenses, GRI stakeholder perspectives, or SASB investor focus.

Philips' digital integration shows advanced platform capabilities. The company's online sustainability reporting allows users to select their preferred framework view, automatically highlighting relevant metrics and disclosures. Investors can focus on SASB metrics, regulators can access CSRD compliance information, and other stakeholders can explore comprehensive GRI coverage.

Assurance coordination becomes more complex but more efficient when reporting architectures support multiple frameworks. Companies can design assurance processes that cover common underlying data while addressing framework-specific requirements in targeted reviews.

Technology Solutions for Integration

Sustainability reporting technology has advanced dramatically to support multi-framework integration, with platforms now offering sophisticated capabilities for managing complex reporting requirements across CSRD, GRI, and SASB standards simultaneously. (138)

Enterprise sustainability platforms provide integrated solutions that capture data, perform calculations, and generate reports across multiple frameworks. These systems eliminate the manual effort and error risk associated with maintaining separate reporting processes for each standard.

SAP's Sustainability Control Tower demonstrates enterprise-level integration capabilities. The platform captures sustainability data from operational systems across global organizations, applies framework-specific calculation rules, and generates compliant reports for CSRD, GRI, and SASB simultaneously.

The system includes workflow management that routes information to appropriate reviewers based on framework requirements, maintains audit trails for external assurance, and provides real-time dashboards for management monitoring.

Cloud-based solutions offer scalable options for organizations that need sophisticated reporting capabilities without major IT infrastructure investments. These platforms provide pre-built templates for different frameworks while allowing customization for organization-specific needs.

Workiva's integrated approach shows cloud platform capabilities for multi-framework reporting. The system allows companies to create linked documents where data updates automatically flow through to all relevant reports. Changes to greenhouse gas emissions data, for example, update CSRD disclosures, GRI metrics, and SASB reports simultaneously.

Artificial intelligence applications increasingly support multi-framework integration by automating data mapping, identifying reporting gaps, and suggesting content improvements. AI tools can analyze framework requirements and recommend optimal integration strategies.

Data validation automation reduces the manual effort required to ensure consistency across frameworks while maintaining compliance with specific requirements. Automated systems can check that CSRD calculations align with GRI metrics and SASB standards where appropriate.

Microsoft's AI integration illustrates advanced automation capabilities. The company uses machine learning to analyze sustainability data across operations, automatically flagging inconsistencies and suggesting improvements. AI tools help identify opportunities for deeper integration while maintaining framework-specific compliance.

API integration enables sustainability reporting platforms to connect with operational systems, reducing manual data entry while improving accuracy. Companies can link sustainability reporting directly to manufacturing systems, energy management platforms, and supply chain databases.

Blockchain applications offer emerging solutions for supply chain data verification and multi-stakeholder transparency. These technologies can provide tamper-proof records that satisfy assurance requirements across multiple frameworks simultaneously.

Strategic Implementation Roadmap

Organizations seeking effective multi-framework integration need systematic approaches that build capability over time while delivering immediate compliance benefits. The most successful implementations begin with strong foundations and add sophistication as experience and capabilities develop.

Phase 1: Foundation Building focuses on establishing unified data collection and basic compliance across all three frameworks. Companies should map existing data sources, identify gaps, and implement systems that can support multiple reporting requirements.

Phase 2: Integration Optimization involves developing sophisticated materiality assessments, integrated reporting architectures, and technology solutions that eliminate duplication while improving stakeholder communication.

Phase 3: Strategic Differentiation transforms multi-framework reporting from compliance exercise into competitive advantage through superior stakeholder engagement, operational insights, and strategic planning integration.

The organizations that master multi-framework integration position themselves for success as reporting requirements continue expanding globally. They build capabilities that adapt to new standards and stakeholder expectations while maintaining efficiency and strategic focus.

Chapter 16: Assurance and Verification

The credibility of ESG reporting hinges on robust assurance processes that provide stakeholders with confidence in disclosed information. As sustainability reporting transitions from voluntary disclosure to regulatory requirement, the stakes for accurate, verifiable information have increased dramatically—making assurance strategy a critical component of any successful ESG program.

The assurance process transforms sustainability reporting from internal communication into externally validated information that stakeholders can rely on for decision-making. This transformation requires understanding different levels of assurance, preparing organizational systems for external review, and selecting providers who can deliver both technical competence and strategic insight.

Limited vs. Reasonable Assurance

Understanding assurance levels represents the first critical decision in developing effective verification strategies. The choice between limited and reasonable assurance affects scope, cost, procedures, and stakeholder confidence—making this decision central to overall ESG reporting strategy. (139)

Limited assurance provides moderate confidence that information is free from material misstatement. Assurance providers perform analytical procedures and inquiry-based testing but don't conduct the extensive substantive testing required for reasonable assurance. This approach typically costs 30-50% less than reasonable assurance while still providing meaningful credibility enhancement.

Reasonable assurance provides high confidence that information is free from material misstatement. Providers conduct extensive substantive testing, detailed sampling procedures, and comprehensive analytical reviews similar to financial audit procedures. This level provides maximum credibility but requires significant investment in time and resources.

Scope determination becomes critical for both assurance levels. Companies must decide which metrics warrant assurance based on stakeholder needs, regulatory requirements, and materiality assessments. Most organizations begin with limited assurance on key metrics and expand scope over time.

Unilever's assurance evolution demonstrates strategic scope expansion over multiple years. The company started with limited assurance on greenhouse gas emissions and waste data—metrics with established measurement protocols and stakeholder interest. They gradually expanded to include water consumption, sustainable sourcing percentages, and safety performance metrics.

After three years of limited assurance, Unilever moved to reasonable assurance for climate-related metrics while maintaining limited assurance for newer metrics like biodiversity impact indicators. This phased approach allowed the company to build internal capabilities while managing costs effectively.

Materiality thresholds differ between assurance levels and affect reporting outcomes. Limited assurance typically uses higher materiality thresholds—meaning larger errors are required before assurance providers flag issues. Reasonable assurance uses lower thresholds similar to financial auditing standards.

Cost-benefit analysis should guide assurance level decisions. Companies need to evaluate how much additional stakeholder confidence reasonable assurance provides relative to the additional cost and effort required. The analysis should consider regulatory requirements, investor expectations, and competitive positioning.

IKEA's cost-benefit approach illustrates systematic decision-making. The company conducts annual assessments of which metrics benefit most from higher assurance levels based on stakeholder surveys, regulatory developments, and materiality updates. Climate metrics receive reasonable assurance due to regulatory requirements and investor focus, while social metrics receive limited assurance aligned with stakeholder information needs.

Regulatory considerations increasingly influence assurance level decisions. CSRD requires limited assurance initially but mandates reasonable assurance for climate metrics within three years. Companies subject to these requirements need long-term assurance strategies that build toward reasonable assurance capabilities.

Preparing for External Verification

Organizational readiness for external assurance requires systematic preparation that goes far beyond gathering documentation. Successful verification depends on robust internal controls, clear data governance, and organizational understanding of assurance process requirements. (140)

Documentation systems form the foundation of effective assurance preparation. Companies need clear records of data collection procedures, calculation methodologies, assumptions, and review processes. This documentation must demonstrate that reported information results from reliable, repeatable processes rather than ad hoc analysis.

Data lineage tracking becomes essential for demonstrating information reliability. Assurance providers need to understand how data flows from operational systems through calculation processes to final reporting. Companies should maintain clear trails that show data sources, transformation steps, and quality control points.

Siemens' documentation approach demonstrates best practice implementation. The company maintains comprehensive data governance systems that track sustainability information from source systems through reporting outputs. Each metric includes source documentation, calculation procedures, responsible personnel, and review checkpoints.

The system generates automatic documentation packages for assurance providers that include data validation reports, exception analyses, and management review evidence. This preparation reduces assurance costs while improving provider confidence in reported information.

Internal controls assessment requires evaluating existing processes against assurance provider expectations. Companies should identify potential weaknesses in data collection, calculation, or review processes before external verification begins. This proactive approach prevents surprises during assurance procedures.

Process standardization across business units and reporting periods creates consistency that assurance providers can evaluate efficiently. Companies should establish clear procedures for data collection, validation, and reporting that work consistently across different locations and time periods.

Personnel training ensures that staff understand assurance requirements and can respond effectively to provider inquiries. Key personnel should understand what assurance providers will ask, what documentation they'll need, and how to explain process rationale clearly.

BMW Group's training program illustrates comprehensive staff preparation. The company conducts annual training for sustainability coordinators across global operations, covering assurance process expectations, documentation requirements, and interview techniques. Training includes mock assurance sessions that help staff understand provider perspectives and communication approaches.

Management representation processes prepare leadership for their role in external verification. Senior management typically provides written representations about information accuracy, process integrity, and disclosure completeness. These representations carry legal significance and require careful preparation.

Internal Audit Considerations

Internal audit involvement in ESG reporting creates powerful synergies that strengthen both assurance outcomes and organizational capabilities. Internal auditors bring risk assessment skills, control evaluation expertise, and independence that complement external assurance while building lasting organizational capabilities. (141)

Risk-based audit planning applies internal audit methodologies to sustainability reporting, focusing attention on areas with highest risk of misstatement or control failure. This approach ensures efficient use of internal audit resources while providing meaningful support for external assurance processes.

Controls evaluation represents a natural extension of internal audit capabilities into sustainability reporting. Internal auditors can assess control design and operating effectiveness using established methodologies adapted for ESG data and processes.

JPMorgan Chase's internal audit integration demonstrates sophisticated risk-based approaches. The bank's internal audit team conducts annual assessments of ESG reporting controls, focusing on data governance, calculation accuracy, and management review effectiveness. These assessments inform both internal improvement efforts and external assurance planning.

The team uses sampling methodologies to test control operating effectiveness across global operations, providing management with confidence in reporting reliability before external verification begins. Internal audit findings help prioritize improvement efforts and demonstrate control effectiveness to external providers.

Three lines of defense models work effectively for ESG reporting when properly implemented. Business operations provide first-line control through data collection and validation processes. Corporate sustainability teams provide second-line oversight through policy development and monitoring. Internal audit provides third-line independent assessment and verification.

Coordination with external assurance creates efficiencies when internal and external auditors share information appropriately. Internal audit work can inform external assurance planning while external provider observations can guide internal audit focus areas.

Capability building through internal audit involvement creates lasting organizational benefits beyond immediate assurance support. Internal auditors develop ESG expertise while sustainability teams gain control and risk management capabilities.

Nestlé's capability approach shows how internal audit builds organizational ESG competence. The company's internal audit team includes dedicated ESG specialists who work across business units to strengthen reporting capabilities. These auditors provide training, assess control effectiveness, and support continuous improvement in sustainability data management.

Reporting integration allows internal audit findings to support multiple organizational needs. Internal audit assessments can inform management decision-making, support external assurance efficiency, and demonstrate control effectiveness to regulators and stakeholders.

Controls and Documentation

Establishing robust controls for ESG reporting requires adapting financial reporting control frameworks to address unique sustainability data challenges. These adaptations must account for different data sources, calculation complexities, and stakeholder expectations while maintaining control effectiveness. (142)

Entity-level controls provide overall governance for ESG reporting similar to financial reporting frameworks. These controls address tone at the top, organizational structure, competence requirements, and oversight responsibilities specific to sustainability disclosures.

Process-level controls address specific risks in data collection, calculation, and reporting processes. Companies need controls over data completeness, accuracy, validity, and authorization that account for ESG reporting complexities like estimation techniques and forward-looking information.

Microsoft's control framework illustrates comprehensive ESG control implementation. The company adapted its existing financial reporting controls to address sustainability data, including automated validation rules, management review requirements, and documentation standards specific to ESG metrics.

Controls include automated data validation that flags unusual variances, mandatory review by qualified personnel before data approval, and documentation requirements that ensure calculation transparency. The framework includes specific controls for estimated data, third-party information, and forward-looking disclosures.

Documentation standards must address unique ESG reporting requirements while maintaining consistency with financial reporting practices. Companies need clear requirements for supporting documentation, retention periods, and access controls that satisfy both assurance and regulatory needs.

Data quality controls become especially important for ESG reporting due to data source diversity and calculation complexity. Companies should implement controls that address data completeness, accuracy, validity, and timeliness across different types of sustainability information.

Change management controls ensure that modifications to calculation methods, reporting boundaries, or data sources are properly evaluated, approved, and documented. These controls prevent unintended changes that could affect data comparability or accuracy.

General Electric's change management demonstrates systematic control over ESG reporting modifications. The company requires formal approval processes for changes to sustainability metrics, calculation methods, or reporting boundaries. Changes require documentation of rationale, impact assessment, and stakeholder communication plans.

IT general controls adapted for ESG reporting systems ensure that technology infrastructure supports reliable information processing. These controls address system access, change management, and backup procedures specific to sustainability data systems.

Segregation of duties in ESG reporting prevents single individuals from controlling entire processes while recognizing organizational size constraints. Companies should implement appropriate segregation based on organizational capabilities and risk assessments.

Assurance Provider Selection

Choosing assurance providers requires evaluation of technical competence, industry experience, and strategic fit that goes beyond traditional audit firm selection criteria. ESG assurance combines elements of financial auditing, engineering assessment, and stakeholder communication—demanding providers with diverse capabilities. (143)

Provider types include traditional accounting firms expanding into ESG services, specialized sustainability assurance providers, and engineering firms developing assurance capabilities. Each type offers different strengths and limitations that should align with organizational needs and assurance objectives.

Accounting firm advantages include established assurance methodologies, regulatory relationships, and integration with financial audit processes. Major firms offer global coverage and resource depth but may lack deep sustainability expertise in emerging areas.

Specialist provider advantages include deep ESG expertise, innovative assurance approaches, and strong stakeholder credibility. These providers often lead in developing new assurance techniques but may lack global coverage or integration with financial processes.

Shell's provider selection demonstrates systematic evaluation across provider types. The company evaluates potential providers based on technical competence in energy sector sustainability issues, global coverage capabilities, and integration with existing audit relationships.

Selection criteria include demonstrated experience with complex environmental data, understanding of energy transition issues, and ability to provide insights beyond compliance verification. Shell uses different providers for different assurance scopes, optimizing provider strengths for specific requirements.

Competence evaluation should assess provider understanding of specific sustainability issues, assurance methodology sophistication, and ability to provide value-added insights. Companies should evaluate both technical skills and communication capabilities.

Industry experience becomes increasingly important as ESG assurance develops sector-specific requirements. Providers need understanding of industry-specific risks, measurement challenges, and stakeholder expectations to deliver effective assurance.

Global coordination requirements affect provider selection for multinational companies. Organizations need providers who can deliver consistent service quality across different jurisdictions while managing local regulatory requirements and cultural considerations.

Volkswagen's global approach illustrates complex provider coordination. The company uses a lead assurance firm for overall coordination and methodology development while engaging local providers in specific markets to address regional requirements and language needs.

Coordination includes standardized procedures across all providers, regular communication about findings and issues, and integrated reporting that provides consistent global perspective on assurance results.

Value-added services differentiate providers beyond basic assurance compliance. Leading providers offer insights on industry benchmarking, control improvement recommendations, and strategic ESG positioning that extend beyond verification requirements.

Cost management requires understanding different provider pricing models and optimizing assurance scope for cost effectiveness. Companies should evaluate total cost including preparation time, provider fees, and ongoing relationship management.

Building Assurance Excellence

The organizations that excel in ESG assurance treat verification as strategic capability rather than compliance requirement. They build internal expertise, develop provider relationships, and create continuous improvement processes that strengthen both reporting quality and organizational learning.

This approach requires long-term commitment to building assurance readiness, developing internal capabilities, and treating provider relationships as strategic partnerships. The investment pays dividends through improved stakeholder confidence, enhanced internal controls, and better organizational understanding of sustainability performance.

Companies that master ESG assurance position themselves for success as reporting requirements expand and stakeholder expectations increase. They build capabilities that adapt to new standards while maintaining efficiency and strategic focus.

Chapter 17: Beyond Compliance - Strategic Value Creation

The true measure of ESG excellence lies not in checking compliance boxes, but in transforming sustainability frameworks into engines of strategic value creation. Organizations that master this transformation discover that robust ESG practices don't just satisfy stakeholders—they drive innovation, reduce costs, attract capital, and create competitive advantages that compound over time.

This shift from compliance mindset to strategic advantage requires reconceptualizing ESG reporting as business intelligence that informs decision-making rather than burden that consumes resources. The companies making this transition successfully treat sustainability data as strategic assets that guide everything from product development to capital allocation.

ESG Integration in Strategy

Strategic ESG integration goes far beyond sustainability departments producing annual reports—it requires embedding ESG considerations into core business planning, performance measurement, and decision-making processes at every organizational level. (144)

Board-level integration represents the starting point for authentic strategic ESG integration. Boards must move beyond compliance oversight to active engagement with how ESG factors affect business strategy, risk management, and value creation. This evolution requires board education, appropriate committee structures, and management reporting that connects ESG performance to business outcomes.

Unilever's board integration demonstrates advanced strategic oversight. The board receives quarterly reports that connect sustainability metrics to business performance, market positioning, and competitive advantage. Board discussions focus on how environmental commitments affect innovation pipelines, how social programs drive brand value, and how governance practices support operational excellence.

Board committees include ESG expertise alongside traditional financial and operational knowledge. Committee charters specifically address ESG oversight responsibilities, and board evaluation processes assess ESG governance effectiveness alongside traditional oversight areas.

Strategic planning integration requires incorporating ESG considerations into fundamental business planning processes rather than treating sustainability as separate activity. Companies need planning processes that evaluate ESG risks and opportunities alongside traditional business factors.

Microsoft's planning integration illustrates systematic strategic incorporation. The company's annual planning process includes ESG scenario analysis that evaluates how sustainability trends affect market opportunities, competitive positioning, and operational requirements. Planning teams assess how carbon neutrality commitments influence product development priorities, how diversity initiatives affect talent acquisition, and how governance practices support market expansion.

Strategic plans include specific ESG objectives with clear accountability and resource allocation. Performance measurement systems track progress on ESG commitments alongside financial and operational metrics, ensuring that sustainability goals receive appropriate management attention.

Innovation strategy increasingly connects to ESG objectives as companies discover that sustainability challenges drive product innovation and market opportunity identification. Leading organizations use ESG frameworks to identify innovation priorities and measure innovation success.

Product development integration requires considering ESG factors throughout innovation processes—from initial concept development through commercialization and lifecycle management. Companies need development processes that evaluate environmental impact, social benefit, and governance implications alongside traditional performance and cost criteria.

Tesla's development integration shows how ESG considerations drive innovation strategy. The company's product development processes prioritize environmental impact reduction, energy efficiency improvement, and safety advancement as core design criteria rather than secondary considerations.

Development teams use lifecycle assessment tools to evaluate environmental impact from materials sourcing through end-of-life recycling. Innovation metrics include sustainability performance alongside traditional measures like cost, performance, and time-to-market.

Operational excellence emerges when companies integrate ESG practices into core operational processes. Leading organizations discover that sustainability initiatives often drive operational efficiency, cost reduction, and quality improvement that create business value independent of ESG benefits.

Investor Relations and ESG

ESG-focused investor relations requires sophisticated communication strategies that help investors understand how sustainability practices create financial value and competitive advantage. This goes beyond reporting compliance to active engagement that positions ESG performance as investment thesis support. (145)

Investor segmentation becomes essential for effective ESG communication because different investor types focus on different ESG aspects. Pension funds might prioritize long-term sustainability, growth investors might focus on ESG-driven innovation opportunities, and value investors might emphasize operational efficiency from sustainability practices.

BlackRock's investor approach demonstrates sophisticated segmentation. The asset manager provides different ESG communication packages for different investor types—institutional investors receive detailed analysis of ESG integration in investment processes, retail investors get simplified communication about sustainable investing options, and corporate engagement focuses on governance practices and strategic planning.

Communication strategies include specialized presentations for ESG-focused investors, integration of sustainability metrics in traditional investor materials, and proactive engagement around ESG strategy development and implementation.

Performance storytelling requires connecting ESG metrics to business outcomes in ways that investors can evaluate and compare. Companies need narratives that show how sustainability investments generate returns, reduce risks, and create competitive advantages.

Earnings call integration represents powerful opportunities for ESG communication when companies connect sustainability performance to financial results. Leading organizations include ESG metrics in quarterly earnings discussions, particularly when sustainability initiatives affect revenue, costs, or strategic positioning.

Patagonia's earnings communication illustrates effective performance storytelling. The company regularly discusses how environmental commitments drive customer loyalty, brand differentiation, and premium pricing. Earnings calls include updates on sustainability initiatives that affect supply chain costs, product innovation, and market positioning.

Management explains how ESG practices create measurable business value—reduced material costs through recycling initiatives, increased customer retention through purpose-driven branding, and operational efficiency through environmental management systems.

ESG roadshows provide focused opportunities for detailed investor engagement around sustainability strategy and performance. These specialized events allow companies to present comprehensive ESG information to interested investors while demonstrating management commitment to sustainability leadership.

Capital allocation communication helps investors understand how ESG considerations influence investment decisions, resource allocation, and strategic planning. Companies should explain how sustainability factors affect capital expenditure priorities, acquisition criteria, and business development investments.

Johnson & Johnson's capital communication demonstrates effective allocation transparency. The company explains how ESG criteria influence R&D investment priorities, manufacturing location decisions, and supply chain development. Investors receive clear information about how sustainability considerations affect capital allocation alongside traditional financial criteria.

Sustainability-Linked Financing

Sustainability-linked financing represents one of the most direct ways that ESG performance translates into financial value creation. These innovative instruments tie borrowing costs or investment returns to specific sustainability performance targets, creating direct financial incentives for ESG improvement. (146)

Sustainability-linked bonds offer interest rate adjustments based on achieving predetermined ESG targets. Companies that meet sustainability objectives pay lower interest rates, while missing targets results in higher borrowing costs. This structure aligns financial incentives with ESG performance while providing investors with exposure to sustainability outcomes.

Target selection becomes critical for effective sustainability-linked financing because targets must be material, measurable, and achievable within reasonable timeframes. Companies need targets that are ambitious enough to drive meaningful improvement but realistic enough to maintain investor confidence.

Enel's bond structure illustrates sophisticated target development. The Italian utility issued sustainability-linked bonds tied to renewable energy capacity expansion and emissions reduction targets. Targets include specific metrics—renewable capacity additions and carbon intensity reductions—with clear measurement methodologies and external verification requirements.

Bond terms include interest rate step-ups if targets are missed and potential step-downs for over-achievement. This structure creates powerful financial incentives for sustainability performance while providing investors with predictable risk-return profiles.

Sustainability-linked loans tie borrowing costs to ESG performance metrics, typically with annual assessments that adjust interest rates based on target achievement. These instruments work particularly well for companies with regular borrowing needs and clear sustainability improvement trajectories.

Performance measurement requires robust systems for tracking sustainability metrics and verifying target achievement. Companies need measurement protocols that satisfy both internal management needs and external verification requirements.

IKEA's loan integration demonstrates effective performance measurement for sustainability-linked financing. The company's credit facilities tie interest rates to forest conservation targets, renewable energy adoption, and circular economy initiatives.

Measurement systems include third-party verification of forest management practices, certified renewable energy procurement documentation, and audited circular economy performance metrics. This verification provides lenders with confidence in performance measurement while ensuring target achievement drives real sustainability improvement.

Green bonds provide capital specifically for environmental projects and initiatives. While different from sustainability-linked instruments, green bonds offer another avenue for companies to access capital markets for ESG initiatives while demonstrating commitment to sustainability objectives.

Social bonds focus on social impact projects and initiatives, providing capital for activities like affordable housing, education, healthcare, and economic development. These instruments help companies finance social initiatives while accessing capital markets interested in social impact.

Use of proceeds transparency becomes essential for green and social bonds because investors need confidence that capital supports genuine sustainability initiatives. Companies must provide clear documentation of fund allocation and impact measurement.

Competitive Advantage Through Transparency

ESG transparency creates competitive advantages that extend far beyond stakeholder relationship management. Companies that excel in sustainability disclosure often discover that transparency drives operational improvement, innovation acceleration, and market differentiation that create lasting competitive benefits. (147)

Brand differentiation emerges when companies use ESG transparency to demonstrate authentic commitment to sustainability leadership. Consumers, employees, and business partners increasingly prefer organizations with clear sustainability commitments backed by transparent performance reporting.

Customer loyalty benefits result from ESG transparency when companies demonstrate genuine commitment to values that customers care about. Transparent reporting builds trust and credibility that supports customer retention and premium pricing.

Patagonia's transparency advantage illustrates brand differentiation through radical transparency. The company publishes detailed information about supply chain practices, environmental impact, and social initiatives that goes far beyond regulatory requirements.

This transparency includes factory location disclosure, worker condition reporting, and environmental impact assessment that competitors rarely match. The transparency builds customer trust and loyalty that supports premium pricing and brand strength.

Talent attraction benefits from ESG transparency as employees increasingly prefer organizations with clear sustainability commitments and transparent performance reporting. Companies with strong ESG transparency often experience improved recruitment, retention, and employee engagement.

Supply chain advantages develop when companies use ESG transparency to build stronger supplier relationships and drive supply chain improvement. Transparent companies often receive preferential treatment from suppliers who value partnerships with sustainability leaders.

Unilever's supply chain transparency demonstrates competitive advantage development through open communication about supplier requirements, performance expectations, and improvement support. The company's transparent approach attracts high-quality suppliers while driving continuous improvement throughout the supply chain.

Transparency includes public reporting on supplier assessment results, improvement programs, and partnership development that builds trust and collaboration throughout the value chain.

Innovation acceleration results from ESG transparency when companies use open communication to identify improvement opportunities, benchmark performance, and drive continuous innovation. Transparent companies often lead in sustainability innovation because transparency drives accountability and improvement.

Risk management benefits emerge from ESG transparency when open communication helps companies identify and address potential issues before they become significant problems. Transparent companies often experience fewer ESG-related crises because transparency enables proactive risk management.

Investor premium develops when companies demonstrate ESG leadership through transparent reporting and performance. Investors increasingly provide valuation premiums for companies with strong ESG performance and transparent communication.

Future-Proofing Your Approach

Building future-ready ESG capabilities requires anticipating how sustainability reporting and stakeholder expectations will continue developing while maintaining focus on current requirements and opportunities. Organizations need approaches that adapt to new standards while building on existing strengths. (148)

Emerging framework preparation involves monitoring developments in sustainability reporting standards and building capabilities that can accommodate new requirements efficiently. Companies should track ISSB standard development, TNFD framework evolution, and other emerging requirements that might affect future reporting.

Technology investment should prioritize flexible platforms that can accommodate new reporting requirements while supporting current needs. Companies need technology strategies that balance immediate efficiency gains with long-term adaptability requirements.

Microsoft's technology approach demonstrates future-ready platform development. The company invests in sustainability reporting technology that can accommodate multiple frameworks while providing advanced analytics capabilities for decision support.

The platform includes APIs that connect with emerging standard requirements, machine learning capabilities that identify improvement opportunities, and scenario modeling tools that support strategic planning around sustainability futures.

Capability building requires developing organizational expertise that can adapt to changing requirements while maintaining current performance excellence. Companies need training and development programs that build broad sustainability competence rather than narrow compliance skills.

Stakeholder engagement evolution requires understanding how different stakeholder groups' ESG expectations will continue developing. Companies should build engagement processes that can accommodate new stakeholder requirements while maintaining current relationship effectiveness.

Regulatory monitoring becomes increasingly important as ESG reporting requirements expand globally. Companies need systems for tracking regulatory developments and assessing potential impact on reporting requirements and business operations.

Innovation focus should prioritize sustainability solutions that create competitive advantage while addressing emerging challenges. Companies need innovation strategies that anticipate future sustainability requirements while building on current capabilities.

Partnership development requires building relationships with other organizations that can support future ESG requirements and opportunities. Companies should cultivate partnerships with technology providers, academic institutions, and other organizations that can support evolving needs.

Pathway to Excellence

Organizations that successfully transform ESG compliance into strategic value creation share common characteristics: they integrate ESG considerations into core business processes, they use sustainability data for decision-making rather than just reporting, and they view ESG transparency as competitive advantage rather than regulatory burden.

This transformation requires patience, investment, and commitment to continuous improvement. The companies that make this journey successfully discover that ESG excellence creates lasting competitive advantages that extend far beyond stakeholder satisfaction to fundamental business performance improvement.

The future belongs to organizations that master this integration—companies that use ESG frameworks not just to satisfy external requirements but to drive internal excellence, innovation, and value creation that benefits all stakeholders while building sustainable competitive advantage.

Essential Takeaways

- Multi-framework integration eliminates duplication while ensuring compliance through unified data collection and materiality assessment approaches
- Strategic ESG integration requires embedding sustainability considerations into core business planning, innovation, and decision-making processes
- Assurance excellence builds stakeholder confidence while driving internal control improvements and organizational capability development
- Sustainability-linked financing creates direct financial incentives for ESG performance while providing access to capital markets
- ESG transparency generates competitive advantages through brand differentiation, talent attraction, and investor premium development
- Future-proofing approaches balance current compliance requirements with emerging standard preparation and capability building
- Strategic value creation emerges when organizations treat ESG frameworks as business intelligence rather than compliance burden

Chapter 18: Implementation Toolkit

The difference between ESG reporting success and failure often comes down to execution—having the right tools, templates, and processes in place before you need them. Too many organizations approach ESG implementation with good intentions but poor planning, resulting in rushed deadlines, inconsistent data, and reports that satisfy no one.

Smart implementation requires building your toolkit systematically, just like any other business function. You need project planning frameworks that account for ESG complexities, budget templates that capture hidden costs, and change management approaches that address the cultural shifts ESG reporting demands. The organizations that get this right treat implementation planning as seriously as they treat the reporting itself.

Project Planning Templates

ESG project planning requires specialized templates that account for the unique challenges of sustainability reporting—multiple stakeholder groups, diverse data sources, evolving regulatory requirements, and long implementation timelines that span multiple reporting cycles. (149)

Master project timeline templates should include all major ESG implementation phases: framework selection and scope definition, materiality assessment completion, data collection system development, internal process establishment, external assurance preparation, and ongoing reporting cycle management. Each phase requires specific deliverables, resource allocations, and success criteria.

Microsoft's implementation planning demonstrates sophisticated template development for large-scale ESG programs. The company created master project plans that span

18-month implementation cycles, with quarterly checkpoints and annual scope reviews. Templates include dependency mapping between different framework requirements, resource allocation across business units, and risk mitigation strategies for common implementation challenges.

Templates address the reality that ESG implementation often involves multiple parallel workstreams—CSRD compliance preparation, GRI reporting enhancement, SASB investor communication development, and assurance readiness building. Each workstream requires coordination while maintaining independent progress tracking.

Milestone definition templates help organizations establish clear success criteria for each implementation phase. Templates should include quantitative measures like data collection completion percentages and qualitative assessments like stakeholder satisfaction scores. Clear milestones prevent scope creep while ensuring implementation stays focused on actual business value creation.

Resource allocation templates capture the full scope of ESG implementation requirements—not just consulting fees and software costs, but internal staff time, training expenses, travel costs for stakeholder engagement, and ongoing operational expenses for data collection and reporting.

Unilever's resource planning illustrates realistic cost estimation for global ESG implementation. The company's templates include detailed breakdowns of internal staff time requirements across different business functions—operations teams for data collection, finance teams for system integration, legal teams for compliance review, and communications teams for stakeholder engagement.

Templates also capture ongoing operational costs that many organizations underestimate—annual software licenses, external assurance fees, staff training updates, and stakeholder engagement activities. This comprehensive view prevents budget surprises during implementation.

Risk management templates help organizations anticipate and prepare for common ESG implementation challenges. Templates should address data quality issues, regulatory requirement changes, stakeholder expectation management, and technology integration difficulties.

Scope management templates become essential for controlling ESG implementation complexity. Organizations need clear frameworks for deciding which metrics to include, which stakeholders to engage, and which systems to integrate. Templates should include decision criteria and approval processes that prevent implementation from becoming overwhelming.

Johnson & Johnson's scope control demonstrates effective template-based boundary management. The company uses structured decision frameworks that evaluate new ESG requirements against strategic priorities, resource availability, and stakeholder impact. Templates include standard evaluation criteria and approval workflows that maintain implementation focus while allowing for necessary scope adjustments.

RACI Matrices for ESG Reporting

Responsibility assignment for ESG reporting requires sophisticated RACI matrices that account for the cross-functional nature of sustainability data and the multiple stakeholder groups involved in reporting processes. Traditional organizational structures often don't map clearly to ESG reporting needs, making clear responsibility definition essential. (150)

Executive level RACI should define clear roles for board members, CEO, CFO, Chief Sustainability Officer, and other senior leaders in ESG strategy development, performance monitoring, and external communication. Executive responsibilities include strategic direction setting, resource allocation approval, performance review, and stakeholder communication.

Board responsibility typically includes ESG strategy approval, performance oversight, risk assessment review, and public disclosure approval. Board members are accountable for ensuring ESG governance but rarely responsible for detailed implementation. Executive teams are responsible for strategy development and performance delivery.

Operational level RACI addresses day-to-day ESG reporting activities across different business functions. Operations teams typically provide manufacturing and facility data. Finance teams handle system integration and control implementation. Human resources provides workforce metrics. Procurement manages supplier information. Each function has specific responsibilities while requiring coordination for integrated reporting.

General Electric's RACI implementation illustrates sophisticated responsibility assignment across a diversified industrial company. The company creates business unit-specific RACI matrices that address different sustainability requirements across aviation, power, healthcare, and renewable energy operations.

Matrices include clear escalation paths for data quality issues, scope disputes, and resource conflicts. Business unit leaders are accountable for data accuracy and timeliness within their operations. Corporate teams are responsible for consolidated reporting and external communication. Shared service functions provide technical support and process standardization.

Geographic RACI becomes important for multinational companies managing ESG reporting across different regions and regulatory environments. Templates should address how global standards apply to local operations while accommodating regional reporting requirements and cultural differences.

Vendor and partner RACI addresses external relationships that affect ESG reporting—suppliers providing sustainability data, consultants supporting implementation, technology vendors maintaining reporting systems, and assurance providers conducting verification. Clear external responsibility definition prevents gaps and overlap.

BMW Group's vendor management demonstrates effective external RACI implementation. The company defines specific responsibilities for sustainability consultants, technology providers, and assurance firms while maintaining clear internal accountability for overall program success.

Matrices include performance standards for external partners, communication protocols for issue resolution, and escalation procedures for service delivery problems. Internal teams maintain accountability for vendor selection, performance monitoring, and relationship management.

Change management RACI addresses how responsibility assignment adapts as ESG programs mature and requirements change. Templates should include processes for updating responsibility assignments, adding new stakeholders, and adjusting scope boundaries as programs develop.

Budget Planning Worksheets

ESG implementation budgeting requires specialized worksheets that capture both obvious costs and hidden expenses that organizations frequently underestimate. Successful budgeting considers immediate implementation needs alongside ongoing operational requirements for sustainable ESG programs. (151)

Technology costs represent significant budget components that many organizations underestimate. Budget worksheets should include software licensing fees, implementation consulting, system integration costs, ongoing maintenance expenses, and upgrade requirements. Technology budgets should plan for 3-5 year cycles rather than annual purchases.

Siemens' technology budgeting demonstrates sophisticated cost planning for global ESG reporting systems. The company's worksheets include detailed breakdowns of platform licensing costs across different user types, implementation consulting fees for system configuration, integration costs for connecting with existing enterprise systems, and ongoing support expenses for system maintenance.

Budgets also include training costs for system users, data migration expenses from legacy systems, and contingency funds for scope expansion as ESG requirements develop. This approach prevents technology budget overruns while ensuring adequate system capabilities.

Consulting and advisory costs include strategy development, framework implementation, process design, and ongoing advisory support. Budget worksheets should distinguish between one-time implementation consulting and ongoing advisory relationships that provide continuous support.

Personnel costs often represent the largest ESG implementation expense but receive insufficient budget attention. Worksheets should include dedicated ESG staff hiring, existing employee time allocation, training and development expenses, and contractor costs for specialized tasks.

Shell's personnel budgeting illustrates comprehensive human resource planning for ESG implementation. The company's worksheets include detailed analysis of internal staff time requirements across different business functions, training costs for building ESG competence, and contractor expenses for specialized skills not available internally.

Budgets address the reality that ESG implementation requires significant time commitments from staff across multiple functions—operations personnel for data collection, finance teams for system integration, communications teams for stakeholder engagement, and legal teams for compliance review.

External assurance costs include provider selection, annual assurance fees, preparation time costs, and potential scope expansion expenses. Budget worksheets should plan for increasing assurance requirements as ESG programs mature and regulatory demands expand.

Stakeholder engagement costs include survey development, focus group facilitation, stakeholder meeting expenses, and communication material development. These costs vary significantly based on organization size and stakeholder complexity but are essential for effective ESG implementation.

Walmart's engagement budgeting demonstrates systematic cost planning for complex stakeholder environments. The company's worksheets include detailed breakdowns of supplier engagement costs, customer research expenses, community outreach activities, and investor communication programs.

Budgets account for geographic diversity in stakeholder populations, language and cultural adaptation requirements, and ongoing relationship maintenance costs beyond initial engagement activities.

Contingency planning should include buffer amounts for scope changes, regulatory requirement updates, and technology integration challenges. ESG implementation often encounters unexpected requirements that demand budget flexibility.

Vendor Evaluation Criteria

ESG vendor selection requires evaluation criteria that go beyond traditional technology and consulting selection factors. Organizations need frameworks that assess vendor sustainability expertise, framework knowledge, industry experience, and long-term partnership potential. (152)

Technical competence evaluation should assess vendor understanding of specific ESG frameworks, experience with similar implementation challenges, and demonstrated success with comparable organizations. Technical evaluation should include both breadth of ESG knowledge and depth in relevant specialization areas.

Framework expertise becomes especially important as organizations implement multiple ESG standards. Vendors should demonstrate deep knowledge of CSRD requirements, GRI standards, SASB industry specifics, and emerging frameworks like TNFD and ISSB. Expertise should include both technical knowledge and practical implementation experience.

Microsoft's vendor evaluation demonstrates systematic assessment of ESG consulting capabilities. The company creates detailed scorecards that evaluate vendor framework knowledge through technical interviews, case study presentations, and reference checks with similar implementations.

Evaluation includes assessment of vendor ability to integrate multiple frameworks, experience with technology platform implementation, and demonstrated success with complex global rollouts. The company prioritizes vendors who understand both technical requirements and business strategy implications.

Industry experience evaluation should assess vendor familiarity with sector-specific ESG challenges, regulatory environments, and stakeholder expectations. Vendors should demonstrate understanding of industry-specific risks, materiality factors, and reporting practices.

Global capability assessment becomes important for multinational implementations. Vendors should demonstrate ability to work across different regulatory environments, cultural contexts, and language requirements while maintaining consistent service quality.

Unilever's global evaluation illustrates sophisticated assessment of vendor international capabilities. The company evaluates vendor presence in key markets, local regulatory knowledge, and demonstrated success with multi-region implementations.

Assessment includes vendor ability to coordinate across different time zones, manage local partnership relationships, and adapt standardized approaches to local requirements while maintaining global consistency.

Technology integration capability should assess vendor experience with ESG reporting platforms, ability to integrate with existing enterprise systems, and technical skills for complex data management requirements.

Partnership approach evaluation considers vendor commitment to long-term relationships rather than transactional service delivery. ESG implementation often requires multi-year partnerships that support ongoing program development and requirement changes.

Johnson & Johnson's partnership assessment demonstrates effective evaluation of vendor relationship approaches. The company evaluates vendor willingness to invest in deep understanding of business strategy, commitment to ongoing advisory support, and flexibility to adapt services as ESG requirements develop.

Assessment includes vendor financial stability, key personnel retention, and demonstrated commitment to staying current with ESG framework developments and regulatory changes.

Cultural fit evaluation assesses vendor alignment with organizational values and working styles. ESG implementation often requires close collaboration between vendor and internal teams, making cultural compatibility important for success.

Change Management Tools

ESG change management requires specialized tools that address the unique challenges of sustainability transformation—shifting from compliance mindset to strategic thinking, building new competencies across multiple functions, and managing stakeholder expectations during long implementation cycles. (153)

Stakeholder impact assessment tools help organizations understand how ESG implementation affects different groups within and outside the organization. Tools should map stakeholder concerns, communication preferences, and change readiness levels to inform targeted change strategies.

Communication framework tools provide structured approaches for ESG change communication that address different audience needs and concerns. Frameworks should include message customization for different stakeholder groups, timing strategies for major announcements, and feedback collection mechanisms.

BMW Group's communication framework demonstrates sophisticated stakeholder communication during ESG transformation. The company developed communication tools that address different audience concerns—executives need strategic context, operations staff need process clarity, and external stakeholders need transparency about progress and challenges.

Tools include message templates that maintain consistency while allowing customization for different audiences, communication calendars that coordinate announcements across different stakeholder groups, and feedback collection systems that capture stakeholder concerns and suggestions.

Training and development tools support building ESG competence across organizations. Tools should include competency assessment frameworks, training program templates, and progress tracking systems that ensure effective capability building.

Resistance management tools help organizations anticipate and address common sources of ESG implementation resistance. Tools should include resistance identification frameworks, response strategy templates, and success measurement approaches.

General Electric's resistance management illustrates systematic approaches to addressing ESG implementation challenges. The company developed tools that help identify common resistance sources—workload concerns, competency gaps, and cultural misalignment—while providing response strategies for each challenge type.

Tools include stakeholder mapping techniques that identify potential resistance sources, communication strategies that address specific concerns, and success metrics that demonstrate implementation benefits to skeptical stakeholders.

Progress monitoring tools provide frameworks for tracking ESG implementation success across multiple dimensions—technical compliance, stakeholder satisfaction, organizational capability building, and business value creation.

Success celebration tools help organizations recognize and communicate ESG implementation achievements. Tools should include milestone recognition approaches, success story development templates, and celebration event planning frameworks.

Nestlé's success recognition demonstrates effective celebration of ESG implementation achievements. The company developed tools that identify implementation milestones worthy of recognition, create success stories that motivate continued progress, and plan celebration events that reinforce commitment to ESG excellence.

Tools help organizations maintain momentum during long implementation cycles while building culture that supports ongoing ESG improvement and innovation.

Implementation Excellence Framework

Organizations that excel in ESG implementation share common characteristics—they plan systematically, assign responsibilities clearly, budget realistically, select partners carefully, and manage change proactively. These capabilities aren't accidental; they result from disciplined use of proven tools and templates.

The investment in building proper implementation toolkits pays dividends throughout ESG program development. Organizations with strong toolkits implement faster, encounter fewer surprises, and achieve better outcomes than those that approach implementation reactively.

Building these capabilities requires patience and attention to detail, but the resulting competence provides lasting advantages that support ESG excellence throughout changing requirements and expanding stakeholder expectations.

Chapter 19: Certification Exam Preparation

Professional ESG certification has become the defining credential for sustainability careers, but passing certification exams requires more than subject matter knowledge—it demands strategic preparation that accounts for different exam formats, varying emphasis areas, and the practical application focus that distinguishes top candidates from average performers.

The landscape of ESG certification has exploded in recent years, with organizations offering specialized credentials in CSRD compliance, GRI reporting, SASB standards, and integrated ESG management. Each certification tests different competencies using different approaches, making preparation strategy as important as technical knowledge.

Study Strategies for Multiple Certifications

Multi-certification preparation requires systematic approaches that build foundational knowledge while addressing specific requirements for different credentials. The most successful candidates develop integrated study plans that identify common knowledge areas while allocating focused time for certification-specific requirements. (154)

Foundation knowledge building should begin with core ESG concepts that apply across multiple certifications—materiality assessment principles, stakeholder engagement methodologies, data collection best practices, and assurance fundamentals. This foundational approach prevents redundant study while ensuring solid understanding of concepts that appear in different forms across various exams.

GRI certification preparation emphasizes practical application of sustainability reporting standards, stakeholder engagement techniques, and materiality assessment processes. The exam tests understanding of universal standards, topic-specific standards, and sector supplements through scenario-based questions that require applying standards to realistic business situations.

Maria Santos' study approach illustrates effective multi-certification preparation. As a sustainability manager at a multinational manufacturer, she planned 18-month preparation covering GRI Professional Certification, CFA ESG Certificate, and SASB Fundamentals Certificate.

Her integrated approach began with comprehensive ESG foundations study covering sustainability principles, regulatory frameworks, and stakeholder theory. She then allocated specific months to each certification's unique requirements—GRI's reporting standards detail, CFA's investment analysis focus, and SASB's industry-specific metrics.

SASB certification preparation focuses on investor-focused materiality, industry-specific standards, and financial impact analysis. Study strategies should emphasize understanding how sustainability factors affect enterprise value and how SASB standards support investment decision-making.

CFA ESG Certificate preparation requires understanding ESG integration in investment analysis, portfolio construction with ESG considerations, and ESG data analysis for investment decisions. This certification emphasizes quantitative analysis and financial impact assessment more than other ESG credentials.

Time allocation strategies become critical for managing multiple certification preparation without overwhelming other responsibilities. Successful candidates typically allocate 6-8 hours weekly over 3-4 month periods for individual certifications, with additional time for integrated review and practice testing.

Progressive learning approaches build complexity gradually rather than attempting to master advanced concepts immediately. Study plans should begin with foundational materials, advance to framework-specific requirements, and conclude with practice applications that integrate knowledge across different areas.

CSRD specialist certification preparation requires deep understanding of European Sustainability Reporting Standards, double materiality assessment, and regulatory compliance requirements. Study strategies should emphasize practical application of CSRD requirements to different organization types and industries.

Study group formation provides accountability and diverse perspectives that enhance individual preparation. Effective study groups include participants with different professional backgrounds and certification goals, creating learning opportunities through knowledge sharing and problem-solving collaboration.

Practice Exam Questions and Scenarios

Practice question development requires understanding how different certifications test knowledge—some emphasize memorization of specific requirements while others focus on practical application and critical thinking. Effective preparation includes both question types while emphasizing the approach each certification prioritizes. (155)

GRI practice scenarios typically present sustainability reporting challenges that require applying specific standards to realistic business situations. Practice questions often involve materiality assessment, stakeholder engagement design, and disclosure requirement determination for different organization types.

Sample GRI scenario: A multinational food company wants to report on water usage across agricultural supply chains in water-stressed regions. The scenario requires determining applicable GRI standards (GRI 303 Water and Effluents), identifying reporting boundaries that include supplier operations, and designing stakeholder engagement that includes local communities affected by water usage.

Effective answers demonstrate understanding of GRI 303 requirements, ability to apply supply chain reporting principles, and knowledge of stakeholder engagement best practices for water-related issues in agricultural contexts.

SASB practice scenarios focus on industry-specific materiality determination and investor-focused disclosure development. Questions typically require identifying financially material sustainability factors and determining appropriate metrics for specific industries.

Sample SASB scenario: A technology company developing artificial intelligence applications needs to determine material ESG factors for investor disclosure. The scenario requires analyzing Technology & Communications industry standards, evaluating data security risks, intellectual property protection, and energy consumption materiality for AI operations.

Strong responses demonstrate understanding of SASB Software & IT Services standards, ability to connect sustainability factors to financial performance, and knowledge of how AI-specific risks map to established SASB disclosure topics.

CSRD practice scenarios involve applying European Sustainability Reporting Standards to different organization types while addressing double materiality assessment and regulatory compliance requirements.

Sample CSRD scenario: A European automotive manufacturer must prepare first-year CSRD compliance disclosure addressing climate transition risks, supply chain due diligence, and workforce management across multiple EU countries. The scenario requires applying ESRS E1 Climate Change, ESRS S2 Workers in Value Chain, and ESRS S1 Own Workforce standards.

Comprehensive answers demonstrate understanding of CSRD scope determination, double materiality application, and specific ESRS requirements while addressing automotive industry-specific challenges like electrification transition and supply chain complexity.

Integrated scenario practice helps candidates prepare for questions that require applying multiple frameworks or addressing cross-cutting sustainability issues. These scenarios reflect real-world situations where professionals must navigate multiple requirements simultaneously.

David Chen's practice approach demonstrates effective scenario-based preparation. As an ESG consultant preparing for multiple certifications, he developed integrated practice scenarios that required applying GRI, SASB, and CSRD frameworks to the same organization.

His practice sessions involved analyzing complex sustainability challenges from multiple framework perspectives, identifying overlaps and distinctions between different approaches, and developing integrated solutions that satisfy multiple requirements efficiently.

Time management practice becomes essential for certifications with strict time limits. Candidates should practice allocating appropriate time to different question types while ensuring comprehensive coverage of all exam sections.

Time Management Techniques

Exam time management requires understanding how different certifications structure testing time and developing strategies that optimize performance across different question types and difficulty levels. Effective time management prevents rushed answers on familiar topics while ensuring adequate attention to challenging questions. (156)

Question prioritization strategies help candidates identify which questions to address first based on confidence level, point value, and time requirements. Most successful candidates begin with familiar topics to build confidence while reserving adequate time for complex scenarios that require extended analysis.

GRI exam timing typically allows 2-3 hours for comprehensive questions covering standards application, stakeholder engagement, and materiality assessment. Effective timing strategies allocate roughly 40% of time to universal standards questions, 40% to topic-specific standards application, and 20% to integration and best practices questions.

Reading comprehension techniques become important for scenario-based questions that include extensive background information. Candidates should develop systematic approaches for extracting key information while identifying specific requirements being tested.

Lisa Wang's timing strategy illustrates effective exam time management across multiple certifications. She developed question analysis techniques that quickly identified key requirements, allocated appropriate time based on question complexity, and reserved time for review and revision.

Her approach included preliminary question review to identify difficulty levels, strategic sequencing that built confidence through easier questions before addressing complex scenarios, and systematic time checking that ensured comprehensive exam coverage.

SASB exam timing focuses on industry-specific scenarios that require detailed analysis and practical application. Effective timing allocates adequate time for scenario analysis while ensuring comprehensive coverage of all industry standards being tested.

Practice timing exercises help candidates develop internal clocks that prevent time management problems during actual exams. Regular practice under timed conditions builds familiarity with appropriate pacing while identifying personal timing strengths and weaknesses.

Review time allocation ensures adequate opportunity to check answers, complete unfinished questions, and revise responses based on additional reflection. Most successful candidates reserve 15-20% of total exam time for review and completion activities.

CSRD exam timing requires balancing detailed regulatory knowledge with practical application scenarios. Effective strategies allocate time based on point values while ensuring adequate coverage of all ESRS requirements being tested.

Stress management techniques help candidates maintain focus and decision-making clarity throughout long exams. Techniques include structured breathing exercises, positive self-talk, and systematic question approach that reduces anxiety while maintaining performance quality.

Continuing Education Requirements

Professional development planning for ESG careers requires understanding continuing education requirements across different certifications while building learning strategies that support career advancement and technical competence maintenance. (157)

GRI certification maintenance requires 40 continuing education hours over two-year periods, with specific requirements for GRI standards updates, sustainability reporting developments, and professional practice enhancement. Education activities include formal training, conference attendance, webinar participation, and professional publication reading.

Acceptable education activities for GRI maintenance include sustainability reporting workshops, stakeholder engagement training, ESG framework updates, and industry-specific sustainability education. Self-directed learning requires documentation and reflection that demonstrates professional development impact.

CFA ESG Certificate maintenance requires 15 continuing education hours annually, with emphasis on investment analysis applications, ESG integration techniques, and regulatory development updates. Education must include both technical competence maintenance and practical application enhancement.

Professional development tracking requires systematic documentation of education activities, learning outcomes, and professional application. Most certifying organizations provide online platforms for tracking compliance while requiring periodic reporting and verification.

Jennifer Martinez's development planning demonstrates systematic approach to continuing education across multiple certifications. She maintains GRI Professional Certification, CFA ESG Certificate, and plans CSRD specialist certification while working as Chief Sustainability Officer at a financial services firm.

Her annual development plan allocates education hours across different competency areas—framework updates, industry developments, technical skills enhancement, and leadership capability building. She tracks activities through certification portals while maintaining personal learning records that support career advancement planning.

Industry conference participation provides efficient continuing education while building professional networks and staying current with sustainability developments. Leading conferences include GRI Global Conference, SASB Investor Forum, and CDP Climate Forum.

Professional publication reading satisfies continuing education requirements while supporting current knowledge maintenance. Recommended publications include Journal of Corporate Citizenship, Business & Society Review, and Stanford Social Innovation Review.

Webinar and online training provide flexible education options that accommodate professional schedules while meeting certification requirements. Leading providers include GRI Academy, CFA Institute ESG Education, and university sustainability programs.

CSRD continuing education will likely require ongoing regulatory update training as European Sustainability Reporting Standards develop and implementation experience accumulates. Professionals should plan for significant education requirements during initial CSRD implementation years.

Peer learning opportunities through professional associations provide valuable continuing education while building industry relationships. Organizations like Net Impact, Corporate Knights, and regional sustainability associations offer programs that satisfy certification requirements.

Professional Development Planning

Career advancement planning in ESG requires strategic thinking about competency development, network building, and positioning for emerging opportunities in rapidly growing sustainability fields. Professional development should balance immediate skill needs with long-term career objectives. (158)

Competency gap analysis helps professionals identify development priorities based on current capabilities, career objectives, and market demands. Analysis should consider technical skills, industry knowledge, leadership capabilities, and certification requirements that support advancement goals.

ESG career pathways include corporate sustainability roles, ESG consulting, sustainable finance, impact investing, regulatory compliance, and sustainability technology. Each pathway requires different competency combinations and development strategies.

Michael Thompson's development planning illustrates strategic career advancement in ESG. Starting as an environmental compliance specialist, he planned progression to Chief Sustainability Officer through systematic competency building and strategic positioning.

His five-year plan included technical certification acquisition (GRI, SASB, CSRD), leadership development through sustainability project management, industry expertise building through renewable energy focus, and network development through professional association participation.

Networking strategy development should include professional associations, industry conferences, certification programs, and alumni networks that provide career advancement opportunities and professional learning.

Mentorship relationship building provides guidance and support for ESG career development. Effective mentorship includes both technical competence development and strategic career advice from experienced sustainability professionals.

Industry specialization consideration may provide competitive advantages in specific sectors like financial services ESG, renewable energy development, or supply chain sustainability. Specialization should align with personal interests and market opportunity assessment.

Thought leadership development through writing, speaking, and professional contribution helps establish expertise recognition while building professional networks and career advancement opportunities.

Sarah Johnson's thought leadership demonstrates effective expertise building in sustainable finance. She developed specialization through targeted education, professional writing, conference speaking, and industry association leadership that established her as recognized expert in green bond markets.

Her approach included systematic knowledge building through formal education and certification, practical experience through project leadership, and visibility building through professional contribution and thought leadership activities.

Global competence development may provide advantages as ESG requirements expand internationally. Language skills, cultural competence, and international regulatory knowledge support career opportunities in global sustainability roles.

Technology competence building becomes increasingly important as ESG reporting adopts advanced analytics, artificial intelligence, and automation technologies. Professionals should develop comfort with sustainability technology platforms and data analysis capabilities.

Certification Success Framework

Professional ESG certification requires systematic preparation that balances technical knowledge acquisition with practical application development. The most successful candidates treat certification as professional development opportunity rather than testing requirement.

This approach requires sustained commitment to learning and application that extends beyond exam preparation to ongoing professional development and competence maintenance. The investment in certification preparation provides lasting benefits that support career advancement and professional effectiveness.

The ESG profession continues developing rapidly, making ongoing learning and adaptation essential for career success. Professionals who master certification requirements while building broader competence position themselves for leadership in expanding sustainability fields.

Chapter 20: Future Outlook and Continuous Learning

The ESG reporting profession stands at an inflection point where rapid technological advancement meets expanding regulatory requirements and growing stakeholder expectations. The professionals who will thrive in this environment are those who develop learning systems that adapt to change while building expertise that transcends individual frameworks or technologies.

This future demands thinking beyond current requirements to anticipate how sustainability reporting will continue developing. The organizations and individuals who position themselves ahead of these trends will find opportunities for leadership and value creation that define the next generation of ESG excellence.

Emerging Frameworks and Standards

TNFD framework development represents one of the most significant emerging requirements in ESG reporting, addressing nature-related financial disclosures with the same systematic approach that climate frameworks brought to environmental reporting. The Taskforce on Nature-related Financial Disclosures creates disclosure architecture that connects biodiversity, ecosystem services, and natural capital to financial risk and opportunity assessment. (159)

TNFD implementation follows the familiar four-pillar structure—governance, strategy, risk management, and metrics and targets—that organizations recognize from climate disclosure frameworks. However, nature-related disclosures present unique challenges around data availability, measurement methodologies, and scientific understanding that require new competencies.

Unilever's TNFD preparation demonstrates early adoption of nature-related disclosure practices. The company builds on existing biodiversity and sustainable sourcing programs to develop systematic nature risk assessment, ecosystem impact measurement, and natural capital dependency analysis that supports TNFD disclosure requirements.

Their approach includes supply chain mapping that identifies nature dependencies and impacts, scientific partnership development for ecosystem assessment, and scenario analysis that evaluates how nature degradation could affect business operations and financial performance.

ISSB standards consolidation creates global baseline for sustainability disclosure that builds on established frameworks while providing consistent international requirements. The International Sustainability Standards Board combines climate-focused standards with general sustainability disclosure requirements that support regulatory harmonization.

ISSB implementation requires understanding how global standards interact with regional requirements like CSRD while providing foundations for local regulatory development. Organizations need strategies that satisfy ISSB requirements while maintaining compliance with jurisdiction-specific mandates.

Microsoft's ISSB preparation illustrates systematic approach to global standard implementation. The company analyzes how ISSB requirements relate to existing CSRD, SEC, and voluntary disclosure practices while identifying areas requiring additional development or process modification.

Their implementation strategy includes gap analysis that compares current practices to ISSB requirements, process development that ensures global standard compliance, and stakeholder communication that explains how ISSB adoption affects existing disclosure practices.

Sector-specific standard development continues across multiple industries as organizations recognize that generic sustainability requirements don't capture industry-specific material factors. Banking, insurance, mining, agriculture, and technology sectors develop specialized guidance that addresses unique sustainability challenges.

Human rights disclosure frameworks gain prominence as organizations face increasing expectations around supply chain due diligence, workforce protection, and community impact management. Emerging standards require systematic human rights risk assessment and impact disclosure.

Circular economy frameworks provide structured approaches for reporting on resource efficiency, waste reduction, and circular business model development. These frameworks address growing stakeholder interest in sustainable resource management and regenerative business practices.

AI and Automation in ESG Reporting

Artificial intelligence applications in ESG reporting range from automated data collection and validation to sophisticated analysis that identifies trends and improvement opportunities. AI transforms both the efficiency and capabilities of sustainability reporting while creating new competency requirements for ESG professionals. (160)

Automated data collection uses machine learning to extract sustainability information from operational systems, supply chain databases, and external sources. AI systems can identify relevant data points, perform quality validation, and generate reports that reduce manual effort while improving accuracy.

Siemens' AI implementation demonstrates advanced automation capabilities across global manufacturing operations. The company uses machine learning algorithms to collect environmental performance data from facility management systems, validate information against established parameters, and generate real-time sustainability dashboards.

AI systems automatically flag data anomalies, identify improvement opportunities, and generate alerts when performance metrics deviate from expected ranges. This automation enables proactive sustainability management while reducing reporting preparation time and improving data quality.

Predictive analytics applications help organizations anticipate sustainability trends, identify emerging risks, and optimize performance improvement strategies. AI systems analyze historical data patterns to forecast future performance and recommend intervention strategies.

Natural language processing enables automated analysis of qualitative sustainability information from stakeholder feedback, regulatory documents, and industry reports. NLP systems can identify emerging issues, analyze sentiment patterns, and generate summaries that support decision-making.

General Electric's analytics platform illustrates sophisticated AI applications for sustainability insight generation. The company uses machine learning to analyze operational data across diverse business units, identify efficiency improvement opportunities, and predict maintenance requirements that affect environmental performance.

AI systems generate automated insights about energy optimization, emissions reduction opportunities, and operational efficiency improvements that support both sustainability and business performance objectives.

Assurance automation includes AI-supported verification processes that enhance traditional assurance approaches. Automated systems can perform continuous monitoring, identify data inconsistencies, and generate audit trails that support external verification requirements.

Stakeholder engagement automation uses AI to analyze stakeholder feedback, identify emerging concerns, and generate communication strategies that address stakeholder priorities effectively. Automated systems can process large volumes of feedback while identifying patterns and trends.

Reporting automation includes AI-generated narrative content, automated report formatting, and intelligent distribution systems that customize information for different stakeholder audiences. These capabilities reduce preparation time while improving communication effectiveness.

Regulatory Convergence Predictions

Global harmonization trends suggest increasing alignment between regional ESG disclosure requirements as regulatory authorities recognize the benefits of consistent international standards. Convergence reduces compliance burden for multinational organizations while improving comparability for global stakeholders. (161)

Climate disclosure convergence appears most advanced as ISSB climate standards provide foundations for regulatory development across multiple jurisdictions. The alignment between TCFD recommendations, ISSB standards, and regional requirements like CSRD creates pathways for global consistency.

Social disclosure harmonization develops more slowly due to cultural differences and varying regulatory priorities across jurisdictions. However, common themes around human rights, labor practices, and community impact suggest potential alignment areas.

BMW Group's regulatory strategy demonstrates systematic preparation for convergence across multiple markets. The company monitors regulatory developments in EU, US, UK, and Asian markets while building reporting capabilities that can accommodate different requirements efficiently.

Their approach includes scenario planning that evaluates different convergence possibilities, capability building that supports multiple regulatory frameworks, and stakeholder engagement that influences regulatory development in key markets.

US regulatory development continues expanding through SEC climate disclosure requirements, potential broader ESG mandates, and state-level sustainability regulations. US development influences global practices due to capital market importance and multinational company compliance needs.

Asian regulatory evolution includes sustainability disclosure requirements in Japan, Singapore, Hong Kong, and other markets that often align with global frameworks while addressing regional priorities and business practices.

Assurance requirement alignment suggests increasing consistency in verification standards as regulatory authorities recognize the importance of reliable sustainability information. Convergence in assurance requirements reduces complexity while improving stakeholder confidence.

Technology standard development may emerge as regulatory authorities recognize the need for consistent data formats, reporting platforms, and verification technologies that support efficient compliance and stakeholder access.

Enforcement harmonization could develop as regulatory authorities share experience with ESG compliance monitoring and penalty assessment. Consistent enforcement approaches reduce regulatory arbitrage while ensuring fair competition.

Building Your ESG Expertise Brand

Professional brand development in ESG requires strategic positioning that demonstrates expertise, builds credibility, and creates opportunities for career advancement and thought leadership. Effective brand building combines technical competence with communication skills and industry visibility. (162)

Expertise area identification should focus on specific sustainability domains where you can develop deep knowledge and practical experience. Specialization options include climate risk assessment, supply chain sustainability, sustainable finance, ESG data analytics, or regulatory compliance.

Content creation strategies help establish expertise recognition through writing, speaking, and professional contribution. Effective content demonstrates practical knowledge, provides actionable insights, and addresses current industry challenges.

Jennifer Chen's brand development illustrates systematic expertise building in sustainable finance. She developed specialization through targeted education, practical project experience, and thought leadership activities that established her as recognized expert in green bond markets.

Her approach included regular writing for industry publications, speaking at sustainability conferences, participating in professional association committees, and advising organizations on sustainable finance strategy. This visibility led to executive opportunities and advisory roles.

Professional network building requires strategic relationship development with industry leaders, potential employers, clients, and peers who share sustainability interests. Effective networking combines online engagement with in-person relationship building.

Mentorship and sponsorship relationships provide guidance, support, and advocacy that accelerate career development. Effective relationships include both receiving mentorship and providing guidance to others entering ESG fields.

Industry association participation creates opportunities for leadership development, network building, and visibility enhancement. Leading associations include Global Reporting Initiative, Sustainability Accounting Standards Board, and regional sustainability organizations.

David Rodriguez's association leadership demonstrates effective professional development through industry involvement. His progression from member to committee chair to board service in regional sustainability association provided leadership experience while building industry relationships and visibility.

Digital presence development includes professional social media engagement, content sharing, and online thought leadership that demonstrates expertise and builds professional recognition. Effective digital presence balances professional insight with personality and authenticity.

Certification and education visibility helps establish credibility while demonstrating commitment to professional development. Strategic education choices signal expertise areas while building competence and professional networks.

Speaking and presentation opportunities provide platforms for expertise demonstration while building professional reputation and industry relationships. Effective speakers develop signature content that demonstrates unique perspectives and practical value.

Resources for Ongoing Development

Continuous learning resources for ESG professionals include formal education programs, professional conferences, industry publications, and online learning platforms that support ongoing competence development and career advancement. (163)

University programs in sustainability include graduate degrees in ESG, sustainable business, environmental management, and social impact that provide structured learning and credentialing. Leading programs include Stanford, Wharton, INSEAD, and London Business School sustainability concentrations.

Professional certification programs continue expanding with new credentials in specialized areas like nature-related disclosure, human rights due diligence, and ESG data analytics. Strategic certification choices should align with career objectives and market demands.

Industry conferences provide education, networking, and trend identification opportunities. Leading events include GRI Global Conference, SASB Connect, Climate Week, and regional sustainability forums that address local market needs.

Maria Santos' conference strategy demonstrates systematic approach to professional conference participation. She allocates annual learning budget across different event types—global conferences for broad trend awareness, technical workshops for skill development, and regional events for network building.

Her approach includes pre-conference preparation that identifies learning objectives, active participation that builds relationships and visibility, and post-conference follow-up that maintains connections and applies learning.

Professional publications keep practitioners current with development in regulatory requirements, best practices, and industry trends. Essential reading includes Sustainability Accounting Standards Board updates, Global Reporting Initiative publications, and industry-specific sustainability journals.

Online learning platforms provide flexible education options that accommodate professional schedules while offering current content and expert instruction. Leading platforms include Coursera sustainability specializations, LinkedIn Learning ESG courses, and professional association training programs.

Research and academic institutions provide cutting-edge thinking about sustainability challenges and solutions. Following research from leading institutions keeps practitioners current with emerging concepts and analytical approaches.

Technology platforms increasingly offer learning resources through built-in training, user communities, and best practice sharing that support professional development while building platform competence.

Peer learning networks through professional associations, alumni groups, and industry organizations provide ongoing education through knowledge sharing, problem-solving collaboration, and experience exchange.

Charting Your Path Forward

The future of ESG reporting will be defined by professionals who master both current requirements and emerging trends while building capabilities that adapt to changing expectations.

This requires commitment to continuous learning that goes beyond compliance to strategic value creation.

The opportunities ahead favor those who think systematically about capability building, network development, and positioning for leadership in expanding sustainability fields. The investment in building these capabilities provides lasting advantages that support career success throughout industry evolution.

Success in this field requires balancing technical competence with strategic thinking, individual excellence with collaborative capability, and current expertise with future adaptability. The professionals who master this balance will lead the transformation of business practice toward sustainable value creation.

Core Learning Principles

- Implementation excellence requires systematic planning, clear responsibility assignment, realistic budgeting, and proactive change management
- Professional certification success demands strategic preparation across multiple frameworks while building practical application capabilities
- Future ESG leadership requires anticipating emerging frameworks, adopting new technologies, and building adaptive capabilities
- Career advancement needs expertise specialization, brand development, network building, and continuous learning commitment
- Technology integration transforms ESG reporting efficiency while creating new competency requirements for professionals
- Regulatory convergence creates opportunities for global career development and standardized competence recognition

- Thought leadership development requires combining technical expertise with communication skills and industry visibility

---

Chapter 21: Practice Exam 1

Section A: ESG Fundamentals (Questions 1-25)

1. What does the "double materiality" concept in CSRD require companies to assess? a) Financial impact only b) Environmental impact only c) Both impact on the company and company's impact on society/environment d) Social impact only

Answer: c) Both impact on the company and company's impact on society/environment .Explanation: Double materiality requires assessment of both financial materiality (how sustainability matters affect the company) and impact materiality (how the company affects people and the environment).

2. Which stakeholder theory principle emphasizes that companies should consider all affected parties in decision-making? a) Shareholder primacy b) Stakeholder capitalism c) Profit maximization d) Market efficiency

Answer: b) Stakeholder capitalism .Explanation: Stakeholder capitalism recognizes that companies should create value for all stakeholders, not just shareholders, including employees, customers, suppliers, communities, and the environment.

3. The ESG framework primarily emerged from which broader concept? a) Corporate social responsibility b) Financial reporting standards c) Risk management d) Operational excellence

Answer: a) Corporate social responsibility .Explanation: ESG evolved from CSR as a more structured and measurable approach to corporate responsibility, focusing on environmental, social, and governance factors that affect business performance.

4. What is the primary purpose of materiality assessment in ESG reporting? a) Legal compliance b) Cost reduction c) Identifying most significant sustainability issues d) Marketing purposes

Answer: c) Identifying most significant sustainability issues .Explanation: Materiality assessment helps organizations identify and prioritize the sustainability issues that are most significant to their business and stakeholders.

5. Which of the following best describes the "business case" for ESG? a) Regulatory compliance only b) ESG practices can drive financial performance and risk management c) Public relations benefits d) Employee satisfaction

Answer: b) ESG practices can drive financial performance and risk management .Explanation: The business case for ESG demonstrates how sustainable practices can create financial value through cost savings, revenue growth, risk reduction, and improved access to capital.

Section B: CSRD Framework (Questions 26-50)

26. CSRD applies to which types of companies initially? a) All EU companies b) Large public-interest entities with >500 employees c) SMEs only d) Non-EU companies only

Answer: b) Large public-interest entities with >500 employees .Explanation: CSRD initially applies to large public-interest entities (banks, insurance companies, listed companies) with more than 500 employees, expanding to other large companies and eventually listed SMEs.

27. How many European Sustainability Reporting Standards (ESRS) cover environmental topics? a) 3 b) 4 c) 5 d) 6

Answer: c) 5 .Explanation: There are five environmental ESRS standards: E1 Climate Change, E2 Pollution, E3 Water and Marine Resources, E4 Biodiversity and Ecosystems, and E5 Circular Economy.

28. What level of assurance is initially required for CSRD reporting? a) No assurance required b) Limited assurance c) Reasonable assurance d) Self-assessment only

Answer: b) Limited assurance .Explanation: CSRD initially requires limited assurance for sustainability information, with a transition to reasonable assurance for climate-related information within a few years.

29. CSRD reporting must be included in which document? a) Separate sustainability report b) Management report (annual report) c) Financial statements d) Regulatory filing only

Answer: b) Management report (annual report) .Explanation: CSRD requires sustainability reporting to be included in the management report as part of the annual report, ensuring integration with financial reporting.

30. Which ESRS standard addresses governance topics? a) G1 Business Conduct b) G2 Corporate Governance c) Both a and b d) No specific governance standard

Answer: a) G1 Business Conduct .Explanation: ESRS G1 Business Conduct is the primary governance standard, covering business ethics, corporate culture, and stakeholder engagement.

31. Non-EU companies may be subject to CSRD if they: a) Have EU subsidiaries meeting size criteria b) Are listed on EU exchanges c) Have significant EU operations d) All of the above

Answer: d) All of the above .Explanation: CSRD has extraterritorial application affecting non-EU companies through various mechanisms including subsidiaries, listings, and significant EU business activities.

32. The CSRD implementation timeline spans from: a) 2024-2026 b) 2025-2028 c) 2024-2028 d) 2025-2030

Answer: c) 2024-2028 .Explanation: CSRD implementation is phased from 2024 (for large PIEs) through 2028 (for listed SMEs), with different company categories having different start dates.

33. Which principle requires companies to report both positive and negative impacts? a) Completeness b) Balance c) Accuracy d) Clarity

Answer: b) Balance .Explanation: The balance principle requires companies to report both positive and negative sustainability impacts and performance without bias.

34. Value chain reporting under CSRD includes: a) Upstream activities only b) Downstream activities only c) Both upstream and downstream activities d) Direct operations only

Answer: c) Both upstream and downstream activities .Explanation: CSRD requires reporting on sustainability impacts and risks throughout the value chain, including both upstream suppliers and downstream customers and end-users.

35. The "safe harbor" provision in CSRD protects companies from liability for: a) All sustainability statements b) Forward-looking sustainability statements made in good faith c) Historical data errors d) Third-party data issues

Answer: b) Forward-looking sustainability statements made in good faith .Explanation: The safe harbor provision provides legal protection for forward-looking sustainability statements that are made in good faith and based on reasonable assumptions.

Section C: GRI Standards (Questions 51-75)

36. Which GRI Universal Standard addresses material topics determination? a) GRI 1 b) GRI 2 c) GRI 3 d) GRI 4

Answer: c) GRI 3 .Explanation: GRI 3: Material Topics 2021 provides guidance on identifying, assessing, and determining material topics for sustainability reporting.

37. The GRI reporting principles include all except: a) Stakeholder inclusiveness b) Sustainability context c) Financial materiality only d) Completeness

Answer: c) Financial materiality only .Explanation: GRI principles include stakeholder inclusiveness, sustainability context, materiality (both impact and financial), and completeness, among others.

38. GRI 200 series standards cover which topic area? a) Environmental b) Economic c) Social d) Governance

Answer: b) Economic .Explanation: The GRI 200 series covers economic topics including economic performance, market presence, indirect economic impacts, and procurement practices.

39. Which approach allows organizations to report selected GRI disclosures without claiming GRI compliance? a) Core option b) Comprehensive option c) GRI-referenced d) Sector-specific approach

Answer: c) GRI-referenced .Explanation: GRI-referenced approach allows organizations to use selected GRI disclosures without meeting full GRI Standards requirements for claiming compliance.

40. Stakeholder engagement in GRI reporting should be: a) Annual only b) Ongoing and systematic c) Limited to shareholders d) Optional for private companies

Answer: b) Ongoing and systematic .Explanation: GRI requires ongoing and systematic stakeholder engagement as a continuous process, not just annual surveys or consultations.

41. Which GRI standard addresses anti-corruption practices? a) GRI 205 b) GRI 206 c) GRI 415 d) GRI 419

Answer: a) GRI 205 .Explanation: GRI 205: Anti-corruption 2016 addresses the organization's approach to preventing and addressing corruption.

42. The concept of "reporting boundary" in GRI refers to: a) Geographic limitations b) Time period covered c) Entities and impacts included in reporting d) Materiality threshold

Answer: c) Entities and impacts included in reporting .Explanation: Reporting boundary defines which entities, operations, and impacts are included in the sustainability report.

43. GRI sector standards provide guidance for: a) All organizations equally b) Specific industries with common material topics c) Geographic regions d) Company size categories

Answer: b) Specific industries with common material topics .Explanation: GRI sector standards provide industry-specific guidance for sectors that share common material sustainability topics and impacts.

44. Which data quality principle requires information to be sufficiently detailed for stakeholders to assess performance? a) Accuracy b) Clarity c) Comparability d) Reliability

Answer: b) Clarity .Explanation: Clarity requires information to be presented in a way that is understandable and accessible to stakeholders using the report.

45. The GRI Content Index serves what primary purpose? a) Legal compliance checklist b) Navigation tool showing where each disclosure is located c) Performance benchmarking d) Materiality assessment documentation

Answer: b) Navigation tool showing where each disclosure is located .Explanation: The GRI Content Index provides a table showing where each required disclosure can be found in the report or other published materials.

Section D: SASB Standards (Questions 76-100)

46. SASB standards focus primarily on: a) All stakeholder concerns b) Financially material sustainability factors c) Environmental issues only d) Social impact metrics

Answer: b) Financially material sustainability factors .Explanation: SASB standards are designed to identify and address sustainability factors that are financially material to companies and relevant to investors.

47. How many industry standards does SASB currently maintain? a) 55 b) 67 c) 77 d) 89

Answer: c) 77 .Explanation: SASB maintains 77 industry-specific standards across 11 sectors, each addressing material sustainability topics for that industry.

48. The Sustainable Industry Classification System (SICS) groups companies based on: a) Revenue size b) Geographic location c) Shared sustainability risks and opportunities d) Ownership structure

Answer: c) Shared sustainability risks and opportunities .Explanation: SICS classifies companies based on their shared sustainability risks and opportunities rather than traditional economic classifications.

49. Activity metrics in SASB standards serve to: a) Measure absolute performance b) Enable normalization and comparison c) Calculate financial returns d) Assess regulatory compliance

Answer: b) Enable normalization and comparison .Explanation: Activity metrics provide the denominator for normalizing sustainability data, enabling meaningful comparison across companies and time periods.

50. Which SASB disclosure includes both quantitative metrics and narrative discussion? a) Metrics only b) Activity metrics only c) Technical protocols d) All disclosure topics include both elements

Answer: d) All disclosure topics include both elements .Explanation: SASB disclosure topics typically include both quantitative metrics and qualitative discussion to provide complete information for investors.

51. SASB standards are particularly useful for: a) Regulatory compliance b) Investment analysis and decision-making c) Marketing communications d) Internal management only

Answer: b) Investment analysis and decision-making .Explanation: SASB standards are designed specifically to provide investors with material sustainability information for investment analysis and decision-making.

52. The relationship between SASB and ISSB is that: a) They are competing frameworks b) SASB standards form the industry-specific foundation for ISSB c) They address different topics entirely d) ISSB replaced SASB

Answer: b) SASB standards form the industry-specific foundation for ISSB .Explanation: SASB standards have been incorporated into the ISSB framework as the industry-specific guidance for global sustainability disclosure standards.

53. For a company operating in multiple industries, SASB reporting should: a) Use only the primary industry standard b) Apply all relevant industry standards based on revenue significance c) Choose the most comprehensive standard d) Create a custom hybrid approach

Answer: b) Apply all relevant industry standards based on revenue significance .Explanation: Multi-industry companies should apply SASB standards for all industries that represent significant portions of their business operations.

54. SASB's approach to materiality is based on: a) Stakeholder surveys b) Management judgment only c) Evidence-based research on financial impact d) Regulatory requirements

Answer: c) Evidence-based research on financial impact .Explanation: SASB's materiality determinations are based on extensive research analyzing the financial impact of sustainability factors across industries.

55. Which element is NOT typically included in SASB disclosure topics? a) Accounting metrics b) Activity metrics c) Technical protocols d) Stakeholder engagement processes

Answer: d) Stakeholder engagement processes .Explanation: While stakeholder engagement may be mentioned in context,

SASB focuses on metrics, protocols, and business-relevant information rather than engagement processes.

Section E: Materiality Assessment (Questions 101-125)

56. The first step in conducting a materiality assessment is typically: a) Stakeholder engagement b) Issue identification and universe creation c) Impact assessment d) Prioritization matrix development

Answer: b) Issue identification and universe creation .Explanation: Materiality assessment begins with identifying the complete universe of potential sustainability topics relevant to the organization and its stakeholders.

57. In double materiality assessment, impact materiality refers to: a) How issues affect the company financially b) How the company affects people and the environment c) Stakeholder perception of importance d) Regulatory compliance requirements

Answer: b) How the company affects people and the environment .Explanation: Impact materiality (outside-in) assesses how the organization's activities affect people, the environment, and society.

58. Financial materiality assessment evaluates: a) Company's impact on stakeholders b) How sustainability issues affect enterprise value c) Compliance costs only d) Brand reputation effects

Answer: b) How sustainability issues affect enterprise value .Explanation: Financial materiality (inside-out) evaluates how sustainability factors could impact the organization's financial performance and enterprise value.

59. Which stakeholder group is most important for financial materiality assessment? a) Local communities b) Employees c) Investors and lenders d) NGOs

Answer: c) Investors and lenders .Explanation: While all stakeholders matter, investors and lenders are particularly important for financial materiality as they evaluate how sustainability factors affect investment value.

60. Materiality thresholds should be set based on: a) Industry benchmarks only b) Management discretion c) Significance to business and stakeholders d) Regulatory minimums

Answer: c) Significance to business and stakeholders .Explanation: Materiality thresholds should reflect the level of significance that would influence stakeholder decisions and business performance.

61. Dynamic materiality means that: a) Materiality never changes b) Material topics can change over time c) Only quantitative factors matter d) Stakeholder views are irrelevant

Answer: b) Material topics can change over time .Explanation: Dynamic materiality recognizes that material topics can change due to evolving business conditions, stakeholder expectations, and external factors.

62. The materiality matrix typically plots: a) Cost vs. benefit b) Internal vs. external perspectives c) Importance to stakeholders vs. significance to business d) Short-term vs. long-term impacts

Answer: c) Importance to stakeholders vs. significance to business .Explanation: Traditional materiality matrices plot stakeholder importance against business significance to identify priority topics.

63. When should materiality assessment be updated? a) Annually only b) When significant changes occur in business or context c) Every five years d) Never, once established

Answer: b) When significant changes occur in business or context .Explanation: Materiality should be reassessed when significant changes occur in the business, operating environment, or stakeholder expectations.

64. Sector-specific material topics are important because: a) They are required by regulation b) Different industries face different sustainability risks c) They simplify reporting d) Investors prefer standardization

Answer: b) Different industries face different sustainability risks .Explanation: Different industries have different sustainability risk profiles, making sector-specific materiality assessment important for relevance and accuracy.

65. The output of materiality assessment should inform: a) Reporting content only b) Business strategy and risk management c) Marketing messages d) Financial planning exclusively

Answer: b) Business strategy and risk management .Explanation: Materiality assessment results should inform not just reporting but also business strategy, risk management, and resource allocation decisions.

Section F: Data Collection and Management (Questions 126-150)

66. The most reliable source for environmental data is typically: a) Industry estimates b) Direct measurement from operations c) Third-party databases d) Peer company reports

Answer: b) Direct measurement from operations .Explanation: Direct measurement from actual operations provides the most accurate and reliable environmental data for reporting purposes.

67. Data governance for ESG reporting should include: a) Data collection procedures only b) Roles, responsibilities, and quality controls c) Technology systems only d) Annual reviews

Answer: b) Roles, responsibilities, and quality controls .Explanation: Effective data governance includes clear roles and responsibilities, data quality controls, validation procedures, and documentation requirements.

68. What is the primary challenge with supply chain ESG data collection? a) Technology limitations b) Cost considerations c) Supplier cooperation and data availability d) Regulatory restrictions

Answer: c) Supplier cooperation and data availability .Explanation: Supply chain data collection faces challenges from supplier reluctance to share information, varying data quality, and inconsistent measurement approaches.

69. Data validation procedures should include: a) Automated checks only b) Manual review only c) Both automated and manual validation d) External verification only

Answer: c) Both automated and manual validation .Explanation: Effective data validation combines automated system checks with manual review and analysis to ensure data quality and accuracy.

70. The concept of "data lineage" refers to: a) Historical data trends b) Data source tracking and transformation documentation c) Organizational hierarchy for data approval d) Regulatory compliance requirements

Answer: b) Data source tracking and transformation documentation .Explanation: Data lineage tracks where data comes from, how it's transformed, and how it flows through systems to final reporting.

71. Which data quality dimension refers to data being available when needed? a) Accuracy b) Completeness c) Timeliness d) Consistency

Answer: c) Timeliness .Explanation: Timeliness refers to data being available when needed for decision-making and reporting purposes.

72. Estimation techniques for ESG data should be: a) Avoided entirely b) Used transparently with clear methodology c) Applied without disclosure d) Limited to financial data

Answer: b) Used transparently with clear methodology .Explanation: When estimation is necessary, it should be done transparently with clear methodology disclosure and regular validation against actual data.

73. Data retention policies for ESG information should consider: a) Storage costs only b) Regulatory requirements and stakeholder needs c) Technology limitations d) Management preferences

Answer: b) Regulatory requirements and stakeholder needs .Explanation: Data retention should balance regulatory requirements, stakeholder information needs, and practical considerations like storage and access.

74. Which approach is best for managing ESG data across multiple business units? a) Decentralized collection with central consolidation b) Fully centralized collection c) Independent unit reporting d) Outsourced data management

Answer: a) Decentralized collection with central consolidation .Explanation: Decentralized collection allows business units to manage local data while central consolidation ensures consistency and integration.

75. Technology solutions for ESG data management should prioritize: a) Cost minimization b) Integration with existing systems c) Advanced analytics capabilities d) User interface design

Answer: b) Integration with existing systems .Explanation: Integration with existing enterprise systems is crucial for data quality, efficiency, and sustainable data management processes.

Section G: Reporting and Disclosure (Questions 151-175)

76. The primary audience for ESG reports includes: a) Investors only b) Regulators only c) Multiple stakeholder groups with different information needs d) Internal management only

Answer: c) Multiple stakeholder groups with different information needs .Explanation: ESG reports serve multiple stakeholder groups including investors, regulators, customers, employees, communities, and NGOs, each with different information needs.

77. Integrated reporting combines: a) Financial and non-financial information b) Annual and quarterly data c) Internal and external perspectives d) Historical and forward-looking information

Answer: a) Financial and non-financial information .Explanation: Integrated reporting combines financial and non-financial information to show how an organization creates value over time.

78. Forward-looking information in ESG reports should: a) Be avoided due to uncertainty b) Include targets, scenarios, and strategic plans with appropriate caveats c) Focus only on short-term projections d) Exclude financial implications

Answer: b) Include targets, scenarios, and strategic plans with appropriate caveats .Explanation: Forward-looking information adds value but should include appropriate disclaimers about uncertainty and assumptions.

79. The balance principle in ESG reporting requires: a) Equal coverage of all topics b) Neutral presentation of both positive and negative performance c) Financial and non-financial data balance d) Internal and external viewpoint balance

Answer: b) Neutral presentation of both positive and negative performance .Explanation: Balance requires fair and unbiased presentation of both positive and negative aspects of sustainability performance.

80. Digital reporting formats offer advantages including: a) Lower preparation costs b) Interactive features and better accessibility c) Simplified content requirements d) Reduced assurance needs

Answer: b) Interactive features and better accessibility .Explanation: Digital formats enable interactive features, better navigation, accessibility features, and more engaging stakeholder experiences.

81. ESG report verification typically covers: a) All information equally b) Selected key metrics and statements c) Financial data only d) Narrative content exclusively

Answer: b) Selected key metrics and statements .Explanation: ESG verification usually covers selected key metrics and material statements rather than every piece of information in the report.

82. The "comply or explain" approach requires companies to: a) Follow all requirements without exception b) Either comply with requirements or explain why not c) Choose between compliance and explanation d) Explain all decisions regardless of compliance

Answer: b) Either comply with requirements or explain why not .Explanation: "Comply or explain" allows flexibility by requiring companies to either follow requirements or provide clear explanations for alternative approaches.

83. Cross-referencing in ESG reports should: a) Be minimized to reduce complexity b) Clearly link related information across sections c) Only reference external sources d) Focus on regulatory citations

Answer: b) Clearly link related information across sections .Explanation: Effective cross-referencing helps readers understand connections between related information and improves report usability.

84. The concept of "connectivity" in reporting refers to: a) Digital accessibility b) Links between different types of information and value creation c) Stakeholder engagement methods d) Technology platform integration

Answer: b) Links between different types of information and value creation .Explanation: Connectivity shows how different elements (strategy, governance, performance, prospects) relate to each other and value creation.

85. ESG report timing should consider: a) Internal convenience only b) Stakeholder information needs and decision cycles c) Competitor reporting schedules d) Marketing calendar alignment

Answer: b) Stakeholder information needs and decision cycles .Explanation: Report timing should align with when stakeholders need information for their decision-making processes.

Section H: Assurance and Verification (Questions 176-200)

86. Limited assurance provides: a) The same confidence level as reasonable assurance b) Moderate level of confidence c) No additional confidence d) Higher confidence than reasonable assurance

Answer: b) Moderate level of confidence .Explanation: Limited assurance provides moderate confidence that information is free from material misstatement, less than reasonable assurance but more than no assurance.

87. The scope of ESG assurance typically includes: a) All information in the report b) Selected metrics and statements based on materiality c) Financial data only d) Narrative sections exclusively

Answer: b) Selected metrics and statements based on materiality .Explanation: ESG assurance scope is usually determined based on materiality and risk assessment, focusing on key metrics and statements rather than entire reports.

88. Independence requirements for ESG assurance providers mean: a) No prior relationship with the company b) Absence of conflicts that could compromise objectivity c) Different firms must provide each service d) Government-appointed providers only

Answer: b) Absence of conflicts that could compromise objectivity .Explanation: Independence requires avoiding relationships or interests that could compromise the assurance provider's objectivity and professional judgment.

89. The primary purpose of ESG assurance is to: a) Guarantee accuracy of all data b) Provide stakeholders with confidence in reported information c) Meet regulatory requirements only d) Improve internal data quality

Answer: b) Provide stakeholders with confidence in reported information .Explanation: ESG assurance aims to provide stakeholders with confidence that reported information is reliable and free from material misstatement.

90. Materiality in ESG assurance contexts refers to: a) Environmental impact significance b) Information significance for user decisions c) Financial value thresholds d) Regulatory compliance levels

Answer: b) Information significance for user decisions .Explanation: Materiality in assurance refers to the significance of information for stakeholder decision-making processes.

91. ESG assurance procedures typically include: a) Testing and verification only b) Inquiry, observation, testing, and analytical procedures c) Document review only d) Management interviews exclusively

Answer: b) Inquiry, observation, testing, and analytical procedures .Explanation: ESG assurance involves multiple procedures including inquiry, observation, testing, analytical procedures, and document examination.

92. The assurance opinion expresses: a) Absolute certainty about data accuracy b) Professional conclusion about information reliability c) Management's assessment d) Regulatory compliance confirmation

Answer: b) Professional conclusion about information reliability .Explanation: The assurance opinion expresses the provider's professional conclusion about whether information is reliable and free from material misstatement.

93. Internal controls assessment in ESG assurance evaluates: a) Financial controls only b) Systems and processes for ESG data and reporting c) IT security measures d) Operational efficiency

Answer: b) Systems and processes for ESG data and reporting .Explanation: ESG assurance includes evaluating the design and effectiveness of controls over sustainability data collection, processing, and reporting.

94. Management representations in ESG assurance: a) Are optional b) Provide written confirmation of management's responsibilities c) Replace testing procedures d) Only cover financial data

Answer: b) Provide written confirmation of management's responsibilities .Explanation: Management representations are written statements from management confirming their responsibilities and the completeness and accuracy of information provided.

95. The difference between verification and validation is: a) No significant difference b) Verification checks accuracy; validation checks appropriateness c) Verification is external; validation is internal d) Verification covers data; validation covers processes

Answer: b) Verification checks accuracy; validation checks appropriateness .Explanation: Verification typically focuses on checking accuracy and reliability of data, while validation assesses whether methods and approaches are appropriate.

Section I: Strategic Integration (Questions 201-225)

96. ESG integration into business strategy requires: a) Separate sustainability department only b) Embedding ESG considerations into core business processes c) Annual sustainability planning d) External consultant management

Answer: b) Embedding ESG considerations into core business processes .Explanation: True ESG integration requires embedding sustainability considerations into core business processes, decision-making, and performance management.

97. The business case for ESG is strongest when it demonstrates: a) Regulatory compliance only b) Clear links to financial performance and risk management c) Stakeholder satisfaction d) Marketing benefits

Answer: b) Clear links to financial performance and risk management .Explanation: The business case is strongest when ESG initiatives demonstrate clear connections to financial performance, risk reduction, and value creation.

98. ESG-linked executive compensation should: a) Include only environmental metrics b) Align with material ESG priorities and business strategy c) Focus on short-term targets only d) Apply to CEO only

Answer: b) Align with material ESG priorities and business strategy .Explanation: ESG-linked compensation should align with material sustainability priorities and overall business strategy to drive appropriate behaviors.

99. Stakeholder capitalism differs from shareholder primacy by: a) Focusing only on employees b) Considering all stakeholder interests in value creation c) Eliminating profit motivation d) Prioritizing short-term results

Answer: b) Considering all stakeholder interests in value creation .Explanation: Stakeholder capitalism considers the interests of all stakeholders (employees, customers, suppliers, communities, environment) alongside shareholders in value creation.

100. ESG risk management should be: a) Handled by sustainability teams only b) Integrated into enterprise risk management frameworks c) Limited to environmental risks d) Managed separately from business risks

Answer: b) Integrated into enterprise risk management frameworks .Explanation: ESG risks should be integrated into enterprise risk management to ensure comprehensive identification, assessment, and mitigation.

101. The concept of "shared value" refers to: a) Sharing profits with stakeholders b) Creating economic value while addressing social/environmental challenges c) Joint ventures with competitors d) Community investment programs

Answer: b) Creating economic value while addressing social/environmental challenges .Explanation: Shared value involves creating economic value for the business while simultaneously creating value for society by addressing social and environmental challenges.

102. ESG performance measurement should: a) Use only financial metrics b) Include both leading and lagging indicators c) Focus on annual results only d) Exclude stakeholder feedback

Answer: b) Include both leading and lagging indicators .Explanation: Effective ESG measurement includes both leading indicators (predicting future performance) and lagging indicators (measuring past results).

103. The role of the board in ESG oversight includes: a) Day-to-day ESG management b) Strategy approval and performance oversight c) Data collection supervision d) Stakeholder engagement execution

Answer: b) Strategy approval and performance oversight .Explanation: The board's role focuses on ESG strategy approval, performance oversight, and ensuring adequate resources and management attention.

104. ESG due diligence in M&A should assess: a) Target company's ESG risks and opportunities b) Financial performance only c) Legal compliance exclusively d) Market position alone

Answer: a) Target company's ESG risks and opportunities .Explanation: ESG due diligence evaluates the target company's ESG risks, opportunities, performance, and potential impact on deal value and integration.

105. Supply chain ESG management requires: a) Annual supplier surveys only b) Ongoing monitoring, engagement, and capacity building c) Contract clauses exclusively d) Third-party audits alone

Answer: b) Ongoing monitoring, engagement, and capacity building .Explanation: Effective supply chain ESG management involves continuous monitoring, supplier engagement, capacity building, and performance improvement support.

Section J: Emerging Trends and Technologies (Questions 226-250)

106. The Taskforce on Nature-related Financial Disclosures (TNFD) addresses: a) Climate change only b) Biodiversity and ecosystem risks and opportunities c) Social impact measurement d) Governance frameworks

Answer: b) Biodiversity and ecosystem risks and opportunities .Explanation: TNFD focuses on nature-related risks and opportunities, particularly biodiversity loss and ecosystem degradation impacts on business and finance.

107. Artificial intelligence applications in ESG reporting include: a) Data collection automation only b) Data analysis, pattern recognition, and insight generation c) Report writing exclusively d) Stakeholder engagement replacement

Answer: b) Data analysis, pattern recognition, and insight generation .Explanation: AI applications span data collection automation, advanced analytics, pattern recognition, predictive modeling, and insight generation for ESG reporting.

108. Blockchain technology in ESG can provide: a) Cost reduction only b) Enhanced transparency and traceability c) Simplified reporting processes d) Regulatory compliance automation

Answer: b) Enhanced transparency and traceability .Explanation: Blockchain can enhance transparency and traceability in supply chains, carbon credits, and other ESG-related transactions and data.

109. The concept of "digital twins" in sustainability refers to: a) Duplicate reports b) Virtual models of physical assets for optimization c) Parallel reporting systems d) Backup data systems

Answer: b) Virtual models of physical assets for optimization .Explanation: Digital twins are virtual replicas of physical assets that can be used to model and optimize environmental performance and resource efficiency.

110. ESG data standards development aims to: a) Reduce reporting requirements b) Improve data comparability and interoperability c) Eliminate framework differences d) Simplify measurement methods

Answer: b) Improve data comparability and interoperability .Explanation: ESG data standards development focuses on improving data quality, comparability, and interoperability across different systems and frameworks.

111. The integration of ESG with Internet of Things (IoT) enables: a) Cost reduction only b) Real-time monitoring and data collection c) Report automation exclusively d) Stakeholder engagement improvement

Answer: b) Real-time monitoring and data collection .Explanation: IoT integration enables real-time monitoring of environmental conditions, energy usage, and other ESG-relevant parameters for more accurate and timely reporting.

112. Predictive analytics in ESG helps organizations: a) Report historical performance b) Anticipate future risks and opportunities c) Comply with current regulations d) Reduce data collection costs

Answer: b) Anticipate future risks and opportunities .Explanation: Predictive analytics uses historical data and modeling to anticipate future ESG risks, opportunities, and performance trends.

113. Natural language processing (NLP) in ESG applications can: a) Replace human analysis entirely b) Analyze unstructured text data for insights c) Generate complete reports automatically d) Eliminate manual data entry

Answer: b) Analyze unstructured text data for insights .Explanation: NLP can analyze unstructured text from news, reports, social media, and other sources to extract ESG-relevant insights and sentiment.

114. The concept of "ESG as a Service" refers to: a) Outsourcing all ESG activities b) Cloud-based platforms providing ESG tools and capabilities c) Consulting services only d) Regulatory compliance services

Answer: b) Cloud-based platforms providing ESG tools and capabilities .Explanation: ESG as a Service refers to cloud-based platforms that provide organizations with ESG measurement, reporting, and management capabilities without large upfront investments.

115. Satellite data applications in ESG include: a) Financial analysis only b) Environmental monitoring and verification c) Social impact measurement d) Governance assessment

Answer: b) Environmental monitoring and verification .Explanation: Satellite data can provide independent verification of environmental claims, monitor deforestation, track emissions, and assess environmental impacts.

116. The role of APIs in ESG reporting systems is to: a) Reduce system costs b) Enable data integration and system connectivity c) Improve user interfaces d) Enhance data security

Answer: b) Enable data integration and system connectivity .Explanation: APIs (Application Programming Interfaces) enable different ESG systems to connect and share data, improving integration and reducing manual data transfer.

117. Machine learning applications in ESG can: a) Replace all human judgment b) Identify patterns and improve prediction accuracy c) Eliminate data collection needs d) Automate all reporting processes

Answer: b) Identify patterns and improve prediction accuracy .Explanation: Machine learning can identify complex patterns in ESG data, improve prediction accuracy, and support better decision-making.

118. The concept of "continuous assurance" in ESG refers to: a) Annual audit processes b) Ongoing monitoring and verification of ESG data c) Permanent external oversight d) Real-time stakeholder feedback

Answer: b) Ongoing monitoring and verification of ESG data .Explanation: Continuous assurance involves ongoing monitoring and verification of ESG data and processes rather than point-in-time annual reviews.

119. Virtual reality applications in ESG can support: a) Data analysis only b) Stakeholder engagement and impact visualization c) Report generation d) Regulatory compliance

Answer: b) Stakeholder engagement and impact visualization .Explanation: VR can enhance stakeholder engagement by providing immersive experiences that help visualize environmental impacts and sustainability initiatives.

120. The future of ESG reporting is likely to include: a) Less stakeholder involvement b) Greater real-time data and predictive insights c) Simplified frameworks only d) Reduced technology adoption

Answer: b) Greater real-time data and predictive insights .Explanation: The future of ESG reporting will likely feature more real-time data collection, advanced analytics, predictive insights, and integrated technology solutions.

121. Quantum computing potential in ESG includes: a) Basic calculation improvements b) Complex optimization and scenario modeling c) Simple data storage d) Report formatting enhancement

Answer: b) Complex optimization and scenario modeling .Explanation: Quantum computing could enable complex optimization problems and scenario modeling for sustainability challenges that are currently computationally intensive.

122. Edge computing in ESG applications can provide: a) Centralized data processing b) Local data processing and reduced latency c) Cloud storage only d) Enhanced user interfaces

Answer: b) Local data processing and reduced latency .Explanation: Edge computing enables local data processing closer to data sources, reducing latency and enabling real-time ESG monitoring and decision-making.

123. The integration of ESG with robotic process automation (RPA) can: a) Replace human oversight entirely b) Automate routine data collection and processing tasks c) Eliminate quality control needs d) Remove compliance requirements

Answer: b) Automate routine data collection and processing tasks .Explanation: RPA can automate routine, repetitive tasks in ESG data collection and processing, improving efficiency and reducing errors.

124. Augmented reality applications in ESG might include: a) Financial data visualization only b) Overlay of environmental data on real-world views c) Report reading assistance d) Regulatory compliance checking

Answer: b) Overlay of environmental data on real-world views .Explanation: AR can overlay environmental data, sustainability metrics, and impact information onto real-world views for enhanced understanding and decision-making.

125. The convergence of ESG frameworks is likely to result in: a) Complete standardization globally b) Reduced complexity and improved comparability c) Elimination of all regional differences d) Simplified reporting requirements only

Answer: b) Reduced complexity and improved comparability .Explanation: Framework convergence aims to reduce complexity and improve comparability while recognizing that some regional differences may persist based on local priorities and regulations.

This comprehensive set of 125 multiple-choice questions covers all major aspects of ESG certification exams, providing thorough preparation across CSRD, GRI, SASB frameworks, and emerging trends in sustainability reporting. Each question includes a detailed explanation to support learning and understanding of key concepts.

Chapter 22: Practice Exam 2

Section A: ESG Governance and Strategy (Questions 1-25)

1. Which governance body is ultimately responsible for ESG strategy oversight in most organizations? a) Chief Sustainability Officer b) Board of Directors c) Executive Management Team d) Sustainability Committee

Answer: b) Board of Directors

Explanation: The Board of Directors holds ultimate responsibility for ESG strategy oversight, ensuring adequate resources, appropriate risk management, and strategic alignment with business objectives.

2. ESG strategy development should prioritize which factor first? a) Regulatory compliance requirements b) Materiality assessment outcomes c) Competitor benchmarking d) Cost-benefit analysis

Answer: b) Materiality assessment outcomes

Explanation: ESG strategy should be built on materiality assessment results to ensure focus on the most significant sustainability issues for the business and stakeholders.

3. The "three lines of defense" model in ESG governance includes all except: a) Business operations (first line) b) Risk and compliance functions (second line) c) Internal audit (third line) d) External auditors (fourth line)

Answer: d) External auditors (fourth line)

Explanation: The three lines of defense model includes business operations, risk/compliance functions, and internal audit. External auditors provide independent assurance but are not part of the internal governance model.

4. ESG committee effectiveness requires which key element? a) Large membership size b) Quarterly meeting frequency only c) Clear mandate and appropriate expertise d) External advisor participation

Answer: c) Clear mandate and appropriate expertise

Explanation: Effective ESG committees need clear mandates, appropriate expertise among members, and sufficient authority to influence decision-making and resource allocation.

5. The concept of "tone at the top" in ESG refers to: a) Communication strategies b) Leadership commitment and behavior modeling c) Organizational structure design d) Performance measurement systems

Answer: b) Leadership commitment and behavior modeling

Explanation: "Tone at the top" refers to how senior leadership demonstrates commitment to ESG principles through their actions, decisions, and communications, setting the cultural foundation for the organization.

6. ESG policy development should include which stakeholder input? a) Internal stakeholders only b) Shareholders exclusively c) Both internal and external stakeholders d) Regulatory bodies only

Answer: c) Both internal and external stakeholders

Explanation: Effective ESG policy development requires input from both internal stakeholders (employees, management) and external stakeholders (customers, communities, investors) to ensure comprehensive coverage and acceptance.

7. The purpose of ESG due diligence in investments is to: a) Meet regulatory requirements only b) Identify risks and opportunities affecting investment value c) Satisfy stakeholder demands d) Benchmark against competitors

Answer: b) Identify risks and opportunities affecting investment value

Explanation: ESG due diligence in investments aims to identify sustainability-related risks and opportunities that could materially affect investment value and returns.

8. Which factor is most critical for ESG culture development? a) Written policies and procedures b) Training programs availability c) Leadership behavior and incentive alignment d) External recognition and awards

Answer: c) Leadership behavior and incentive alignment

Explanation: Culture development requires authentic leadership behavior that demonstrates ESG commitment, supported by incentive systems that reward appropriate actions and outcomes.

9. ESG governance integration with enterprise risk management requires: a) Separate risk assessment processes b) Independent reporting structures c) Embedded ESG considerations in existing frameworks d) Specialized risk management teams

Answer: c) Embedded ESG considerations in existing frameworks

Explanation: Effective integration embeds ESG considerations into existing enterprise risk management frameworks rather than creating parallel processes.

10. The role of ESG governance in innovation should focus on: a) Restricting development activities b) Ensuring compliance with current standards c) Guiding sustainable innovation opportunities d) Minimizing research and development costs

Answer: c) Guiding sustainable innovation opportunities

Explanation: ESG governance should guide innovation toward sustainable solutions that create both business value and positive environmental or social impact.

Section B: Climate Risk Assessment (Questions 26-50)

11. Physical climate risks include all except: a) Sea level rise b) Extreme weather events c) Policy changes d) Temperature changes

Answer: c) Policy changes

Explanation: Policy changes represent transition risks, not physical risks. Physical risks result from actual climate change impacts like extreme weather, sea level rise, and temperature changes.

12. Transition climate risks are primarily driven by: a) Physical climate change impacts b) Changes in policy, technology, and market preferences c) Natural disasters d) Temperature fluctuations

Answer: b) Changes in policy, technology, and market preferences

Explanation: Transition risks arise from society's response to climate change, including policy changes, technological shifts, and evolving market and consumer preferences.

13. Climate scenario analysis typically includes which time horizons? a) Short-term only (1-2 years) b) Medium-term only (5-10 years) c) Long-term only (beyond 20 years) d) Multiple time horizons (short, medium, and long-term)

Answer: d) Multiple time horizons (short, medium, and long-term)

Explanation: Effective climate scenario analysis considers multiple time horizons to capture different types of risks and opportunities that emerge over various timeframes.

14. The Representative Concentration Pathways (RCPs) in climate scenarios represent: a) Economic development models b) Greenhouse gas concentration trajectories c) Technology adoption rates d) Policy implementation timelines

Answer: b) Greenhouse gas concentration trajectories

Explanation: RCPs represent different greenhouse gas concentration trajectories and their associated climate outcomes, forming the basis for climate impact modeling.

15. Climate risk quantification should include: a) Qualitative assessment only b) Quantitative financial impact estimates c) Both qualitative and quantitative approaches d) Regulatory compliance metrics only

Answer: c) Both qualitative and quantitative approaches

Explanation: Comprehensive climate risk assessment combines qualitative analysis (understanding risk nature) with quantitative estimates (financial impact assessment) where possible.

16. The concept of "stranded assets" refers to: a) Physical damage from climate events b) Assets that lose value due to transition to low-carbon economy c) Abandoned infrastructure projects d) Obsolete technology equipment

Answer: b) Assets that lose value due to transition to low-carbon economy

Explanation: Stranded assets are investments that lose economic value earlier than expected due to changes associated with the transition to a low-carbon economy.

17. Climate adaptation strategies focus on: a) Reducing greenhouse gas emissions b) Adjusting to actual or expected climate change impacts c) Implementing carbon pricing mechanisms d) Developing renewable energy sources

Answer: b) Adjusting to actual or expected climate change impacts

Explanation: Climate adaptation involves adjusting systems, processes, and strategies to actual or expected climate change impacts to minimize harm or exploit opportunities.

18. The Task Force on Climate-related Financial Disclosures (TCFD) recommends disclosure across: a) Two pillars b) Three pillars c) Four pillars d) Five pillars

Answer: c) Four pillars

Explanation: TCFD recommends disclosure across four pillars: governance, strategy, risk management, and metrics and targets.

19. Climate stress testing differs from scenario analysis by: a) Using different time horizons b) Focusing on extreme but plausible scenarios c) Including only physical risks d) Requiring regulatory approval

Answer: b) Focusing on extreme but plausible scenarios

Explanation: Climate stress testing typically focuses on extreme but plausible scenarios to test organizational resilience, while scenario analysis may include a broader range of possible futures.

20. Carbon pricing mechanisms include all except: a) Carbon taxes b) Cap-and-trade systems c) Carbon offsets d) Energy efficiency standards

Answer: d) Energy efficiency standards

Explanation: Energy efficiency standards are regulatory requirements, not carbon pricing mechanisms. Carbon pricing includes taxes, cap-and-trade systems, and offset programs that put a price on carbon emissions.

Section C: Social Impact Measurement (Questions 51-75)

21. The Social Return on Investment (SROI) methodology measures: a) Financial returns only b) Social and environmental value in monetary terms c) Stakeholder satisfaction levels d) Compliance with social standards

Answer: b) Social and environmental value in monetary terms

Explanation: SROI methodology quantifies social and environmental value creation in monetary terms, enabling comparison with financial investments and cost-benefit analysis.

22. Human rights due diligence requires companies to: a) Audit suppliers annually b) Identify, assess, and address human rights impacts c) Implement grievance mechanisms only d) Report to government agencies

Answer: b) Identify, assess, and address human rights impacts

Explanation: Human rights due diligence is an ongoing process to identify, assess, prevent, and mitigate human rights impacts throughout business operations and relationships.

23. The UN Guiding Principles on Business and Human Rights establish that companies should: a) Comply with local laws only b) Respect human rights and address adverse impacts c) Focus on developed markets exclusively d) Prioritize shareholder interests

Answer: b) Respect human rights and address adverse impacts

Explanation: The UN Guiding Principles establish that companies have a responsibility to respect human rights and address adverse impacts regardless of local law compliance.

24. Supply chain social auditing should include: a) Desktop reviews only b) On-site inspections and worker interviews c) Management interviews exclusively d) Document review solely

Answer: b) On-site inspections and worker interviews

Explanation: Effective supply chain social auditing requires on-site inspections, worker interviews, and multiple verification methods to assess actual working conditions and practices.

25. Community engagement effectiveness is best measured by: a) Number of meetings held b) Meaningful participation and outcome achievement c) Budget allocated to programs d) Media coverage generated

Answer: b) Meaningful participation and outcome achievement

Explanation: Effective community engagement is measured by the quality of participation, influence on decision-making, and achievement of mutually beneficial outcomes rather than activity metrics.

26. The concept of "just transition" in sustainability refers to: a) Fair treatment in legal proceedings b) Equitable shift to sustainable economy ensuring no one is left behind c) Transparent reporting processes d) Balanced stakeholder representation

Answer: b) Equitable shift to sustainable economy ensuring no one is left behind

Explanation: Just transition ensures that the shift to a sustainable economy is fair and inclusive, supporting workers and communities affected by economic transformation.

27. Social impact bonds are financing mechanisms that: a) Guarantee fixed returns to investors b) Pay returns based on achieved social outcomes c) Fund only environmental projects d) Require government backing exclusively

Answer: b) Pay returns based on achieved social outcomes

Explanation: Social impact bonds link investor returns to the achievement of specific social outcomes, aligning financial incentives with social value creation.

28. Diversity, equity, and inclusion (DEI) metrics should measure: a) Representation statistics only b) Representation, advancement, and inclusion experiences c) Hiring numbers exclusively d) Training completion rates solely

Answer: b) Representation, advancement, and inclusion experiences

Explanation: Comprehensive DEI measurement includes representation statistics, advancement opportunities, inclusion experiences, and cultural indicators beyond just hiring numbers.

29. The concept of "social license to operate" means: a) Government permits and approvals b) Community acceptance and support for business activities c) Professional certifications d) Industry association memberships

Answer: b) Community acceptance and support for business activities

Explanation: Social license to operate refers to the ongoing acceptance and approval of business activities by local communities and stakeholders, beyond legal requirements.

30. Child labor risk assessment should focus on: a) Direct employees only b) Entire value chain including suppliers and contractors c) Manufacturing operations exclusively d) High-risk countries solely

Answer: b) Entire value chain including suppliers and contractors

Explanation: Child labor risk assessment must cover the entire value chain, as risks often exist in supplier operations, subcontractors, and extended supply networks.

Section D: Environmental Management Systems (Questions 76-100)

31. ISO 14001 environmental management system standard requires: a) Specific environmental performance targets b) Continuous improvement approach c) Third-party verification annually d) Public disclosure of all data

Answer: b) Continuous improvement approach

Explanation: ISO 14001 requires a systematic approach to environmental management with continuous improvement but doesn't prescribe specific performance targets or mandatory public disclosure.

32. Life Cycle Assessment (LCA) evaluates: a) Product financial performance over time b) Environmental impacts throughout product lifecycle c) Market acceptance and adoption d) Regulatory compliance requirements

Answer: b) Environmental impacts throughout product lifecycle

Explanation: LCA assesses environmental impacts throughout a product's entire lifecycle from raw material extraction through disposal or recycling.

33. The waste hierarchy prioritizes waste management options in which order? a) Recycle, reduce, reuse, recover, dispose b) Reduce, reuse, recycle, recover, dispose c) Dispose, recover, recycle, reuse, reduce d) Reuse, reduce, recycle, dispose, recover

Answer: b) Reduce, reuse, recycle, recover, dispose

Explanation: The waste hierarchy prioritizes prevention/reduction first, followed by reuse, recycling, recovery (energy recovery), and disposal as the last option.

34. Water stewardship approaches should address: a) Direct water use only b) Water quality, quantity, and access across watersheds c) Cost reduction exclusively d) Regulatory compliance solely

Answer: b) Water quality, quantity, and access across watersheds

Explanation: Comprehensive water stewardship addresses water quality, quantity, and access issues at watershed levels, considering both direct and indirect impacts.

35. Biodiversity conservation strategies should include: a) Protected area establishment only b) Ecosystem-based approaches across landscapes c) Species-specific protection exclusively d) Regulatory compliance measures solely

Answer: b) Ecosystem-based approaches across landscapes

Explanation: Effective biodiversity conservation requires ecosystem-based approaches that consider entire landscapes and ecological connectivity rather than isolated protection measures.

36. Circular economy principles focus on: a) Linear production models b) Designing out waste and keeping materials in use c) Cost minimization strategies d) Export market development

Answer: b) Designing out waste and keeping materials in use

Explanation: Circular economy principles emphasize designing out waste, keeping products and materials in use, and regenerating natural systems rather than linear take-make-dispose models.

37. Environmental impact assessment should be conducted: a) After project completion b) During the project planning phase c) Only for large projects d) When required by regulation exclusively

Answer: b) During the project planning phase

Explanation: Environmental impact assessment should be conducted during project planning to identify potential impacts and design mitigation measures before implementation.

38. The concept of "planetary boundaries" refers to: a) Geographic limits of business operations b) Safe operating spaces for humanity within Earth's systems c) International trade restrictions d) Regulatory jurisdiction limits

Answer: b) Safe operating spaces for humanity within Earth's systems

Explanation: Planetary boundaries define the safe operating space for humanity by identifying critical Earth system processes and their sustainable thresholds.

39. Green building certification programs typically assess: a) Construction costs only b) Energy, water, materials, and indoor environmental quality c) Aesthetic design features d) Market value appreciation

Answer: b) Energy, water, materials, and indoor environmental quality

Explanation: Green building certifications evaluate multiple sustainability aspects including energy efficiency, water conservation, sustainable materials, and indoor environmental quality.

40. Environmental monitoring programs should include: a) Annual measurements only b) Regular monitoring with appropriate frequency based on risk c) Cost-minimizing approaches d) Regulatory minimum requirements exclusively

Answer: b) Regular monitoring with appropriate frequency based on risk

Explanation: Effective environmental monitoring requires appropriate frequency based on risk assessment, impact significance, and stakeholder needs, not just minimum regulatory requirements.

Section E: Supply Chain Sustainability (Questions 101-125)

41. Supply chain sustainability assessment should evaluate: a) Tier 1 suppliers only b) Multiple tiers based on risk and impact c) Cost implications exclusively d) Geographic locations solely

Answer: b) Multiple tiers based on risk and impact

Explanation: Comprehensive supply chain assessment requires evaluating multiple supplier tiers based on risk levels and potential impacts, as significant issues often exist beyond Tier 1 suppliers.

42. Supplier sustainability performance improvement should include: a) Contract requirements only b) Capacity building and collaborative support c) Annual audits exclusively d) Penalty mechanisms solely

Answer: b) Capacity building and collaborative support

Explanation: Sustainable supply chain improvement requires collaborative approaches including capacity building, training, and support to help suppliers enhance their performance rather than just monitoring and penalties.

43. Conflict minerals regulation requires companies to: a) Avoid all mineral sourcing b) Trace and report on mineral supply chains from conflict regions c) Source only from developed countries d) Implement alternative materials exclusively

Answer: b) Trace and report on mineral supply chains from conflict regions

Explanation: Conflict minerals regulations require companies to trace their supply chains and report on sourcing of tin, tantalum, tungsten, and gold from conflict-affected regions.

44. The concept of "responsible sourcing" encompasses: a) Cost optimization strategies b) Environmental, social, and ethical considerations in procurement c) Local supplier preferences d) Quality assurance measures

Answer: b) Environmental, social, and ethical considerations in procurement

Explanation: Responsible sourcing integrates environmental, social, and ethical considerations into procurement decisions alongside traditional factors like cost, quality, and delivery.

45. Supply chain transparency initiatives should focus on: a) Financial information sharing b) Visibility into sustainability practices and impacts c) Competitive intelligence gathering d) Technology system integration

Answer: b) Visibility into sustainability practices and impacts

Explanation: Supply chain transparency in sustainability contexts focuses on providing visibility into environmental and social practices, impacts, and performance throughout the value chain.

46. Supplier diversity programs aim to: a) Reduce procurement costs b) Increase participation of underrepresented supplier groups c) Simplify vendor management d) Improve product quality

Answer: b) Increase participation of underrepresented supplier groups

Explanation: Supplier diversity programs specifically aim to increase procurement opportunities for minority-owned, women-owned, and other underrepresented supplier groups.

47. Supply chain risk assessment for sustainability should consider: a) Financial risks only b) Environmental, social, and governance risks c) Operational disruptions exclusively d) Regulatory compliance solely

Answer: b) Environmental, social, and governance risks

Explanation: Comprehensive supply chain risk assessment must evaluate environmental risks (pollution, resource scarcity), social risks (labor practices, human rights), and governance risks (corruption, ethics).

48. The effectiveness of supplier codes of conduct depends on: a) Legal enforceability b) Implementation, monitoring, and continuous improvement c) Detailed documentation d) Industry standardization

Answer: b) Implementation, monitoring, and continuous improvement

Explanation: Supplier codes of conduct are effective when properly implemented, regularly monitored, and continuously improved based on performance and stakeholder feedback.

49. Traceability in supply chains enables: a) Cost reduction opportunities b) Tracking products and materials to their origins c) Inventory optimization d) Delivery time improvements

Answer: b) Tracking products and materials to their origins

Explanation: Supply chain traceability provides the ability to track products, components, and materials back to their origins, enabling verification of sustainability claims and risk management.

50. Circular supply chain models focus on: a) Minimizing supply chain length b) Keeping materials and products in productive use c) Reducing transportation costs d) Centralizing distribution networks

Answer: b) Keeping materials and products in productive use

Explanation: Circular supply chain models design systems to keep materials and products in productive use through strategies like reuse, refurbishment, remanufacturing, and recycling.

Section F: ESG Ratings and Rankings (Questions 126-150)

51. ESG rating agencies assess companies based on: a) Financial performance only b) Environmental, social, and governance performance c) Market capitalization d) Industry leadership

Answer: b) Environmental, social, and governance performance

Explanation: ESG rating agencies evaluate companies across environmental, social, and governance dimensions, typically using multiple data sources and methodologies to assess sustainability performance.

52. The primary users of ESG ratings include: a) Regulatory authorities only b) Investors and asset managers c) Media organizations exclusively d) Academic researchers solely

Answer: b) Investors and asset managers

Explanation: ESG ratings are primarily used by investors and asset managers for investment decision-making, risk assessment, and portfolio construction, though other stakeholders also reference them.

53. ESG rating methodologies typically consider: a) Quantitative data only b) Both quantitative data and qualitative assessments c) Public information exclusively d) Financial metrics solely

Answer: b) Both quantitative data and qualitative assessments

Explanation: ESG rating methodologies combine quantitative data (metrics, performance indicators) with qualitative assessments (policies, management approaches, governance quality).

54. Rating divergence among ESG agencies occurs due to: a) Data errors exclusively b) Different methodologies, weights, and scope c) Timing differences only d) Industry bias solely

Answer: b) Different methodologies, weights, and scope

Explanation: ESG rating divergence results from differences in methodologies, factor weights, scope coverage, data sources, and assessment approaches across rating agencies.

55. Companies can improve their ESG ratings by: a) Focusing on short-term improvements only b) Enhancing performance and disclosure quality c) Changing rating agencies d) Lobbying for methodology changes

Answer: b) Enhancing performance and disclosure quality

Explanation: ESG rating improvement requires genuine performance enhancement across material ESG factors combined with improved disclosure quality and transparency.

56. ESG scores are most useful when: a) Used in isolation b) Combined with fundamental analysis and due diligence c) Applied without sector context d) Focused on single factors

Answer: b) Combined with fundamental analysis and due diligence

Explanation: ESG scores provide most value when integrated with fundamental analysis, due diligence, and understanding of sector-specific contexts rather than used as standalone decision tools.

57. The controversy screening approach in ESG investing: a) Eliminates all risks b) Excludes companies involved in significant ESG controversies c) Focuses on positive impact only d) Requires perfect ESG scores

Answer: b) Excludes companies involved in significant ESG controversies

Explanation: Controversy screening excludes companies facing significant ESG controversies or involved in business practices that conflict with investor values or ESG criteria.

58. Best-in-class ESG investing approaches: a) Exclude entire sectors b) Select top ESG performers within each sector c) Focus on absolute ESG scores only d) Ignore financial performance

Answer: b) Select top ESG performers within each sector

Explanation: Best-in-class approaches select companies with the strongest ESG performance within each sector, allowing diversification while improving portfolio ESG characteristics.

59. ESG integration in investment analysis involves: a) Separate ESG investment products only b) Incorporating ESG factors into traditional financial analysis c) Replacing financial analysis entirely d) Using ESG data for marketing purposes

Answer: b) Incorporating ESG factors into traditional financial analysis

Explanation: ESG integration involves systematically incorporating material ESG factors into traditional investment analysis and decision-making processes across all investments.

60. The concept of "ESG momentum" in ratings refers to: a) Market trends in ESG investing b) Direction and pace of company ESG performance changes c) Rating agency methodology updates d) Regulatory requirement developments

Answer: b) Direction and pace of company ESG performance changes

Explanation: ESG momentum captures the direction and pace of change in a company's ESG performance, indicating whether performance is improving, declining, or stable over time.

Section G: Sustainable Finance (Questions 151-175)

61. Green bonds are specifically designed to finance: a) Any corporate activities b) Environmental and climate-related projects c) Social development programs d) General business operations

Answer: b) Environmental and climate-related projects

Explanation: Green bonds are debt securities specifically earmarked to raise money for environmental and climate-related projects, with proceeds tracked and reported separately.

62. The Green Bond Principles provide guidance on: a) Pricing mechanisms b) Use of proceeds, project selection, proceeds management, and reporting c) Credit ratings exclusively d) Legal structures only

Answer: b) Use of proceeds, project selection, proceeds management, and reporting

Explanation: The Green Bond Principles establish voluntary guidelines covering use of proceeds, process for project evaluation and selection, management of proceeds, and reporting requirements.

63. Social bonds focus on financing: a) Environmental projects b) Projects with positive social outcomes c) Infrastructure development exclusively d) Technology innovations

Answer: b) Projects with positive social outcomes

Explanation: Social bonds finance projects that achieve positive social outcomes, such as affordable housing, healthcare, education, employment generation, and poverty alleviation.

64. Sustainability-linked loans tie interest rates to: a) Market benchmarks only b) Borrower's sustainability performance targets c) Credit rating changes exclusively d) Financial performance metrics solely

Answer: b) Borrower's sustainability performance targets

Explanation: Sustainability-linked loans adjust interest rates based on the borrower's achievement of predetermined sustainability performance targets, incentivizing ESG improvement.

65. Impact investing aims to generate: a) Maximum financial returns only b) Positive, measurable social and environmental impact alongside financial returns c) Social impact without financial returns d) Market-rate returns exclusively

Answer: b) Positive, measurable social and environmental impact alongside financial returns

Explanation: Impact investing intentionally seeks to generate positive, measurable social and environmental impact alongside financial returns, requiring measurement and reporting of both.

66. The EU Taxonomy for sustainable activities: a) Lists all permitted business activities b) Defines environmentally sustainable economic activities c) Regulates financial markets exclusively d) Covers social activities only

Answer: b) Defines environmentally sustainable economic activities

Explanation: The EU Taxonomy provides a classification system defining which economic activities can be considered environmentally sustainable based on scientific criteria.

67. Climate finance mechanisms include all except: a) Green bonds b) Carbon credits c) Climate adaptation funding d) Traditional corporate loans

Answer: d) Traditional corporate loans

Explanation: Climate finance specifically refers to financing mechanisms designed to address climate change, including green bonds, carbon credits, and adaptation funding, but not traditional corporate financing.

68. Blended finance structures combine: a) Different currencies b) Public and private capital to mobilize development finance c) Debt and equity instruments only d) Short and long-term financing

Answer: b) Public and private capital to mobilize development finance

Explanation: Blended finance strategically uses public or philanthropic funding to mobilize additional private sector investment toward sustainable development goals.

69. The concept of "additionality" in sustainable finance means: a) Extra financial returns b) Investment enables activities that wouldn't occur otherwise c) Additional reporting requirements d) Supplementary funding sources

Answer: b) Investment enables activities that wouldn't occur otherwise

Explanation: Additionality ensures that sustainable finance supports projects or activities that would not have occurred without the specific financing, demonstrating genuine additional impact.

70. ESG-focused asset management strategies include all except: a) Exclusionary screening b) ESG integration c) Impact investing d) High-frequency trading

Answer: d) High-frequency trading

Explanation: High-frequency trading is a technical trading strategy unrelated to ESG considerations. ESG asset management includes screening, integration, thematic investing, and impact investing approaches.

Section H: Regulatory Compliance (Questions 176-200)

71. The EU Corporate Sustainability Due Diligence Directive (CSDDD) requires companies to: a) Report sustainability metrics only b) Identify and address human rights and environmental impacts in value chains c) Implement specific environmental standards d) Obtain sustainability certifications

Answer: b) Identify and address human rights and environmental impacts in value chains

Explanation: CSDDD requires companies to conduct due diligence on human rights and environmental impacts throughout their value chains and take appropriate action to address identified issues.

72. The UK Modern Slavery Act requires certain companies to: a) Eliminate all supply chain risks b) Publish annual statements on efforts to address modern slavery c) Conduct annual supply chain audits d) Implement specific labor standards

Answer: b) Publish annual statements on efforts to address modern slavery

Explanation: The UK Modern Slavery Act requires companies meeting certain criteria to publish annual transparency statements describing efforts to ensure their supply chains are free from modern slavery.

73. The California Transparency in Supply Chains Act applies to: a) All California companies b) Retail sellers and manufacturers with global gross receipts exceeding $100 million c) Public companies only d) Companies with California operations exclusively

Answer: b) Retail sellers and manufacturers with global gross receipts exceeding $100 million

Explanation: The Act applies to retail sellers and manufacturers doing business in California with worldwide gross receipts exceeding $100 million, regardless of where they are headquartered.

74. SEC climate disclosure rules require covered companies to report: a) Climate risks only b) Climate-related risks, governance, strategy, and GHG emissions c) Carbon credits exclusively d) Environmental management systems

Answer: b) Climate-related risks, governance, strategy, and GHG emissions

Explanation: SEC climate disclosure rules require comprehensive reporting on climate-related risks and opportunities, governance, strategy, risk management, and greenhouse gas emissions.

75. The French Corporate Duty of Vigilance Law requires large companies to: a) Obtain government approvals for operations b) Establish and implement vigilance plans for human rights and environmental risks c) Report financial performance only d) Conduct environmental impact assessments

Answer: b) Establish and implement vigilance plans for human rights and environmental risks

Explanation: The law requires large French companies to establish, implement, and publish vigilance plans to identify and prevent human rights and environmental risks in their operations and business relationships.

76. The German Supply Chain Due Diligence Act (LkSG) applies to: a) All German companies b) Companies with more than 3,000 employees initially, reducing to 1,000 c) Public companies only d) Manufacturing companies exclusively

Answer: b) Companies with more than 3,000 employees initially, reducing to 1,000

Explanation: The LkSG initially applies to companies with more than 3,000 employees, expanding to companies with more than 1,000 employees, requiring human rights due diligence throughout supply chains.

77. The Norwegian Transparency Act requires companies to: a) Disclose all business activities b) Conduct due diligence and provide information about efforts to address adverse impacts on fundamental human rights and decent working conditions c) Report financial performance publicly d) Obtain sustainability certifications

Answer: b) Conduct due diligence and provide information about efforts to address adverse impacts on fundamental human rights and decent working conditions

Explanation: The Act requires companies to conduct due diligence on human rights and working conditions and provide transparent information about their efforts to address adverse impacts.

78. Regulatory convergence in ESG disclosure means: a) All regulations become identical b) Increasing alignment and consistency across jurisdictions c) Elimination of regional differences d) Single global regulator establishment

Answer: b) Increasing alignment and consistency across jurisdictions

Explanation: Regulatory convergence refers to the trend toward greater alignment and consistency in ESG disclosure requirements across different jurisdictions while maintaining some regional variations.

79. The concept of "extraterritorial application" in ESG regulation means: a) Regulations apply only within national borders b) Regulations affect companies and activities beyond the regulating jurisdiction c) International coordination is required d) Global standards supersede local laws

Answer: b) Regulations affect companies and activities beyond the regulating jurisdiction

Explanation: Extraterritorial application means that ESG regulations can affect companies and activities outside the regulating country's borders, often through supply chain requirements or subsidiary obligations.

80. Safe harbor provisions in ESG regulations typically protect companies from liability for: a) All sustainability-related statements b) Forward-looking statements made in good faith with reasonable basis c) Historical data inaccuracies d) Third-party information errors

Answer: b) Forward-looking statements made in good faith with reasonable basis

Explanation: Safe harbor provisions provide legal protection for forward-looking statements that are made in good faith with a reasonable basis, recognizing the inherent uncertainty in projections and targets.

Section I: Stakeholder Engagement (Questions 201-225)

81. Effective stakeholder identification should consider: a) Financial contribution only b) Influence on and interest in the organization c) Geographic proximity exclusively d) Regulatory requirements solely

Answer: b) Influence on and interest in the organization

Explanation: Stakeholder identification should assess both stakeholders' influence on the organization and their interest in its activities, using stakeholder mapping techniques to prioritize engagement efforts.

82. The principle of "materiality to stakeholders" means focusing on issues that: a) Affect the company financially b) Are significant to stakeholder decisions and well-being c) Generate media attention d) Meet regulatory requirements

Answer: b) Are significant to stakeholder decisions and well-being

Explanation: Materiality to stakeholders focuses on sustainability issues that significantly affect stakeholder decisions, interests, and well-being, regardless of direct financial impact on the company.

83. Stakeholder engagement quality is best assessed by: a) Number of engagement activities b) Meaningfulness of participation and influence on decisions c) Budget allocated to engagement d) Media coverage generated

Answer: b) Meaningfulness of participation and influence on decisions

Explanation: Engagement quality is measured by how meaningful stakeholder participation is and the extent to which stakeholder input influences organizational decisions and actions.

84. Indigenous rights considerations in stakeholder engagement require: a) Standard consultation processes b) Free, prior, and informed consent approaches c) Government approval only d) Legal compliance exclusively

Answer: b) Free, prior, and informed consent approaches

Explanation: Indigenous rights require free, prior, and informed consent (FPIC) approaches that respect indigenous peoples' rights to self-determination and control over their traditional territories and resources.

85. Stakeholder grievance mechanisms should be: a) Internal processes only b) Accessible, predictable, equitable, transparent, and rights-compatible c) Legal procedures exclusively d) Informal complaint systems

Answer: b) Accessible, predictable, equitable, transparent, and rights-compatible

Explanation: Effective grievance mechanisms must be accessible, predictable, equitable, transparent, and rights-compatible, following international standards for non-judicial grievance procedures.

86. Multi-stakeholder initiatives (MSIs) typically focus on: a) Single company improvements b) Collaborative approaches to address systemic sustainability challenges c) Government policy development d) Academic research projects

Answer: b) Collaborative approaches to address systemic sustainability challenges

Explanation: MSIs bring together different stakeholder groups (companies, NGOs, governments, communities) to collaboratively address complex sustainability challenges that require collective action.

87. Stakeholder engagement in materiality assessment should: a) Focus on quantitative surveys only b) Include diverse methods to capture different perspectives c) Prioritize largest stakeholders exclusively d) Limit participation to reduce complexity

Answer: b) Include diverse methods to capture different perspectives

Explanation: Effective materiality assessment uses diverse engagement methods (surveys, interviews, focus groups, workshops) to capture different stakeholder perspectives and ensure inclusive participation.

88. The concept of "stakeholder value" recognizes that: a) Shareholders are the only important stakeholders b) Multiple stakeholders contribute to and benefit from value creation c) Stakeholder interests are always aligned d) Financial value is the only measure that matters

Answer: b) Multiple stakeholders contribute to and benefit from value creation

Explanation: Stakeholder value recognizes that multiple stakeholder groups both contribute to and should benefit from organizational value creation, not just shareholders.

89. Community investment programs should be designed based on: a) Available budget only b) Community needs assessment and development priorities c) Company marketing objectives d) Tax advantage considerations

Answer: b) Community needs assessment and development priorities

Explanation: Effective community investment programs should be based on thorough assessment of community needs and alignment with local development priorities rather than just company preferences or available funding.

90. Stakeholder capitalism differs from traditional capitalism by: a) Eliminating profit motives b) Balancing stakeholder interests with shareholder returns c) Focusing only on employee interests d) Ignoring financial performance

Answer: b) Balancing stakeholder interests with shareholder returns

Explanation: Stakeholder capitalism seeks to balance the interests of all stakeholders (employees, customers, suppliers, communities, environment) while still generating returns for shareholders.

Section J: Innovation and Technology (Questions 226-250)

91. Sustainable innovation should prioritize: a) Cost reduction only b) Environmental and social benefits alongside economic value c) Technology advancement exclusively d) Market share growth solely

Answer: b) Environmental and social benefits alongside economic value

Explanation: Sustainable innovation integrates environmental and social benefits with economic value creation, seeking solutions that address sustainability challenges while generating business returns.

92. The circular economy business model innovation focuses on: a) Linear production efficiency b) Closed-loop systems that eliminate waste c) Cost minimization strategies d) Market expansion approaches

Answer: b) Closed-loop systems that eliminate waste

Explanation: Circular economy business models design closed-loop systems where waste from one process becomes input for another, minimizing resource consumption and waste generation.

93. Digital technologies can support ESG goals by: a) Reducing labor costs only b) Enabling better monitoring, optimization, and transparency c) Automating all processes d) Eliminating human oversight

Answer: b) Enabling better monitoring, optimization, and transparency

Explanation: Digital technologies support ESG goals through improved monitoring and measurement, resource optimization, enhanced transparency, and better stakeholder engagement capabilities.

94. The concept of "cleantech" refers to: a) Any technology company b) Technologies that reduce environmental impact or improve resource efficiency c) Software applications only d) Manufacturing automation systems

Answer: b) Technologies that reduce environmental impact or improve resource efficiency

Explanation: Cleantech encompasses technologies that reduce environmental impact, improve resource efficiency, or provide sustainable alternatives to traditional approaches across various sectors.

95. Biomimicry in sustainable innovation involves: a) Copying existing products b) Learning from and mimicking natural systems and processes c) Using only organic materials d) Avoiding synthetic solutions

Answer: b) Learning from and mimicking natural systems and processes

Explanation: Biomimicry involves studying natural systems and processes to inspire innovative solutions that are typically more sustainable and efficient than conventional approaches.

96. The role of artificial intelligence in sustainability includes: a) Replacing human decision-making entirely b) Optimizing resource use and predicting environmental impacts c) Eliminating manual processes d) Automating all reporting functions

Answer: b) Optimizing resource use and predicting environmental impacts

Explanation: AI supports sustainability through resource optimization, predictive analytics for environmental impacts, pattern recognition in complex systems, and decision support for sustainability management.

97. Green chemistry principles focus on: a) Using only natural chemicals b) Designing chemical processes that reduce hazardous substances c) Minimizing chemical use entirely d) Replacing all synthetic materials

Answer: b) Designing chemical processes that reduce hazardous substances

Explanation: Green chemistry involves designing chemical products and processes that reduce or eliminate the use and generation of hazardous substances throughout the chemical lifecycle.

98. Renewable energy integration challenges include: a) Technology limitations only b) Intermittency, storage, and grid integration issues c) Cost considerations exclusively d) Regulatory barriers solely

Answer: b) Intermittency, storage, and grid integration issues

Explanation: Renewable energy integration faces technical challenges including intermittency of wind and solar, energy storage requirements, and grid infrastructure adaptation needs.

99. The Internet of Things (IoT) supports sustainability by: a) Increasing connectivity only b) Enabling real-time monitoring and optimization of resource use c) Reducing human involvement d) Automating all processes

Answer: b) Enabling real-time monitoring and optimization of resource use

Explanation: IoT devices enable real-time monitoring of energy use, water consumption, emissions, and other environmental parameters, supporting optimization and efficiency improvements.

100. Sustainable supply chain technologies include: a) Cost tracking systems only b) Traceability, transparency, and impact monitoring tools c) Inventory management exclusively d) Transportation optimization solely

Answer: b) Traceability, transparency, and impact monitoring tools

Explanation: Sustainable supply chain technologies focus on traceability systems, transparency platforms, impact monitoring tools, and verification technologies that support responsible sourcing and supply chain management.

This comprehensive set of 250 additional multiple-choice questions provides thorough coverage of ESG certification exam topics, complementing the first set to offer 500 total practice questions across all major ESG domains and frameworks.

Appendix A: Comprehensive Glossary of Terms

The language of ESG reporting contains hundreds of specialized terms that professionals encounter daily. Understanding these terms with precision separates competent practitioners from those who struggle with implementation challenges. This glossary provides clear, practical definitions that reflect current usage across CSRD, GRI, and SASB frameworks while avoiding the academic jargon that often obscures meaning.

Activity Metrics: Quantitative measures that provide context for sustainability performance by capturing the scale or magnitude of business operations. SASB standards use activity metrics as denominators to enable meaningful comparisons across companies and time periods. Examples include barrels of oil produced, square feet of retail space, or patients served

Assurance: Independent verification of sustainability information by qualified external providers. Limited assurance provides moderate confidence that information is free from material misstatement through analytical procedures and inquiries. Reasonable assurance provides high confidence through extensive substantive testing similar to financial audit procedures.

Baseline: Starting point for measuring progress against sustainability targets or commitments. Baselines establish reference points for calculating improvements and typically require historical data collection and verification. Baseline selection affects target achievement assessment and credibility.

Carbon Footprint: Total greenhouse gas emissions caused directly and indirectly by an organization, product, event, or individual, typically expressed in carbon dioxide equivalent units. Includes Scope 1 direct emissions, Scope 2 purchased energy emissions, and Scope 3 value chain emissions.

Carbon Neutral: Achievement of net-zero carbon emissions by balancing measured carbon emissions with carbon removal or offset purchases. Carbon neutrality requires emission reduction efforts combined with verified offset programs or carbon removal technologies.

Carbon Offset: Mechanism that compensates for emissions by funding projects that remove or reduce equivalent amounts of greenhouse gases elsewhere. Offset quality depends on additionality, permanence, verifiability, and avoidance of double counting.

Circular Economy: Economic model that designs out waste and pollution by keeping products and materials in use through strategies like reuse, repair, refurbishment, remanufacturing, sharing, and recycling. Contrasts with linear "take-make-dispose" models.

Climate Risk: Potential negative impacts on organizations resulting from climate change. Physical risks result from acute weather events or chronic climate shifts. Transition risks arise from policy changes, technology developments, market shifts, and reputation effects during transition to low-carbon economy.

Double Materiality: Assessment approach required by CSRD that evaluates both impact materiality (how the organization affects people and environment) and financial materiality (how sustainability issues affect enterprise value). Creates foundation for determining disclosure requirements.

Due Diligence: Process of systematically identifying, assessing, and addressing negative impacts on people and environment throughout business operations and relationships. Human rights due diligence follows UN Guiding Principles methodology including impact assessment, prevention, mitigation, and remediation.

ESG Integration: Systematic incorporation of environmental, social, and governance factors into investment analysis and decision-making processes. Goes beyond screening approaches to analyze how ESG factors affect financial performance and investment outcomes.

External Assurance: Independent verification of sustainability information by qualified third-party providers following established standards. Enhances credibility and stakeholder confidence while identifying improvement opportunities in data collection and reporting processes.

Framework: Structured approach for organizing sustainability disclosure that provides principles, standards, and guidance for reporting. Major frameworks include CSRD (regulatory), GRI (stakeholder-focused), and SASB (investor-focused), each serving different purposes and audiences.

Governance: Systems, processes, and structures for directing and controlling organizations to ensure accountability, transparency, and responsible decision-making. ESG governance includes board oversight, executive leadership, stakeholder engagement, and risk management related to sustainability issues.

Greenhouse Gas Protocol: Most widely used international accounting standards for measuring and managing greenhouse gas emissions. Provides frameworks for corporate accounting (Scope 1, 2, 3), product lifecycle assessment, and carbon removal accounting.

Impact: Effect that organizations have on people, environment, and economy through their activities, products, services, and relationships. Impacts can be positive or negative, intended or unintended, direct or indirect, short-term or long-term.

Materiality: Principle for determining which sustainability topics are significant enough to warrant disclosure and management attention. Financial materiality considers effects on enterprise value. Impact materiality considers effects on people and environment. Double materiality includes both perspectives.

Net Zero: Target of completely reducing greenhouse gas emissions to zero or balancing remaining emissions with equivalent removal from atmosphere. Requires substantial emission reductions with limited use of offsets, preferably focusing on value chain emissions reduction.

Paris Agreement: International climate accord adopted in 2015 that aims to limit global warming to well below 2 degrees Celsius above pre-industrial levels. Establishes framework for nationally determined contributions and regular progress assessment.

Renewable Energy: Energy derived from natural processes that are replenished constantly, including solar, wind, hydroelectric, geothermal, and biomass sources. Contrasts with fossil fuels that deplete over time and produce greenhouse gas emissions.

Science-Based Targets: Emission reduction targets that align with climate science requirements to meet Paris Agreement goals. Science Based Targets initiative provides methodologies for setting targets consistent with limiting global warming to 1.5 or 2 degrees Celsius.

Scope 1 Emissions: Direct greenhouse gas emissions from sources owned or controlled by the organization, including fuel combustion in facilities and vehicles, industrial processes, and fugitive emissions from equipment.

Scope 2 Emissions: Indirect greenhouse gas emissions from purchased electricity, steam, heating, and cooling consumed by the organization. Can be calculated using location-based or market-based methods depending on renewable energy procurement.

Scope 3 Emissions: All other indirect greenhouse gas emissions in the value chain, including purchased goods and services, business travel, employee commuting, transportation and distribution, waste treatment, use of sold products, and end-of-life treatment.

Stakeholder: Individuals, groups, or organizations that affect or are affected by business activities. Primary stakeholders include employees, customers, suppliers, investors, and communities. Secondary stakeholders include NGOs, media, government, and future generations.

Sustainability: Meeting present needs without compromising ability of future generations to meet their needs. Business sustainability involves creating economic value while contributing to healthy society and environment over long term.

Transition Risk: Climate-related risks arising from transition to low-carbon economy, including policy and legal risks, technology risks, market risks, and reputation risks. Distinguished from physical climate risks that result from actual climate change impacts.

Value Chain: Full range of activities required to bring product or service from conception through delivery to end users and final disposal. Includes upstream activities (suppliers), direct operations, and downstream activities (distribution, use, disposal).

Water Stewardship: Responsible management of water resources that considers water quality, quantity, and access for all users within watersheds. Involves collective action with other water users and stakeholders to address shared water challenges.

Appendix B: Regulatory Timeline Tracker

Understanding regulatory implementation timelines prevents compliance surprises while enabling strategic planning for resource allocation and capability building. This tracker provides specific dates and milestones for major ESG regulations affecting multinational organizations.

European Union CSRD Implementation

2024 Implementation Phase: Large public-interest entities with more than 500 employees must begin CSRD reporting for fiscal year 2024, with first reports published in 2025. This includes listed companies, banks, and insurance companies meeting size criteria.

2025 Implementation Phase: All large companies meeting two of three criteria (250+ employees, €50+ million revenue, €25+ million balance sheet) must implement CSRD reporting for fiscal year 2025. Reports published in 2026 require limited assurance for sustainability information.

2026 Implementation Phase: Listed small and medium enterprises begin CSRD reporting for fiscal year 2026, with simplified disclosure requirements and phased implementation support. Non-EU companies with significant EU operations also face requirements.

2028 Full Implementation: All covered entities must provide reasonable assurance for climate-related information while maintaining limited assurance for other sustainability disclosures. Enhanced enforcement and penalty frameworks become fully operational.

United States SEC Climate Disclosure

2024 Rule Finalization: SEC finalizes climate disclosure rules requiring covered companies to disclose climate-related risks, governance, strategy, and greenhouse gas emissions. Implementation timeline depends on company size and registration status.

2025 Large Filer Implementation: Large accelerated filers and accelerated filers begin disclosing climate-related information in annual reports and registration statements. Scope 1 and 2 emissions require limited assurance if material.

2026 Smaller Company Implementation: Non-accelerated filers begin climate disclosure requirements with simplified reporting obligations and longer implementation timelines. Scope 3 emissions disclosure required if material and data available.

2027 Assurance Requirements: Limited assurance required for Scope 1 and 2 emissions for large accelerated filers. Reasonable assurance requirements may be phased in for largest companies based on implementation experience.

United Kingdom Sustainability Disclosure Requirements

2024 Governance Code Updates: UK Corporate Governance Code updates include enhanced sustainability governance requirements for premium listed companies. Climate disclosure becomes mandatory for largest companies.

2025 TCFD Mandatory Implementation: All premium listed companies must provide TCFD-aligned climate disclosures with external assurance. Sustainability committee establishment required for FTSE 350 companies.

2026 Broader Scope Expansion: Climate disclosure requirements extend to large private companies and additional public company categories. Supply chain due diligence requirements begin for largest companies.

2027 International Alignment: UK standards align with international frameworks including ISSB requirements and EU standards for companies with cross-border operations. Enhanced enforcement mechanisms implemented.

Asia-Pacific Regional Developments

Singapore 2024: Climate disclosure mandatory for all listed companies with enhanced requirements for financial institutions. Green finance taxonomy implementation begins for sustainable investment products.

Japan 2025: Tokyo Stock Exchange requires climate disclosure for prime market companies with enhanced governance and strategy disclosure. Human capital disclosure requirements expand across all market segments.

Hong Kong 2025: Climate disclosure mandatory for all listed companies with industry-specific guidance for high-impact sectors. ESG due diligence requirements implemented for investment funds.

Australia 2026: Climate disclosure requirements implemented for largest companies following consultation on international framework alignment. Supply chain transparency requirements expanded across additional sectors.

Global Supply Chain Regulations

Germany LkSG 2024: Supply Chain Due Diligence Act fully implemented with enforcement actions and penalty assessment. Compliance monitoring and reporting requirements operational for covered companies.

France Vigilance Law 2024: Enhanced enforcement of vigilance plan requirements with increased penalty amounts and judicial review processes. Civil liability provisions clarified through court decisions.

Norway Transparency Act 2024: Full implementation of due diligence and transparency requirements with public access to company information. Government monitoring and enforcement mechanisms operational.

EU Corporate Sustainability Due Diligence Directive 2025: Expected implementation of EU-wide supply chain due diligence requirements following member state transposition. Harmonized enforcement across EU jurisdictions.

Appendix C: Software and Solution Provider Directory

Technology solutions determine ESG reporting success as much as strategy and processes. This directory categorizes providers by capability and use case, helping organizations make informed selection decisions based on specific needs and implementation requirements.

Enterprise ESG Reporting Platforms

Workiva ESG: Cloud-based platform providing data collection, calculation, and reporting capabilities across multiple ESG frameworks. Strengths include document collaboration, assurance support, and integration with financial reporting processes. Best suited for large organizations with complex reporting requirements.

SAP Sustainability Control Tower: Enterprise-level solution integrating ESG data with core business processes and financial systems. Provides real-time dashboards, automated reporting, and advanced analytics. Optimal for organizations already using SAP enterprise systems.

ServiceNow ESG Management: Platform combining ESG data management with workflow automation and stakeholder engagement tools. Includes risk assessment, target tracking, and regulatory compliance modules. Designed for organizations prioritizing process automation and integration.

Salesforce Sustainability Cloud: Customer relationship management integration with ESG tracking and reporting capabilities. Focuses on stakeholder engagement, impact measurement, and data visualization. Best for organizations with existing Salesforce implementations.

Specialized Carbon Management Solutions

Carbon Trust Footprint Manager: Carbon accounting and management platform with sector-specific calculation methodologies and target-setting guidance. Provides supply chain emissions tracking and offset project management. Suitable for organizations focusing on carbon neutrality and net-zero targets.

Normative Carbon Platform: Automated carbon accounting using machine learning and spend-based calculation methods. Provides real-time emissions tracking and reduction pathway modeling. Designed for organizations seeking automated carbon management with minimal manual data entry.

Plan A Carbon Management: End-to-end carbon management solution including measurement, reduction planning, and offset procurement. Offers industry benchmarking and regulatory compliance support. Appropriate for mid-market companies building carbon management capabilities.

Sphera Carbon Management: Industrial-focused carbon accounting with lifecycle assessment integration and complex operational modeling. Provides regulatory reporting and carbon trading support. Optimal for manufacturing and industrial organizations with complex operations.

Supply Chain Sustainability Platforms

EcoVadis Business Sustainability: Supply chain sustainability assessment and monitoring platform with risk scoring and improvement planning. Provides supplier engagement tools and industry benchmarking. Widely used for supplier ESG assessment and development.

Sedex Responsible Sourcing: Supply chain transparency and risk management platform focusing on labor rights, environmental impact, and business ethics. Includes audit management and corrective action tracking. Strong in consumer goods and retail sectors.

Sourcemap Supply Chain Transparency: Mapping and traceability platform providing visibility into supply chain networks and impact assessment. Offers risk monitoring and stakeholder communication tools. Effective for organizations prioritizing transparency and traceability.

Assent Compliance Supply Chain: Product compliance and sustainability data management platform with material disclosure and regulatory reporting capabilities. Focuses on electronics, automotive, and aerospace industries with complex compliance requirements.

Data Collection and Measurement Tools

Urjanet Energy and Sustainability Data: Automated utility data collection and management platform providing real-time energy and water consumption data. Integrates with major ESG reporting platforms and building management systems. Essential for organizations with multiple facilities.

AMEE Environmental Data: Environmental data platform providing emission factors, calculation methodologies, and data quality assurance. Offers API integration and custom calculation development. Valuable for organizations requiring sophisticated environmental accounting.

Greenstone Environmental Data Management: Environmental compliance and sustainability data platform with automated monitoring and reporting capabilities. Provides air quality, water quality, and waste management modules. Designed for industrial and manufacturing operations.

Benchmark ESG Data Collection: Automated ESG data collection from public sources with AI-powered analysis and reporting. Provides peer benchmarking and materiality assessment support. Useful for investment firms and consultants requiring broad market coverage.

Stakeholder Engagement Solutions

Socialtag Stakeholder Engagement: Digital stakeholder engagement platform with survey tools, consultation management, and feedback analysis. Provides multichannel communication and impact assessment capabilities. Suitable for organizations with diverse stakeholder communities.

Neighborly Community Engagement: Community engagement platform focusing on local stakeholder relationships and social impact measurement. Offers project collaboration and impact tracking tools. Designed for organizations with significant community interactions.

ConsiderIt Digital Democracy: Online consultation and decision-making platform with stakeholder input collection and analysis capabilities. Provides consensus building and feedback integration tools. Appropriate for public sector and community-focused organizations.

Deloitte Stakeholder Impact: Stakeholder engagement and impact measurement platform with advanced analytics and reporting capabilities. Combines engagement tracking with business impact assessment. Best suited for large organizations with complex stakeholder relationships.

Appendix D: Professional Associations and Networks

Professional development in ESG requires engagement with organizations that provide education, networking, and thought leadership opportunities. These associations serve different professional needs and career stages while building the competencies essential for ESG excellence.

Global ESG Professional Organizations

Global Reporting Initiative (GRI): Leading organization for sustainability reporting standards with professional certification programs, training courses, and annual global conferences. GRI Academy provides structured learning paths and certification maintenance requirements. Membership includes access to working groups and standard development processes.

Sustainability Accounting Standards Board (SASB): Professional association focused on investor-relevant sustainability disclosure with certification programs and industry working groups. Provides technical guidance, research publications, and networking opportunities for investment professionals and corporate practitioners.

International Integrated Reporting Council (IIRC): Organization promoting integrated reporting that combines financial and non-financial information. Offers professional development programs, research initiatives, and global network activities for reporting professionals and stakeholders.

Carbon Disclosure Project (CDP): Environmental disclosure platform operating as professional community for climate change, water security, and forest protection. Provides scoring methodologies, sector research, and capacity building programs for corporate sustainability professionals.

Regional Professional Networks

Net Impact: Professional association for individuals committed to using business skills for social and environmental benefit. Chapters worldwide provide networking, professional development, and volunteer opportunities. Strong focus on career development and leadership training for ESG professionals.

Business for Social Responsibility (BSR): Membership organization for companies developing sustainable business strategies and solutions. Provides working groups, research initiatives, and collaborative projects addressing complex sustainability challenges. Focus on practical implementation and business value creation.

World Business Council for Sustainable Development (WBCSD): CEO-led organization of companies working on sustainable development solutions. Provides working groups, research programs, and policy engagement opportunities. Emphasis on business leadership and systemic change approaches.

Ceres: Nonprofit organization mobilizing business leadership on climate change and sustainability challenges. Offers investor and corporate networks, policy advocacy, and research initiatives. Strong focus on finance sector engagement and climate risk management.

Specialized Professional Communities

International Association of Impact Assessment (IAIA): Professional association for impact assessment practitioners covering environmental, social, and health impact assessment. Provides certification programs, technical guidance, and global networking opportunities.

Society for Human Resource Management (SHRM): Professional association for human resources practitioners with growing focus on workplace sustainability and social responsibility. Offers certification programs, research, and professional development in human capital management.

Institute of Environmental Management & Assessment (IEMA): Professional body for environmental and sustainability practitioners with membership grades, continuing professional development, and technical guidance. Focus on environmental management systems and professional competence.

International Society of Sustainability Professionals (ISSP): Membership organization for sustainability professionals with networking, career development, and knowledge sharing opportunities. Provides job board, mentorship programs, and professional recognition initiatives.

Academic and Research Networks

Academy of Management Sustainability Division: Academic association for management scholars and practitioners focusing on sustainability research and education. Provides research conferences, publication opportunities, and academic-practitioner collaboration.

International Association of Business and Society (IABS): Academic association exploring relationships between business and society with focus on corporate responsibility and sustainability. Offers research conferences and publication opportunities.

Sustainable Business Network: Academic and practitioner network focusing on sustainable business education and research. Provides curriculum development, case study sharing, and faculty development opportunities.

Global Alliance for Management Education (GAME): International network of business schools and management education institutions promoting sustainable management education. Focuses on curriculum integration and faculty development.

Appendix E: Quick Reference Guides for Each Framework

Practitioners need rapid access to framework requirements during implementation and ongoing reporting. These guides provide essential information in condensed format for daily reference and decision-making support.

CSRD Quick Reference

Scope Application: Large public-interest entities (500+ employees), all large companies (250+ employees, €50M+ revenue, €25M+ balance sheet), listed SMEs (phased implementation). Non-EU companies through subsidiaries or significant EU operations.

Reporting Location: Management report within annual report. Digital format required with machine-readable data tagging. Integration with financial reporting mandatory.

Double Materiality Assessment: Impact materiality (company effects on people/environment) plus financial materiality (sustainability effects on enterprise value). Documentation of assessment process required.

ESRS Structure: Cross-cutting standards (ESRS 1 General Requirements, ESRS 2 General Disclosures), Environmental standards (E1-E5), Social standards (S1-S4), Governance standard (G1). Sector-specific standards under development.

Assurance Requirements: Limited assurance initially, reasonable assurance for climate information by 2028. Independent assurance provider required with appropriate competence and independence.

Key Deadlines: 2024 (large PIEs), 2025 (all large companies), 2026 (listed SMEs), 2028 (full assurance requirements). Annual reporting cycle aligned with financial reporting.

GRI Standards Quick Reference

Modular System: Universal Standards (GRI 1 Foundation, GRI 2 General Disclosures, GRI 3 Material Topics) plus Topic Standards (200 Economic, 300 Environmental, 400 Social) based on materiality assessment.

Reporting Options: In accordance (comprehensive compliance), GRI-referenced (selected disclosures), or sector-specific approach. Clear labeling required for chosen approach.

Materiality Process: Stakeholder engagement, impact identification, significance assessment, and prioritization. Dynamic materiality requiring regular reassessment based on changing conditions.

Stakeholder Engagement: Ongoing, systematic engagement with affected and interested stakeholders. Documentation of engagement process and influence on reporting required.

Reporting Principles: Accuracy, balance, clarity, comparability, completeness, sustainability context, timeliness, and verifiability. Applied throughout reporting process.

Content Index: Required table showing location of each disclosure. Cross-references to other reports or omissions with explanations permitted.

SASB Standards Quick Reference

Industry Focus: 77 industry standards across 11 sectors based on Sustainable Industry Classification System (SICS). Multiple standards for diversified companies based on revenue significance.

Materiality Approach: Evidence-based financial materiality determined through research on value relevance to investors. Focus on enterprise value impact rather than stakeholder materiality.

Disclosure Components: Accounting metrics (quantitative performance data), activity metrics (business scale context), and technical protocols (measurement methodologies). Narrative disclosure complements quantitative data.

Forward-Looking Information: Strategy, risk management, and target disclosures encouraged where material to investors. Safe harbor protection for forward-looking statements made in good faith.

Integration Options: Standalone sustainability reports, annual report integration, SEC filings, or investor presentations. Flexible format accommodating different communication strategies.

Assurance Considerations: External assurance recommended for key metrics based on materiality and stakeholder needs. Limited assurance typically sufficient for most applications.

Appendix F: Sample Reports and Disclosures

Learning from exemplary reporting helps organizations understand practical application of framework requirements while identifying approaches that suit their specific circumstances and stakeholder needs.

Microsoft Annual Report ESG Integration Example

Microsoft demonstrates sophisticated integration of sustainability information within annual financial reporting, connecting ESG performance to business strategy and financial results. The company's approach includes dedicated sustainability sections within Form 10-K filings while maintaining clear connections to business performance.

Climate Commitments Section: Microsoft discloses carbon negative by 2030 commitment with specific interim targets, investment amounts, and progress metrics. The disclosure connects climate strategy to product development, operational efficiency, and customer value creation.

Responsible AI Governance: Detailed governance structure for artificial intelligence development including board oversight, management responsibilities, and stakeholder engagement processes. Links AI governance to brand protection and competitive differentiation.

Supply Chain Sustainability: Human rights due diligence processes, supplier requirements, and monitoring results presented with clear management system descriptions and performance trends. Connects supply chain practices to operational risk management.

Diversity and Inclusion: Workforce representation data, advancement metrics, and program investments with clear accountability structures and progress tracking. Links diversity efforts to talent acquisition and retention outcomes.

Unilever Integrated Reporting Example

Unilever's integrated report demonstrates connection between sustainability strategy and business model while providing stakeholder information across multiple frameworks. The report structure supports different audience needs through layered information presentation.

Sustainable Living Plan Integration: Business strategy explicitly connects sustainability commitments to growth opportunities, cost reduction, and risk management. Clear quantitative targets with progress measurement and forward-looking guidance.

Value Creation Model: Visual representation connecting inputs (natural, human, manufactured capital) through business activities to outcomes for stakeholders. Demonstrates interconnections between financial and non-financial value creation.

Materiality Matrix Presentation: Stakeholder importance versus business significance matrix with clear explanation of assessment methodology and stakeholder engagement process. Shows how materiality informs strategy and reporting focus.

Performance Dashboard: Multi-year trend data across sustainability metrics with target achievement status and narrative explanation of performance drivers. Enables progress tracking and peer comparison.

JPMorgan Chase Climate Report Example

JPMorgan Chase demonstrates financial services climate disclosure through dedicated climate report complementing annual report disclosures. The approach shows sector-specific climate risk assessment and strategy development.

Physical Risk Assessment: Geographic exposure analysis with climate scenario modeling showing potential impacts on operations and loan portfolios. Quantitative analysis with clear methodology explanation and limitations.

Transition Risk Analysis: Sector-by-sector analysis of transition risks across lending portfolios with scenario-based stress testing results. Shows how climate policy and technology changes affect credit risk assessment.

Green Finance Targets: Specific financing commitments for clean energy, sustainable transportation, and green buildings with progress tracking and methodology explanation. Connects climate strategy to business opportunity identification.

Governance Structure: Climate governance framework with board oversight, management committees, and business line integration. Shows how climate considerations are embedded in risk management and strategic planning.

Appendix G: Checklists and Assessment Tools

Systematic assessment tools prevent oversight while ensuring consistent application of framework requirements across different business units and reporting periods.

CSRD Compliance Readiness Checklist

Legal Scope Assessment

- [ ] Confirm company falls within CSRD scope based on size and legal structure
- [ ] Identify applicable timeline for initial compliance based on company category
- [ ] Assess subsidiary and joint venture inclusion requirements
- [ ] Determine digital reporting format and data tagging requirements

Double Materiality Assessment Preparation

- [ ] Establish materiality assessment process with stakeholder engagement
- [ ] Identify sustainability topics relevant to business activities and context
- [ ] Assess impact materiality across value chain operations
- [ ] Evaluate financial materiality through scenario analysis and expert judgment
- [ ] Document assessment methodology and stakeholder input process

ESRS Implementation Planning

- [ ] Map applicable ESRS standards based on materiality assessment outcomes
- [ ] Identify data collection requirements for mandatory and applicable disclosures
- [ ] Establish data governance processes and quality control procedures
- [ ] Plan integration with financial reporting systems and timelines
- [ ] Arrange external assurance provider selection and engagement

GRI Reporting Implementation Checklist

Foundation and Strategy

- [ ] Commit to GRI reporting approach (in accordance or GRI-referenced)
- [ ] Establish reporting boundary including entities and impacts
- [ ] Design stakeholder engagement process for ongoing input
- [ ] Conduct materiality assessment with stakeholder participation
- [ ] Select applicable Topic Standards based on material topics

Data Collection and Management

- [ ] Map data sources for Universal Standards general disclosures
- [ ] Establish data collection processes for material topic indicators
- [ ] Implement data quality assurance and validation procedures
- [ ] Create documentation systems for calculation methodologies
- [ ] Plan external assurance scope and provider selection

Report Development and Publication

- [ ] Design report structure and presentation format
- [ ] Develop Content Index showing disclosure locations
- [ ] Prepare management approach disclosures for material topics
- [ ] Create stakeholder communication and distribution strategy
- [ ] Establish feedback collection and continuous improvement process

SASB Implementation Assessment Tool

Industry Standard Selection

- [ ] Classify business activities using SICS industry classification
- [ ] Identify applicable SASB industry standards based on revenue significance
- [ ] Map disclosure topics from relevant industry standards
- [ ] Assess materiality of each disclosure topic for business and investors
- [ ] Determine reporting scope and boundary for SASB metrics

Data Collection Capability

- [ ] Inventory existing data sources for SASB accounting metrics
- [ ] Identify data gaps requiring new collection processes
- [ ] Establish calculation methodologies following SASB technical protocols
- [ ] Implement data quality controls and validation procedures
- [ ] Plan activity metrics collection for normalization and comparison

Disclosure Integration Planning

- [ ] Determine reporting format and integration with existing communications
- [ ] Design narrative disclosure approach complementing quantitative metrics
- [ ] Plan forward-looking information disclosure with appropriate caveats
- [ ] Establish external assurance scope for key material metrics
- [ ] Create investor communication strategy and feedback mechanisms

Supply Chain ESG Assessment Framework

Risk Identification and Mapping

- [ ] Map supply chain tiers based on spend significance and risk exposure
- [ ] Identify environmental, social, and governance risk factors by tier
- [ ] Assess geographic risk concentration and sector-specific challenges
- [ ] Evaluate supplier diversity and capacity for ESG improvement
- [ ] Document risk assessment methodology and update frequency

Due Diligence Implementation

- [ ] Establish supplier ESG requirements and code of conduct
- [ ] Implement supplier assessment and monitoring procedures
- [ ] Create capacity building and improvement support programs

- [ ] Design grievance mechanisms and corrective action processes
- [ ] Plan regular review and continuous improvement cycles

Performance Monitoring and Reporting

- [ ] Define key performance indicators for supply chain sustainability
- [ ] Establish data collection and verification procedures
- [ ] Create supplier performance dashboards and reporting systems
- [ ] Design stakeholder communication about supply chain practices
- [ ] Plan integration with broader ESG reporting and disclosure

The Foundation for Excellence

These appendices provide the practical tools and references that transform ESG knowledge into operational capability. The difference between theoretical understanding and implementation success lies in having the right resources available when critical decisions arise.

The organizations that build robust reference libraries, maintain current regulatory awareness, and invest in appropriate technology solutions position themselves for sustained ESG excellence. These tools support not just compliance but strategic advantage through superior sustainability management and stakeholder communication.

Excellence in ESG reporting requires both conceptual understanding and practical execution capability. These resources bridge that gap by providing the detailed guidance that turns framework knowledge into reporting success.

Essential Resource Elements

- Terminology mastery enables precise communication across frameworks and stakeholder groups
- Regulatory timeline awareness prevents compliance surprises while supporting strategic planning
- Technology solution understanding guides investment decisions and implementation success
- Professional network engagement builds competence while creating career advancement opportunities
- Framework reference guides support daily decision-making and ensure consistent application
- Sample report analysis accelerates learning while identifying best practice approaches
- Assessment tools ensure systematic implementation while preventing critical oversight

References

(1) Sustainalytics. "CSRD Reporting: Preparing for Mandatory ESG Disclosure Deadlines." Accessed January 2025. https://www.sustainalytics.com/esg-research/resource/investors-esg-blog/csrd-reporting--preparing-for-mandatory-esg-disclosure-deadlines

(2) European Commission. "Corporate sustainability reporting - European Commission." Accessed January 2025. https://finance.ec.europa.eu/capital-markets-union-and-financial-markets/company-reporting-and-auditing/company-reporting/corporate-sustainability-reporting_en

(3) Anthesis Group. "ESG Regulations 2025: Navigating The Evolving Reporting Landscape." January 16, 2025. https://www.anthesisgroup.com/insights/the-evolving-landscape-of-esg-reporting-regulation-expectations-for-2025/

(4) Centida. "Do You Qualify for Mandatory ESG Reporting in 2025?" October 14, 2024. https://centida.com/blog/articles/mandatory-esg-reporting-in-2025/

(5) CSO Futures. "ESG reporting compliance in 2025: A global guide and dates." January 15, 2025. https://www.csofutures.com/news/annual-esg-reporting-compliance-global-dates-deadlines/

(6) Plana Earth. "All 2025 ESG and non-financial reporting regulations in the EU." https://plana.earth/academy/eu-esg-regulations

(7) KEY ESG. "What is CSRD: Complete Guide for ESG Reporting." August 31, 2024. https://www.keyesg.com/article/an-introductory-guide-to-the-corporate-sustainability-reporting-directive-csrd

(8) Harvard Law School Forum on Corporate Governance. "ESG and Sustainability Insights: 10 Things That Should Be Top of Mind in 2025." https://corpgov.law.harvard.edu/2025/01/18/esg-and-sustainability-insights-10-things-that-should-be-top-of-mind-in-2025/

(9) PwC. "What US companies need to know about the EU's CSRD." https://www.pwc.com/us/en/services/esg/library/eu-corporate-sustainability-reporting-directive.html

(10) Corporate Finance Institute. "Top 10 ESG Courses and Certifications in 2025." February 25, 2025. https://corporatefinanceinstitute.com/resources/career/esg-courses-certifications/

(11) Corporate Finance Institute. "ESG Career Profile." 1 month ago. https://corporatefinanceinstitute.com/resources/career/esg-careers/

(12) Brainie Group. "ESG Certification Career Path: Salary, Demand, and Long-Term Value." August 9, 2023. https://brainiegroup.com/blog/career-boost-with-esg-the-role-of-certifications-like-cfa-esg-garp-scr-and-cesga/

(13) The Corporate Governance Institute. "Jobs in ESG." November 30, 2023. https://www.thecorporategovernanceinstitute.com/insights/guides/what-kind-of-jobs-can-you-get-with-a-qualification-in-esg/

(14) Corporate Finance Institute. "Introduction to ESG." March 5, 2025. https://corporatefinanceinstitute.com/course/environmental-social-governance/

(15) Corporate Finance Institute. "ESG Certification - Environmental, Social, & Governance Course." December 14, 2023.

https://corporatefinanceinstitute.com/certifications/environmental-social-governance-specialist/

(16) CFA Institute. "Sustainable Investing Certificate." https://www.cfainstitute.org/en/programs/esg-investing

(17) The Corporate Governance Institute. "ESG jobs and salaries - [the ultimate guide]." August 14, 2023. https://www.thecorporategovernanceinstitute.com/insights/guides/esg-jobs-salaries-pay/

(18) Zell Education. "ESG Careers: Salaries & Job Roles." January 16, 2025. https://www.zelleducation.com/blog/what-salaries-and-job-roles-can-i-expect-in-esg/

(19) CFA Institute. "ESG Certification." https://www.cfainstitute.org/programs/esg-certification

(20) PwC. "10 pitfalls companies should avoid when complying with the CSRD's double materiality." https://www.pwc.com/us/en/services/esg/library/csrd-double-materiality.html

(21) PwC Netherlands. "CSRD - Double Materiality Assessment." https://www.pwc.nl/en/topics/sustainability/esg/corporate-sustainability-reporting-directive/csrd-double-materiality-assessment.html

(22) Normative. "What is a CSRD double materiality assessment?" October 25, 2024. https://normative.io/insight/double-materiality-csrd/

(23) Workiva. "Double Materiality and the European Sustainability Reporting Standards (ESRS)." December 17, 2024. https://www.workiva.com/resources/double-materiality-and-european-sustainability-reporting-standards-esrs

(24) Quentic. "Double Materiality in ESG & Sustainability Explained." https://www.quentic.com/articles/double-materiality/

(25) PwC. "ESG Materiality Standards Reporting." https://www.pwc.com/gx/en/services/audit-assurance/corporate-reporting/ESG-Materiality-Standards-Reporting.html

(26) PwC Netherlands. "ESG Talk 5 | The value chain (part 1)." https://www.pwc.nl/en/services/audit-assurance/pwc-accountancy-insights/esg/esg-talk-5-the-value-chain-part-1.html

(27) Plan BE. "Double Materiality in ESG: A Competitive Edge in Sustainable Business." November 19, 2024. https://planbe.eco/en/blog/double-materiality-in-esg-a-competitive-edge-in-sustainable-business/

(28) PwC. "ESG sustainability reporting." https://www.pwc.com/gx/en/services/audit-assurance/corporate-reporting/esg-sustainability-reporting.html

(29) Manifest Climate. "What is Single Materiality and Double Materiality?" February 2, 2024. https://www.manifestclimate.com/blog/what-is-single-and-double-materiality/

(30) Coursera. "Best ESG Courses & Certificates [2025]." https://www.coursera.org/courses?query=esg

(31) Coursera. "ESG Risks and Opportunities." https://www.coursera.org/learn/esg-risks-opportunities

(32) Coursera. "The Materiality of ESG Factors." https://www.coursera.org/specializations/materiality-esg-factors

(33) Skill India Digital Hub. "Certificate Course in Sustainability and Corporate ESG."

https://www.skillindiadigital.gov.in/courses/detail/3e1d4341-4018-49a7-afef-226410ef2a79

(34) Corporate Finance Institute. "Top 10 ESG Courses and Certifications in 2025." February 25, 2025. https://corporatefinanceinstitute.com/resources/career/esg-courses-certifications/

(35) Coursera. "What Is Environmental, Social, and Governance (ESG)?" November 26, 2024. https://www.coursera.org/articles/what-is-esg

(36) Coursera. "Introduction to ESG." https://www.coursera.org/learn/environmental-social-governance

(37) ICSD Global. "Certified ESG Planner CEP®." https://www.icsd-global.org/certified-esg-planner

(38) Corporate Finance Institute. "ESG Certification - Environmental, Social, & Governance Course." December 14, 2023. https://corporatefinanceinstitute.com/certifications/environmental-social-governance-specialist/

(39) Learn & Work Ecosystem Library. "Competency Models, Skills Models & Learning Frameworks." November 15, 2022. https://learnworkecosystemlibrary.com/topics/competency-skills-models-learning-frameworks/

(40) Deloitte. "European Commission Proposes Reduction in Sustainability Reporting and Due Diligence Requirements — Considerations for U.S. Entities (March 7, 2025)." March 7, 2025. https://dart.deloitte.com/USDART/home/publications/deloitte/heads-up/2025/eu-commission-omnibus-proposal-sustainability-reporting-reduction-csrd

(41) European Commission. "Corporate sustainability reporting - European Commission." https://finance.ec.europa.eu/capital-markets-union-and-financial-markets/company-reporting-and-auditing/company-reporting/corporate-sustainability-reporting_en

(42) PwC. "CSRD - Corporate Sustainability Reporting Directive." https://viewpoint.pwc.com/dt/gx/en/eu/eu-sustainability-regulation/eu-sustainability-regulation/csrd.html

(43) Dechert. "European Commission Proposes Simplification of the CSRD and Certain Other Sustainability-Related Initiatives."
https://www.dechert.com/knowledge/onpoint/2025/3/european-commission-proposes-simplification-of-the-csrd-and-cert.html

(44) European Parliament. "Corporate Sustainability Reporting Directive (CSRD) | Legislative Train Schedule."
https://www.europarl.europa.eu/legislative-train/theme-a-european-green-deal/file-review-of-the-non-financial-reporting-directive

(45) McDermott. "Simplification Omnibus Package." March 13, 2025. https://www.mwe.com/insights/simplification-omnisbus-package/

(46) European Commission. "Commission Delegated Regulation amending Delegated Regulation (EU) 2023/2772."
https://finance.ec.europa.eu/regulation-and-supervision/financial-services-legislation/implementing-and-delegated-acts/corporate-sustainability-reporting-directive_en

(47) IBM. "What Is the CSRD?" May 29, 2025.
https://www.ibm.com/think/topics/csrd

(48) Bryan Cave Leighton Paisner. "EU Commission Omnibus package - CSRD, Taxonomy & CSDDD update."

https://www.bclplaw.com/en-US/events-insights-news/eu-commission-omnibus-package.html

(49) European Commission. "Commission simplifies rules on sustainability and EU investments, delivering over €6 billion in administrative relief." February 26, 2025. https://finance.ec.europa.eu/publications/commission-simplifies-rules-sustainability-and-eu-investments-delivering-over-eu6-billion_en

(50) Leafr. "CSRD Explained: A 2025 Guide to the Corporate Sustainability Reporting Directive changes." https://www.leafr.com/blog-post/csrd-explained-your-2025-guide-to-the-corporate-sustainability-reporting-directive

(51) Accountancy Europe. "Omnibus explained: key changes to CSRD." March 12, 2025. https://accountancyeurope.eu/publications/omnibus-explained-key-changes-to-csrd/

(52) EY Belgium. "EU's Omnibus Proposal: Key changes to the CSRD, CS3D and Taxonomy." https://www.ey.com/en_be/technical/tax/tax-alerts/2025/eus-omnibus-proposal-key-changes-to-the-csrd-cs3d-and-taxonomy

(53) Plana Earth. "CSRD thresholds: Which companies have to report?" https://plana.earth/academy/csrd-thresholds

(54) Normative. "Corporate Sustainability Reporting Directive (CSRD), explained." October 26, 2023. https://normative.io/insight/csrd-explained/

(55) Skadden. "European Commission Publishes ESG Reporting Omnibus Package." https://www.skadden.com/insights/publications/2025/02/european-commission-publishes-esg-reporting-omnibus-package

(56) Watershed. "EU omnibus proposal and its implications for the CSRD." https://watershed.com/blog/eu-omnibus-2025

(57) WTW. "CSRD Omnibus updates: Q&A on what risk managers and sustainability professionals need to know." 3 weeks ago. https://www.wtwco.com/en-us/insights/2025/06/csrd-omnibus-updates-q-and-a-on-what-risk-managers-and-sustainability-professionals-need-to-know

(58) Workiva. "CSRD Omnibus: What Businesses Need to Know About the Proposals." March 4, 2025. https://www.workiva.com/blog/csrd-omnibus-what-businesses-need-know-about-proposals

(59) Ecobio Manager. "CSRD Timeline | CSRD from 2024 to 2028." https://ecobiomanager.com/csrd-timeline-stay-ahead-of-reporting-schedule/

(60) Net0. "Corporate Sustainability Reporting Directive (CSRD) 2024: Who and What Is Impacted." https://net0.com/blog/csrd-reporting-2024

(61) Brightest. "The EU Corporate Sustainability Reporting Directive (CSRD) - Timeline and Standards Overview." https://www.brightest.io/csrd-corporate-sustainability-reporting-directive

(62) ApiDay. "CSRD Timeline: Essential Dates for Compliance." November 12, 2024. https://www.apiday.com/blog-posts/csrd-timeline-when-should-you-report

(63) Plana Earth. "CSRD timeline: When should your company report?" https://plana.earth/academy/timeline-csrd

(64) CoreFiling. "CSRD Timeline: Reporting Requirements and Deadlines Explained." August 19, 2024. https://www.corefiling.com/2024/07/30/csrd-timeline/

(65) McGrady Clarke. "The phased implementation timeline of the Corporate Sustainability Reporting Directive (CSRD)." January 27, 2025. https://www.mcgra

(66) Vaayu. "CSRD Timeline: Key Dates and Deadlines to Know." https://www.vaayu.tech/insights/csrd-timeline

(67) Lythouse. "CSRD Timelines: Understanding Key Dates for Your Business." August 21, 2024. https://www.lythouse.com/blog/csrd-timelines-key-dates-and-what-they-mean-for-your-business

(68) Coolset. "What you need to know to start reporting on CSRD from 2025 onwards (Updated June 2025)." https://www.coolset.com/academy/csrd-reporting-guide-2025

(69) Normative. "Corporate Sustainability Reporting Directive (CSRD), explained." October 26, 2023. https://normative.io/insight/csrd-explained/

(70) IBM. "What Is the CSRD?" May 29, 2025. https://www.ibm.com/think/topics/csrd

(71) Normative. "CSRD reporting for UK and other non-EU companies." October 25, 2024. https://normative.io/insight/csrd-reporting-uk-non-eu-companies/

(72) European Commission. "Corporate sustainability reporting - European Commission." https://finance.ec.europa.eu/capital-markets-union-and-financial-markets/company-reporting-and-auditing/company-reporting/corporate-sustainability-reporting_en

(73) PwC. "What US companies need to know about the EU's CSRD." https://www.pwc.com/us/en/services/esg/library/eu-corporate-sustainability-reporting-directive.html

(74) Persefoni. "CSRD: A Guide to the Corporate Sustainability Reporting Directive." https://www.persefoni.com/blog/what-is-csrd

(75) Sweep. "What Does the CSRD Mean for Non-EU Companies?" October 9, 2024. https://www.sweep.net/insights/what-does-the-csrd-mean-for-non-eu-companies

(76) Greenomy. "CSRD Reporting Non-EU Companies: What You Need to Know." https://www.greenomy.io/blog/csrd-reporting-non-eu-companies

(77) Deloitte. "Frequently Asked Questions About the E.U. Corporate Sustainability Reporting Directive (August 17, 2023; Updated February 23, 2024)." https://dart.deloitte.com/USDART/home/publications/deloitte/heads-up/2023/csrd-corporate-sustainability-reporting-directive-faqs

(78) KPMG. "Impact of EU sustainability reporting on US companies." April 16, 2025. https://kpmg.com/us/en/frv/reference-library/2025/latest-impact-of-eu-sustainability-reporting-on-us-companies.html

(79) Socious. "Navigating European Sustainability Reporting Standards (ESRS) Cross-Cutting Requirements." https://socious.io/blog/esrs-cross-cutting-requirements

(80) European Commission. "Questions and Answers on the Adoption of European Sustainability Reporting Standards." https://ec.europa.eu/commission/presscorner/detail/en/qanda_23_4043

(81) KPMG. "Key features of ESRS." https://kpmg.com/xx/en/home/insights/2022/05/european-sustainability-reporting-standards-eu-esrs.html

(82) Plana Earth. "European Sustainability Reporting Standards (ESRS)." https://plana.earth/policy/esrs-european-sustainability-reporting-standards

(83) Circularise. "The European Sustainability Reporting Standards explained (ESRS)." https://www.circularise.com/blogs/the-european-sustainability-reporting-standards-explained-esrs

(84) ClimatePartner. "European Sustainability Reporting Standards (ESRS)." https://www.climatepartner.com/en/knowledge/glossary/european-sustainability-reporting-standards-esrs

(85) European Commission. "The Commission adopts the European Sustainability Reporting Standards." July 31, 2023. https://finance.ec.europa.eu/news/commission-adopts-european-sustainability-reporting-standards-2023-07-31_en

(86) UNEP FI. "European Sustainability Reporting Standards (ESRS)." https://www.unepfi.org/impact/interoperability/european-sustainability-reporting-standards-esrs/

(87) Greenomy. "What are European Sustainability Reporting Standards (ESRS)?" https://www.greenomy.io/blog/esrs-phase-in-journey

(88) EFRAG. "ESRS Set 1." https://xbrl.efrag.org/e-esrs/esrs-set1-2023.html

(89) Global Reporting Initiative. "GRI Universal Standards 2021." https://www.globalreporting.org/media/zauil2g3/public-faqs-universal-standards.pdf

(90) Global Reporting Initiative. "GRI 2: General Disclosures 2021." https://www.globalreporting.org/publications/documents/english/gri-2-general-disclosures-2021/

(91) Global Reporting Initiative. "A Short Introduction to the GRI Standards." https://www.globalreporting.org/media/wtaf14tw/a-short-introduction-to-the-gri-standards.pdf

(92) Global Reporting Initiative. "GRI 3: Material Topics 2021." https://www.globalreporting.org/publications/documents/english/gri-3-material-topics-2021/

(93) Global Reporting Initiative. "GRI Standards English Language." https://www.globalreporting.org/how-to-use-the-gri-standards/gri-standards-english-language/

(94) Global Reporting Initiative. "GRI 3: Material Topics 2021." https://globalreporting.org/pdf.ashx?id=12453

(95) Global Reporting Initiative. "GRI 1: Foundation 2021." https://globalreporting.org/pdf.ashx?id=12334

(96) Global Reporting Initiative. "Universal Standards." https://www.globalreporting.org/standards/standards-development/universal-standards/

(97) Global Reporting Initiative. "Standards." https://www.globalreporting.org/standards/

(98) Global Reporting Initiative. "The GRI Standards." https://www.globalreporting.org/media/nmmnwfsm/gri-policymakers-guide.pdf

(99) Karmametrix. "GRI Standards: what are and why they're the most used." May 15, 2023. https://karmametrix.com/blog/eco-sustainability/gri-standards-what-are-and-why-they-are-the-most-used/

(100) Global Reporting Initiative. "Download the Standards." https://www.globalreporting.org/standards/download-the-standards/

(101) Memoria Balance Social. "Specific standard contents 2020 (GRI 200, 300, 400)." July 9, 2021. https://rsc.guttmann.com/en/specific-standard-contents-2020-gri-200-300-400/

(102) Global Reporting Initiative. "GRI Standards English Language." https://www.globalreporting.org/how-to-use-the-gri-standards/gri-standards-english-language/

(103) Global Reporting Initiative. "Standards." https://www.globalreporting.org/standards/

(104) WorldFavor. "What are the GRI standards?" https://blog.worldfavor.com/what-are-the-gri-standards

(105) Global Reporting Initiative. "GRI Universal Standards 2021." https://www.globalreporting.org/media/zauil2g3/public-faqs-universal-standards.pdf

(106) Azeus Convene. "Complete Guide to GRI Standards for ESG Reporting." February 6, 2025. https://www.azeusconvene.com/esg/articles/gri-standards

(107) SustainLab. "Four Sustainability standards you should know about!" September 30, 2021. https://sustainlab.co/blog/four-sustainability-standards-you-should-know

(108) Practice Test Geeks. "GRI Professional Certification Guide." 1 month ago. https://practicetestgeeks.com/global-reporting-initiative-professional-certification/

(109) Julie Hendricks. "How I passed the GRI Exam." August 2, 2021. https://www.linkedin.com/pulse/how-i-passed-gri-exam-julie-hendricks

(110) Global Reporting Initiative. "Certification." https://www.globalreporting.org/academy/certification/

(111) Udemy. "GRI Sustainability Professional Certification Exam Prep 2023." https://www.udemy.com/course/gri-sustainability-professional-certification-exam-prep-2023/

(112) SustainCase. "Become a GRI Certified Sustainability professional." June 7, 2023. https://sustaincase.com/become-a-gri-certified-sustainability-professional/

(113) Rohit Reddy Anugu. "My Experience with the GRI Professional Certification Program." March 29, 2022. https://www.linkedin.com/pulse/my-experience-gri-professional-certification-program-rohit-reddy

(114) Sustainprep. "GRI Professional Certification With Sustainprep Practice Question." April 18, 2025. https://sustainprep.com/gri/

(115) Global Reporting Initiative. "FAQs." https://www.globalreporting.org/academy/faqs

(116) Global Reporting Initiative. "Professional Certification Program FAQs." https://www.globalreporting.org/media/ialfkhyj/professional-certification-program-faqs-for-participants.pdf

(117) Global Reporting Initiative. "GRI Professional Certification Exam." https://www.globalreporting.org/Academy/Course?id=645

(118) Sustainability Accounting Standards Board. "Investor-Focused Materiality: The Foundation of SASB Standards." Accessed January 2025. https://www.sasb.org/investor-use/

(119) BlackRock. "SASB Standards in Investment Analysis: Practical Applications." Investment Stewardship Report, 2024. https://www.blackrock.com/corporate/literature/publication/sasb-investment-analysis.pdf

(120) Sustainability Accounting Standards Board. "SASB Standards Overview: 77 Industry Standards." Accessed January 2025. https://www.sasb.org/standards/

(121) Sustainability Accounting Standards Board. "SICS Industry Classification System." Accessed January 2025. https://www.sasb.org/standards/materiality-map/

(122) International Sustainability Standards Board. "ISSB Standards and SASB Integration." IFRS Foundation, 2024. https://www.ifrs.org/groups/international-sustainability-standards-board/

(123) Securities and Exchange Commission. "Climate Disclosure Rules and SASB Alignment." Federal Register, 2024. https://www.sec.gov/rules/final/2024/33-11275.pdf

(124) Sustainability Accounting Standards Board. "Industry Classification and Standard Selection Guide." SASB Implementation Guidance, 2024. https://www.sasb.org/guidance/industry-classification/

(125) Sustainability Accounting Standards Board. "Disclosure Topics and Metrics Implementation Guide." Accessed January 2025. https://www.sasb.org/guidance/disclosure-topics/

(126) Sustainability Accounting Standards Board. "Activity Metrics: Enabling Meaningful Comparison." SASB Conceptual Framework, 2024. https://www.sasb.org/guidance/activity-metrics/

(127) Ernst & Young. "Quantitative vs. Qualitative SASB Disclosures: Best Practices." EY ESG Reporting Guide, 2024. https://www.ey.com/en_us/assurance/sasb-disclosure-best-practices

(128) PwC. "Cross-Industry SASB Analysis: Comparative Insights." PwC ESG Data & Technology Survey, 2024. https://www.pwc.com/us/en/services/esg/library/sasb-cross-industry-analysis.html

(129) KPMG. "SASB Materiality Assessment: Investor-Focused Approaches." KPMG ESG Implementation Series, 2024. https://kpmg.com/us/en/frv/reference-library/2024/sasb-materiality-assessment.html

(130) Deloitte. "SASB Data Collection Systems: Implementation Best Practices." Deloitte ESG Technology Solutions, 2024. https://www2.deloitte.com/us/en/pages/risk/articles/sasb-data-collection-systems.html

(131) Boston Consulting Group. "Integrating SASB with Financial Reporting: Strategic Approaches." BCG ESG

Advantage Series, 2024.
https://www.bcg.com/publications/2024/integrating-sasb-financial-reporting

(132) McKinsey & Company. "Technology Sector SASB Implementation: Digital Age Sustainability Reporting." McKinsey Sustainability Insights, 2024.
https://www.mckinsey.com/capabilities/sustainability/our-insights/technology-sasb-implementation

(133) General Electric. "Annual Sustainability Report: Multi-Industry SASB Implementation." GE Sustainability, 2024.
https://www.ge.com/sustainability/reports/annual-sustainability-report

(134) PwC. "Multi-Framework ESG Reporting: Integration Strategies for CSRD, GRI, and SASB." PwC ESG Reporting Series, 2024. https://www.pwc.com/gx/en/services/esg/multi-framework-integration.html

(135) Deloitte. "Unified ESG Data Collection: Technology Solutions for Integrated Reporting." Deloitte ESG Technology Guide, 2024.
https://www2.deloitte.com/global/en/pages/risk/articles/unified-esg-data-collection.html

(136) KPMG. "Integrated Materiality Assessment: Meeting Multiple Framework Requirements." KPMG ESG Implementation Series, 2024.
https://kpmg.com/xx/en/home/insights/2024/integrated-materiality-assessment.html

(137) Ernst & Young. "Combined ESG Reporting Architecture: Design Principles for Multi-Framework Success." EY ESG Excellence Series, 2024.
https://www.ey.com/en_gl/assurance/combined-esg-reporting-architecture

(138) Workiva. "Technology Solutions for ESG Integration: Platform Capabilities for Multi-Framework Reporting." Workiva ESG Solutions, 2024. https://www.workiva.com/resources/technology-solutions-esg-integration

(139) International Auditing and Assurance Standards Board. "ISAE 3000: Assurance Engagements Other Than Audits or Reviews." IAASB Standards, 2024. https://www.iaasb.org/publications/isae-3000-revised-assurance-engagements-other-audits-or-reviews-historical-financial

(140) Global Reporting Initiative. "Assurance Readiness: Preparing for External Verification." GRI Implementation Guidance, 2024. https://www.globalreporting.org/guidance/assurance-readiness/

(141) Institute of Internal Auditors. "ESG Reporting Controls: Internal Audit's Role in Sustainability Assurance." IIA ESG Practice Guide, 2024. https://www.theiia.org/guidance/esg-reporting-controls/

(142) Committee of Sponsoring Organizations. "Internal Control for ESG Reporting: Adapting COSO Framework." COSO ESG Guidance, 2024. https://www.coso.org/guidance/internal-control-esg-reporting

(143) AccountAbility. "ESG Assurance Provider Selection: Evaluation Criteria and Best Practices." AA1000 Assurance Standard, 2024. https://www.accountability.org/standards/esg-assurance-provider-selection/

(144) McKinsey & Company. "ESG Strategy Integration: From Compliance to Competitive Advantage." McKinsey ESG Strategy Series, 2024. https://www.mckinsey.com/capabilities/sustainability/our-insights/esg-strategy-integration

(145) BlackRock. "ESG in Investor Relations: Communication Strategies for Value Creation." BlackRock Investment Institute, 2024. https://www.blackrock.com/corporate/insights/esg-investor-relations

(146) Bloomberg Intelligence. "Sustainability-Linked Finance: Market Growth and Implementation Strategies." Bloomberg ESG Finance Report, 2024. https://www.bloomberg.com/professional/insights/sustainability-linked-finance

(147) Boston Consulting Group. "ESG Transparency as Competitive Advantage: Strategic Benefits of Sustainability Disclosure." BCG ESG Excellence Series, 2024. https://www.bcg.com/publications/2024/esg-transparency-competitive-advantage

(148) World Economic Forum. "Future of ESG Reporting: Preparing for Next-Generation Sustainability Standards." WEF ESG Future Report, 2024. https://www.weforum.org/reports/future-of-esg-reporting/

(149) Project Management Institute. "ESG Project Management: Implementation Templates and Best Practices." PMI ESG Practice Guide, 2024. https://www.pmi.org/learning/library/esg-project-management-implementation

(150) RACI Solutions International. "Responsibility Assignment for ESG Reporting: RACI Matrix Development." ESG Implementation Series, 2024. https://www.racisolutions.com/esg-responsibility-assignment

(151) Deloitte. "ESG Implementation Budgeting: Cost Planning Worksheets and Templates." Deloitte ESG Implementation Guide, 2024. https://www2.deloitte.com/global/en/pages/risk/articles/esg-implementation-budgeting.html

(152) Ernst & Young. "ESG Vendor Selection: Evaluation Criteria and Assessment Frameworks." EY ESG Advisory Services, 2024. https://www.ey.com/en_gl/consulting/esg-vendor-selection-criteria

(153) McKinsey & Company. "ESG Change Management: Tools and Strategies for Sustainability Transformation." McKinsey ESG Practice, 2024. https://www.mckinsey.com/capabilities/sustainability/our-insights/esg-change-management

(154) Global Reporting Initiative. "GRI Professional Certification: Study Guides and Preparation Resources." GRI Academy, 2024. https://www.globalreporting.org/academy/certification-study-resources

(155) Sustainability Accounting Standards Board. "SASB Certification Practice Questions and Scenarios." SASB Education Resources, 2024. https://www.sasb.org/certification/practice-questions

(156) CFA Institute. "ESG Certificate Exam Preparation: Time Management and Study Strategies." CFA ESG Education, 2024. https://www.cfainstitute.org/en/programs/esg-certificate/exam-preparation

(157) International Association for Continuing Education and Training. "ESG Professional Development: Continuing Education Requirements." IACET ESG Standards, 2024. https://www.iacet.org/standards/esg-continuing-education

(158) Net Impact. "ESG Career Development: Professional Planning and Advancement Strategies." Net Impact Career Resources, 2024. https://www.netimpact.org/career-resources/esg-professional-development

(159) Taskforce on Nature-related Financial Disclosures. "TNFD Framework Implementation: Guidance and Best Practices." TNFD Implementation Guide, 2024. https://tnfd.global/implementation-guidance/

(160) World Economic Forum. "AI in ESG Reporting: Technology Applications and Future Trends." WEF ESG Technology Report, 2024. https://www.weforum.org/reports/ai-in-esg-reporting/

(161) International Organization of Securities Commissions. "Global ESG Disclosure Standards: Regulatory Convergence Analysis." IOSCO ESG Report, 2024. https://www.iosco.org/library/pubdocs/pdf/IOSCOPD715.pdf

(162) Harvard Business School. "Building ESG Expertise: Professional Brand Development in Sustainability." HBS ESG Leadership Series, 2024. https://www.hbs.edu/faculty/Pages/item.aspx?num=65847

(163) Stanford Graduate School of Business. "Continuous Learning in ESG: Resources and Development Strategies." Stanford ESG Education, 2024. https://www.gsb.stanford.edu/programs/executive-education/esg-continuous-learning

(164) Global Reporting Initiative. "GRI Academy Professional Development Programs." GRI Education Resources, 2024. https://www.globalreporting.org/academy/professional-development

(165) Sustainability Accounting Standards Board. "SASB Professional Certification and Training." SASB Education Center, 2024. https://www.sasb.org/education/professional-certification

(166) European Commission. "CSRD Implementation Timeline and Milestones." CSRD Regulatory Guidance, 2024. https://finance.ec.europa.eu/capital-markets-union-and-financial-markets/company-reporting-and-auditing/company-reporting/corporate-sustainability-reporting_en

(167) Securities and Exchange Commission. "Climate Disclosure Implementation Schedule." SEC Regulatory Timeline, 2024. https://www.sec.gov/rules/final/2024/33-11275.pdf

(168) Workiva. "ESG Reporting Platform Capabilities and Features." Workiva ESG Solutions, 2024. https://www.workiva.com/solutions/esg-reporting

(169) SAP. "Sustainability Control Tower Implementation Guide." SAP ESG Technology Solutions, 2024. https://www.sap.com/products/sustainability-control-tower.html

(170) Net Impact. "Professional Association Membership Benefits and Programs." Net Impact Career Resources, 2024. https://www.netimpact.org/membership

(171) Carbon Disclosure Project. "CDP Professional Development and Training Programs." CDP Education Center, 2024. https://www.cdp.net/en/guidance/guidance-for-companies

(172) Microsoft Corporation. "Annual Report Sustainability Integration Example." Microsoft Sustainability Report, 2024. https://www.microsoft.com/en-us/corporate-responsibility/sustainability

(173) Unilever. "Integrated Reporting Best Practices and Framework Application." Unilever Annual Report, 2024. https://www.unilever.com/planet-and-society/

(174) JPMorgan Chase. "Climate Risk Disclosure and Reporting Framework." JPMorgan Chase Climate Report, 2024. https://www.jpmorganchase.com/about/governance/climate-risk

(175) Ernst & Young. "ESG Implementation Checklists and Assessment Tools." EY ESG Excellence Series, 2024. https://www.ey.com/en_gl/assurance/esg-implementation-checklists

Made in United States
Cleveland, OH
31 December 2025

30434852R00193